THINKING THROUGH METHODS

Thinking Through Methods

A SOCIAL SCIENCE PRIMER

John Levi Martin

The University of Chicago   Chicago and London

The University of Chicago Press, Chicago 60637
The University of Chicago Press, Ltd., London
© 2017 by The University of Chicago
Published 2017.

Printed in the United States of America

26 25 24 23 22 21 20 19 18 17   1 2 3 4 5

ISBN-13: 978-0-226-43169-7 (cloth)
ISBN-13: 978-0-226-43172-7 (paper)
ISBN-13: 978-0-226-43186-4 (e-book)
DOI: 10.7208/chicago/9780226431864.001.0001

Library of Congress Cataloging-in-Publication Data

Names: Martin, John Levi, 1964– author.
Title: Thinking through methods : a social science primer / John Levi Martin.
Description: Chicago ; London : The University of Chicago, 2017. | Includes
bibliographical references and index.
Identifiers: LCCN 2016025207 | ISBN 9780226431697 (cloth : alk. paper) | ISBN
9780226431727 (pbk. : alk. paper) | ISBN 9780226431864 (e-book)
Subjects: LCSH: Sociology—Research—Methodology. | Social
sciences—Research—Methodology.
Classification: LCC HM511 .M357 2017 | DDC 301.072—dc23 LC record available at
https://lccn.loc.gov/2016025207

♾ This paper meets the requirements of ANSI/NISO Z39.48–1992
(Permanence of Paper).

Contents

Preface

This is a book about methods in sociology and kindred social sciences. It is different from most other methods books in two ways. First, it has a pretty strong "line" regarding what is the right thing to do across situations. Second, despite treating a variety of methods, it has a single unifying theme—namely, that you can be far more rigorous than most sociologists if you really understand where the data you are working with come from, and how they sit in a space of all the possible data you *could* have gathered. This book has something to offer about pretty much every method, but isn't attempting to give you the ABCs of any. Rather, it is going to help you use the method in question to come away with something good, and not something bad, from all your hard work.

You might wonder how I am able to dispense such useful information about practically every major method in sociology, given that I myself haven't, of course, become an expert in each and every one. It's a good question. Most of my knowledge doesn't come from my own practice. Instead, it comes from being in a great position to watch others fail or succeed. You don't need to have ridden on the space shuttle to figure out why they blow up. You just need to sift through the wreckage.

Most of my knowledge comes from graduate and undergraduate students I advised, including historical sociologists, ethnographers, interviewers, statistical analysts, experimentalists—the gamut. Because I generally lacked first-hand familiarity with their methods and topics, I gave them advice based on what I'd learned from reading texts and the exemplary works I'd come across, often peppered with common sense and social psychology, and most (though not all) of that advice was excellent. Fortunately for me, my advisees aren't very easily cowed, and so they always did whatever the hell they wanted. Which meant that I got to see the results of approaches that I hadn't known about.

And I had a great comparison group, as I reviewed dozens of flawed manuscripts and watched plenty of other people (not my students, thankfully!) crash and burn. Watching others' education is mostly rewarding, but all too often, it becomes like that slow-motion feeling you have in a car accident—seeing that window pane coming closer and closer and knowing nothing is going to keep your forehead off of it. Graphic, I know. But that's why I wrote this book. Not to make sociology perfect but to prevent the huge carnage that comes from students embarking in preventably fatal directions.

There are other good methodology books for students out there, though there are few that try to cover the range this one does. Most focus on a single method or perhaps two, and go into greater depth than this book can. I'll be sure to mention those that I think are going to be most useful for you if you want to explore a method further. But here, I have a simple argument that can help us across all methods, and it's this: that when we think through what we are doing—where we are now, how we got here, where we are likely to end up if we go in one direction as opposed to another—we'll do a lot better. And although *this* part of methods is a lot harder than it seems, it's something that can be learned.

I'll show how this point informs our practice at different stages of research design. I'm going to spend a lot of time talking about what you *shouldn't* do. That might seem really negative. It's not. It's because although I could tell you how *I* do things, chances are, it won't work for you. For better or worse, you're going to need to do things *your* way. To steal a phrase from Jennifer Margulis, it's gonna be your baby, so you might as well do it your way. It's just that your way shouldn't totally stink like a monkey's butt.

Your baby, Your way

Luckily, there *are* different fine ways of doing things. And even more luckily, they have something in common, which is that they involve researchers trying *really hard* to think through what they're doing at any time. Of course, if I can save you thinking, I will. And so there are still plenty of juicy tips I can give you, collected from other books, personal experience, or watching others, that can serve as reminders for general principles of good practice.

I also strongly urge you to read the whole book—don't assume you know in advance what is important for your research. "A chapter on talking to people? I'm not planning on doing in-depth interviews, so I can skip that." Well, if you're an ethnographer, you're talking to people; if you're using survey data, it probably came from someone *else* talking to people, and so on. Further, there's a good chance that some day you might want to be able to help someone else with *her* project, even if it doesn't use the methods you know best. So read up, and in order.

Acknowledgments

Benjamin Merriman was the first reader of the first draft of this manuscript—his encouragement and wise thoughts were pivotal in me going forward. Thanks, Ben. Other readers I'd like to thank include Graham Patterson, Ellis Monk, and, especially, Sophie Fajardo, who wielded scalpel over the whole. I'm grateful for the impressive work on the manuscript—and enjoyable dialogue on both the philosophy and the vagaries of the written word—by Yvonne Zipter, as well as Ashley Pierce, Matt Avery, and Skye Agnew at the press. And especial thanks to reviewers, to Kyle Wagner, and to Doug Mitchell for shepherding this through.

This book certainly is intended as a companion to *Thinking Through Theory*. The perfect marriage of theory and method is, of course, elusive. But I was trained by just that. This book started with the methods class that I took, taught by Claude Fischer, when I started my graduate career. This work comes from a quarter-century engagement with that class, as I adapted it when I began teaching, and adapted the adaptation, and so on. I think he'd agree with most of the points that I make here, even though they only came after years of advising *others*. But anyway, about the perfect marriage of theory and research, Claude's wife, Ann Swidler, taught my theory class at the same time and became my adviser. Thanks to both of you.

But this book is dedicated to the memory of one other person who taught me what to do: Sylvia Schneider Martin. Lots of love.

Now, we begin.

* 1 *

Sharpen Your Tools

Methods are means to an end, and you control them by using things in your brain, like concepts, which are mental tools. You don't want hand-me-down tools that are rusty with neglect. Know what you are doing and be willing to defend it.

What Are Methods of Sociological Research?

What Is Research?

This is a book about how to do sociological research. And so I think it is appropriate to talk about what research is. It is, first and foremost, *work*. One does not do work for nothing. Why do it? Even if you think it is only done for self-centered reasons (e.g., to get an A in a class, to get an article published, to get a job, or to get tenure), that begs the question of why there is a system in which this work is required.

The answer is that social science is one of the types of knowledge that require work to be done right, often very hard work, over long stretches of time, often on the part of many different people. Methods are about the how of this work. That means that if you're not interested in methods, it's like being a violinist and not being interested in playing. This is what you do all day... if you're really doing something. And to get these methods to do something for us, we need to use them seriously, not ritualistically, and think them through.

How Do We Use Our Brains?

One of the things about our partition of sociology into theory, methods, and substance is that we forget that we can use our brains not just in the theory part but also in the methods part. In fact, the key argument of this book is that we need to "theorize" our own practice... not in the sense that most folks mean by "theorize," which is basically to toss a lot of fancy abstractions around hither and thither. I mean the opposite—we need to really have a scientifically defensible understanding of what we are doing before we give much credence to the results. If you were a contaminant ecologist attempting to see whether fish in some lake had too many toxins, you wouldn't just stop by a fish fry some folks are having and take a nibble, would you? So why do the equivalent as a sociologist?

In order to understand what our data—our experiences and interactions with the world—mean for us, we need to spend a fair amount of time understanding "where" in the world we are, and what we are really doing. We're going to be trying to think about both the planned and the unplanned aspects of research. Let's start with the planned parts. The most straightforward way that we use our brains in research is to construct a research *design*—a plan for future research that guides our data *collection* efforts so that we can compile our data usefully, and that guides our data *compilation* efforts so that we can bring our data to bear on the questions we're interested in. The key to research design is understanding which kinds of problems are most likely to be relevant to our proposed case of research and seeing if we can be clever enough to avoid a head-on collision with them.

A good research design can avoid many problems, but not all. Much of the difficult work comes in ways that our research design didn't anticipate or wasn't relevant for. For this reason, we will find that we need to think through—carefully, rigorously, and without mystification or wishful thinking—*all* the steps that go into making our claims (also see Latour 2005, 133), starting from the very first: "How did I get interested in this question? Where did I get the concepts I use to think about it?" And then on to: "How did I end up at this particular site? Why am I talking to these people and not those?" Or, "Why am I looking at these documents and not those?" And then on to things like: "When someone says, 'Yes, I approve of Obama's foreign policy' to me, what is going on? What did *I* say to provoke this? What was the setting in which this was embedded?" and so on. If you do this, you have a remarkably good chance of doing something worthy of being called social science.

In other words, the process of producing knowledge can be understood impressionistically as a meeting between your mind and some part of the world (perhaps a particular person at a particular place saying a particular thing). To understand what this interaction produces, to make it truly a *datum*, as opposed to a profound mystery, requires reconstructing, as best as we can, the nature of the meeting. Figure 1 gives a schematic rendition of this process. The rectangle you are in represents all the "places" (analogically speaking) you could have this interaction. The solid line represents your path, and the broken line that of the part of the world.

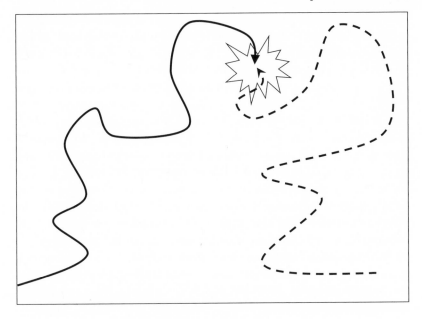

What is your path? Perhaps something very simple: you wanted to study young Americans' attitudes toward sexual preference—do they see it as genetic or not? Already, in a way, you have started moving down one path, merely by thinking of this question and not others, and in formulating the terms in which you are thinking about it (perhaps you are assuming that "biological" and "genetic" mean the same thing to people). But then you make other choices. First, you stayed in the city where your own school is, as opposed to going to one of the other twenty-five thousand towns and cities in the United States. Second, you got permission to pass out flyers in the lunchroom at two high schools, as opposed to the other two hundred schools in the area. And then you waited.

Some parts of the process happened behind the scenes, as far as you were concerned. Students got the flyers. Some immediately became paper airplanes. Others were the subject of guffaws in the cafeteria. Some were carefully folded and put in a back pocket, sometimes by a guffawer. Others were stuffed into textbooks. Some of those folded and stuffed flyers were only found months later. Some were found soon, and here and there, a student pondered whether to volunteer. More decided to volunteer than actually called you. Some called, but when you weren't there, they didn't leave a message; perhaps especially those without their own phones. Some made plans to meet with you but never showed. And when they did, you asked some particular questions (among others)—a few out of the near infinite number you could have asked. And only *then* did you get your (potential) information in response. This answer is only a datum when it can be placed, with great imprecision, of course, in this overall landscape of acts of choice and selection.

I will be emphasizing this selection and selectivity throughout. We often now may associate this issue with causal estimation. That's only one teeny part of selectivity. It's about the choices that we make, and those that others make. We can't control others' choices, but we can theorize them. And we can control our own. So make good choices. To do this, we need to pursue our investigations with symmetry, with impartiality (*sine ira et studio*, as Weber would say), and without bad behavior on our side. I'm going to be arguing that you need to really pursue this ideal, and not simply in some vague lip-service, recognize-it's-best-but-not-plausible-for-mere-mortals way, but as in, when someone draws your attention to a lapse here, you fix it. Sure, smart aleck reader, I also read the philosophy of science, and I admit that I can't *prove* to students that this is necessary, if you are going to do valid social research. But students have proven it to *me*.

To orient ourselves, let's back up, and see what we're doing with this whole "methods" thing.

Methods in General

There are some things that are—or should be—common to *all* sociological methods. First, sociological methods are, I believe, driven by a *question*. That might sound funny or obvious, but it's not; in fact, most sociologists seem to disagree with me here. But I think that things we do that *aren't* driven by a question aren't methods—they're not a means to an intellectual end. They're dressing, ritual, whatever.

Second, sociological methods involve a good faith attempt to find a *fair sample* of the universe at question. Not a "representative" one, but a *fair* one. A question has multiple places where it can be answered, and your answer may depend on which place you examine. For example, say you start with the question, "Does strong leadership increase or decrease members' attachment to the group?" You might get a different question if you looked at army platoons than if you looked at the history of the British monarchy.

There are two implications. The first is that if you have an answer you *want* to find, it isn't *fair* to choose a site that's likely to give you the answer you want. The second implication (which I'll discuss more in the next chapter) is that if it really seems like your answer completely depends on where you look, you don't yet have a proper question.

Third, sociological methods push us to be *systematic* in answering the question, allowing for disconfirmation of our hunches as opposed to selectively marshaling the evidence we want. In the most satisfying cases, we construct a "research design" like the mousetrap in that board game—a whole elaborate machinery is set up, then we pull the switch (by collecting our data), and see what happens.

It's rare for research to unfold so mechanically. And for that reason, sometimes we need to be "unsystematically systematic." That is, we have to figure out what's the sort of evidence that we *haven't* seen yet and that might lead to a different conclusion. (This is what Mitchell Duneier [2011] calls "inconvenience sampling.")

Fourth, sociological methods tend—if only for rhetorical reasons—to stress comparison and hence variation. It's hard to know if you're right or wrong in explaining something that doesn't vary—something that's always there. So some of the most interesting questions get ignored. Questions like "Why do people use language?" or "What causes patriarchy?" aren't ones we can do much with. Something that does vary, however, is amenable to explanation via comparison. I'm not actually so sure a focus on comparison is always a good idea, but it is a central aspect of sociological methods, so we would do well to understand it.

Those four traits are basic to most methods. Past these commonalities, we will find that different methods have different advantages depending on, most important, what the *process* is (or was) that is of interest to us. Is it social-psychological? Institutional? A historical development? Second, which method is most appropriate will turn on whether the effects of this process are... repeatable or not? Generalizable to all people or only to a group? Conscious or not conscious (can you get the information by asking or must you watch)?

Depending on what we think we're studying, we're going to take a different approach. And—silly though it sounds, I know—to know what we think we're studying, we're going to need to make a few provisional decisions about what we think is out there in the world.

Things and Concepts

What Is Real? What Can Act? What Is a Concept?

Theory is a funny thing. Among the tricks it can play on us is leading us to devote long periods of our lives to the examination of things that, in our saner moments, we would concede do not exist.

Do you want to argue about what "real" means and start a rumble over realism? I don't. All we need to do is to use the word "real" to denote the stuff we're absolutely committed to defending. That means something that probably has most of the following properties. First, we think it'll still be there if we come back tomorrow (it's "obdurate"—though we don't deny that some phenomena are transitory). Second, we think that other people will be able to see it too (it's "intersubjectively valid"—though we don't deny that sometimes you have to learn to notice certain phenomena). Third, you can study it via a number of different methods (it's "robust under triangulation"—though we recognize that sometimes we don't yet have ways of getting information on people's thoughts other than talking to them, and so on). Something that lacks one of these properties might still deserve our commitment. But something that lacks *all* of them—it comes and goes, not everybody can see it, and only some methods reveal it—that doesn't seem like the kind of thing we call "real," does it? It sounds more like a ghost.

Sometimes we end up chasing ghosts because we are enamored of a theory that makes strong claims about the world. The simplest way in which this messes with our heads comes from what is called "reification" or "the fallacy of misplaced concreteness." In our case, that means that we take a "theoretical" phrase or a concept—something that should really be a shorthand that helps us organize our thoughts about the world—and treat it as if it were a thing. Once it becomes a thing, it is easy for us to imagine that it can "do things" that we include in our explanation. For example, many sociologists are interested in capitalism as a mode of production rooted in the private appropriation of productive capital. Even if we assume that there is a utility to this theoretical construct (which I'll continue to use as an example below), it doesn't mean that capitalism is really a thing that exists somewhere.

There are times when it is going to help to decide, before you begin, what you think is real enough to make things happen. The reason is simple—that's the stuff you need to get data on. Once we've done *that*, we can begin to think methodologically. I'm going to start laying out the conventional understanding of sociological methods. I don't think that this understanding is defensible in *all* aspects, but it is important that you understand it, and appreciate its strengths and limitations, before we go much further.

What Is a Unit of Analysis?

Let me start by quickly going through some pretty conventional language that we'll need. Most folks will tell you that any sociological investigation involves a choice of the *unit of analysis* (UOA). These days, we frequently do comparisons across more than one *case* (or *instantiation*) of the unit of analysis.[1] We generally have a *question* about some sort of variation or

1. This isn't necessarily so; many early sociologists took "society" as the UOA, and they took there to be a single society of interest to them, nineteenth-century European society, within which they made no distinctions. I'm only going to focus on multiple UOA designs here.

differences among instantiations of our UOA. Here are examples: does labor unrest affect a *nation's* employment insurance policies? Do *cities* with higher levels of income inequality have higher rates of crime? Are religiously orthodox *individuals* more or less hostile to immigration?

Very frequently UOAs are nested, in that there are distinct levels of analysis. For example, nations are composed of states or provinces, which are composed of counties, which include towns. And sometimes it helps to see all of these as composed of individuals. Because of this, we frequently refer to the question of the choice of UOA as a choice of the "level" of analysis.

Obviously, the choice of UOA determines the research design. If you're going to compare UOAs, for example, you will miss everything if your choice is wrong. For example, imagine that income inequality *does* lead to increased crime at the level of the *nation* but *not* at the level of the city— say, because the processes have to do with cultural senses of fairness and opportunity and not material opportunism. You could come up with a null finding if you compare cities within the United States. Obvious, true, but still the sort of obvious thing that we overlook as we rush to "get started."

Finally, there may be theories or questions that we believe to hold at more than one UOA. For example, we may say that increasing income inequality leads to increased crime at *any* level of analysis: town, county, state, or nation, say. While there might be times when this makes sense, it's usually a worrisome signal that we're tossing words around somewhat randomly. Since it's unlikely that the *processes* involved at these different levels could be the same, it seems like we haven't gotten concrete enough yet to know what we should actually be studying. It isn't "theoretical" to be indifferent to the nature of your UOAs.

What Can Act?

This seems like an awful lot of time to spend on such simple terminology, but an ounce of methodological prevention is worth a pound of cure. I emphasized that we need to focus not only on what we are committed to treating as real, but also on what units can *make things happen*. This is important in thinking through the relation between our question, our method, and our units of analysis. What you mean by this "making things happen" is perhaps up to you. If you think in terms of action, you need to ask "what can act here?" If you're thinking in terms of external causality (some things causally affect others), you need to ask: "What is an effective cause here?" And if you think of cascades of linked events, you need to ask: "Which events are part of the chain I care about?"

This is a second part of the fundamental reality check, and even more important, because many of our theoretical shorthands involve attributing efficacy or causality to things that aren't real, or that are attributes of other things. As we get more concrete, we may realize that our UOAs aren't the entities that we consider to be responsible for making things happen.

In such cases, we frequently designate as "mechanisms" those entities or processes that lead to the differences in our UOAs. For example, we may be interested in why some countries have more militant labor movements than others. Thus the nation is our UOA. We may suspect that it is due to differences in how workers are *paid*. So we want to compare strike hours by payment types. Thus the *firm* becomes our unit of measurement; firms are (or were) nested in countries, in that there are many firms in one country. For each country, we examine the total strike hours (summed over firms) and relate this to the percentage of workers (aggregated over firms) who are paid hourly as opposed to by the piece. Now a firm is a pretty real thing, and the way workers are paid is indeed an *attribute* of the firm. But this attribute cannot itself produce strikes. Only something real can do that, not the attribute of a real thing. It seems silly to say that the firm itself creates the strikes.

So what can act in this scenario? Presumably only the workers at the firms. Note that they are neither our *unit of measurement* (UOM) nor our UOA, but they play a vital role in our investigation. Even though we can't demonstrate it, we need to think about *how* the workers make the relation appear on the level of the nation. Then we may realize that, for example, the firm-level configurations might be only *necessary* (but not sufficient) for strikes. Patterns that would otherwise be confusing or disheartening will make sense to us.

That was an easy example (it's also a real one, from a wonderful book by Richard Biernacki [1997]). But harder ones mess up many decent theoretical projects. For example, we argue that capitalism's need to dispose of surplus products led to the rise of modern advertising. But is capitalism a real thing? Even if it is, it's "need" is an *attribute* of capitalism, and an attribute cannot itself do anything. Does capitalism itself produce modern advertising? What could this mean? Shouldn't we first identify something that is capable of, say, setting up an advertising agency and pounding the pavement to get clients before we make this kind of argument?

At this stage, it's easy to despair and think that the solution is to ignore all theoretical terms and simply operate on the most obvious level possible. That's a mistake; methodological failures come as often from the obvious as from the imaginary. But now we need to turn around, and stop asking "what is real," and ask...

What Is a Concept?

There are some things that are enormously useful in sociological investigations even though they are not real. Some of these we will call concepts.

For our purposes, we can define a concept as a communicable mental heuristic that allows us to process commonalties and differences among real things. In simpler terms, it's something that we use in our heads to process our data—and something we can *share* with others. In sociology, we tend to rely on one type of concept, and a very straightforward type at that. This is the sort of general concept that is produced via *selective abstraction*. This means we select a few features of some existing thing or things, and we exaggerate these features or at least ignore all others. When we use the concept "table," we focus on an object's size, shape, and functionality—not what it is made out of. When we use the concept "wood," however, we are paying attention *only* to what it is made out of.

Now in some cases, we are able to give a formal definition for our concept: "a mammal is any vertebrate the female of which nurses its young via mammary glands." In other cases, we appear to have *prototypes* that we use to ground the concept, and we link various empirical cases to concepts according to the prototype to which they are closest. It's actually pretty hard to define what we mean by "tree"—it includes multitrunked woody-stem plants and some grasses (like the palm). But we know what's a good example of a tree and what's a bad one.

There's nothing intrinsically wrong with informal concepts like tree. Nor is there anything intrinsically wrong with folk concepts (like "depression"), nor with specialist ones that actors don't recognize (like "hegemony"). The problems come not when we construct concepts, but when we let them do heavy lifting that they aren't capable of. They can *organize* our data. But they can't, by themselves, explain it, and they certainly can't *do stuff* out there in the world. The "hegemony" of the ruling class, or a person's "depression," can't actually do anything, except, perhaps, help us organize our thoughts to answer our questions.

In sociology, we tend to ignore the difference between very abstract concepts like "hegemony" and seemingly more concrete ones like "depression." Whether that's a good thing or a bad thing, I don't know, but I want to give some attention to how we try to link these concepts to data, because, when you try to support a claim about concepts using data, your argument is never stronger than its weakest link.

Hypothetico-Deductionism

It's good not to flee from any encounter with the concrete—something like everyday people's everyday problems. Still, sociology is a science of generalization. It's going to involve putting concrete observations in some general conceptual structure. In sociology, we often understand a set of linkages between abstractions (or sometimes between more concrete terms) as a "model." The idea of a model is that it is a stripped down and simplified version of reality. So a model necessarily leaves a lot of stuff out, but that doesn't make it "wrong." If it "gets at" something (according to criteria to be determined later), then it's OK.

I think the reason this idea of models became so well loved is that it really works with the way in which we often teach methods, which is a philosophy of science idea called hypothetico-deductivism. According to this vision of science, there is a fundamental difference between theoretical terms and observational terms. We make a hypothesis that pertains to a relation between *theoretical* terms (e.g., "social dislocation leads to existential anxiety"). We then want to *test* whether this is true using data, but to do this, we need to *link* our theoretical terms to observational terms. In America, this last act is often called operationalization.

While this isn't necessarily the most air-tight theory of science, it has some advantages for sociologists when it comes to thinking through a research design. Most importantly, it should make us realize that just because we *claim* to be measuring something abstract, this doesn't mean we really are. The link needs to be defended. For example, imagine that you are interested in changes in the political climate of the United States. How can you measure this climate? Perhaps you decide to use newspaper articles. Does a newspaper really reflect the underlying political climate? It's possible, but it requires a bit more study before making this an assumption.

The hypothetico-deductive system has another advantage for research design. Since we aim to test a theory by the observable results, it tends to force us to think about the consequences of our theoretical claims. In this light, a claim that makes no difference isn't a very strong one. That doesn't mean that theories that don't have consequences that are observably different from their rivals might not have use. But it does mean that this isn't what *you* want to be doing, at least not now.

But there are disadvantages to hypothetico-deductivism, especially when it becomes ritualized. If others let us get away with piss-poor linkages ("we operationalized alienation by whether or not children had two or more unexcused absences"), we forget about what we are really doing. And in fact, sociology has often thought that just labeling one thing as another magically transubstantiated it. Don't bother me with reciting history of science. If most of your conclusions come from your labeling, forget it.

And this turns out to be a very common problem for us. This is in part because of our way of thinking about concepts. As I've emphasized elsewhere (2015), sociologists are strong believers in nominalism. That means we think that we need to define our terms, as opposed to discovering what they mean (which is how "realists" think). Thus, in a typical sociology paper we will start out: "In this paper, 'depression' will be defined as a persistent mood disorder the severity of which interferes...."

Yet (like most people) we tend to have mental images (prototypes) that affect our interpretation of our categories. The problem is that the way we define our terms can produce a group of observations that is very different from how we think about them. As Joel Best has said, when we think about the gun deaths of children, we're likely to envision something like two six-year-olds playing with Daddy's gun. But if we define "child" as "under eighteen," most of gun deaths are going to be young men who are seventeen years old, with the next most being sixteen-year-olds, then some fifteen-year-olds, and then fourteen, and so on (Best 2012).

For this reason, it's sometimes easy for us to work with a real dislocation between our theoretical vision on the one hand, and our actual measures on the other... and therefore, confusing our labeling of our data with the data themselves. I don't know if I can *prove* to you that this is avoidable. But I'm going to teach you how to avoid it, and the best way to do this is to spend some serious time thinking about measurement instead of "operationalization."

Variables and Measurement

Measurement

At least in my day, bringing up the notion of measurement was often interpreted by many sociologists to mean "stop listening now." Because we thought that talk about measurement certainly wasn't relevant to historical sociologists, ethnographers, interviewers, and so on, and even a quantitative sociologist who talked about measurement was some sort of atavistic mental caveman. It sounded like we were pretending to do some sort of white-lab-coat science that we weren't *really* doing. And we often confused *measures* with *numbers*. But most numbers in sociology don't come from measuring, they come from counting, and many of the measures that we do make aren't numbers at all.

So what is measurement? Measurement is when we interact with the world so that we come back with information. The information is usually about attributes of *units* that we are measuring. In sociology, these are often (not always) people (or people-at-some-particular-time). So the information has something to do with the people we are studying, but it also has to do with how we are reaching out to them. For this reason, research is the outcome of interactions, usually between researcher and research subject. These interactions take place in situations that have their own particular features, and in order to understand the measurements, we need to understand these particular features and what they imply about the process of interaction.

It helps to think of the people we are interacting with as presenting us with *profiles of potentialities for interaction*. We trigger these with our data collection efforts and record the results. That's all well and good, but that means we can't necessarily treat the resulting outcomes as if they were fixed *propensities for action*. That would mean ignoring what *we* did to trigger the response. It's a bit like smacking someone in the back of the head and then, when he turns around red-faced and shouts at you, recording on your chart "person A tends to shout." Even worse would be treating the results as qualities of individuals that they carry around with them all the time ("person A is an angry sort of person").

Does this mean that everything is relative? Sure, in a way, but relativity isn't opposed to objectivity. We want to be writing down that "person A yells when smacked," because this does tell us something about him. Person B might burst into tears and run away, person C turn around and throw a punch, and so on. Interactions produce objective information only when we don't ignore the nature of the interaction. It's a bit similar to a "scratch test" used in mineralogy. You can rank rocks in order of hardness by seeing if *this* one can leave a scratch mark on *that*. It wouldn't be any more objective if you tried to ignore which rock you were scratching with. In our case, this means that, without decent theories of interaction, we could never understand our results. Fortunately, when it comes to theories of interaction, we have some good ones. But as these are going to depend on the specific type of interaction, I'll introduce them as we go through different methods. Here, I'm going to stick with the most general issues having to do with measurement.

> **Measurements are relative to the situation that provoked them. That's precisely why they're objective.**

Units of Measurement

I have emphasized that we need to ask what attributes of our units of analysis (UOAs) are of interest to us. For one example, if our units are cities, we might be interested in their degree of economic inequality. We then must ask, are these attributes measureable at this level of analysis? In the example here, the answer is no. To get information about the degree of income inequality, we don't examine the city itself. We examine the people living in this city, get their individual income levels, and then construct a number that tells us the degree of inequality.

Thus we need also to think about a *unit of measurement* (UOM). These aren't always the same thing as our units of analysis. Very often, the relation between our UOAs and UOMs is one of "nesting"—a "one to many" (or "many to one") relation. That is, it may be that the UOMs are "below" the UOAs (in other words, there are many UOMs within any UOA), and we use the UOMs in aggregate form to construct something we consider to be an "attribute" of the UOA. I'd wager that this is the most common relation between UOMs and UOAs (outside of identity) for sociology, partly because, being sociologists, we're often interested in groups, classes, and other forms of aggregations. Indeed, Durkheim basically thought that sociology as a science would take off because of our capacity to compose averages based on measurements of individuals. We frequently refer to such constructions as measures, but in the interest of consistency, I'll assume than anything is only a measure "once," that is, only one unit can be measured for any attribute.[2]

But in other cases, the UOMs are "above" the UOAs (which is to say, there are many UOAs within any UOM). For example, John Markoff (1996) was interested in whether distance from Paris increased the likelihood of peasants' revolting. Our theoretical unit may be individual peasants, but their distance from Paris may only be computed as an attribute of the village they are in.

Finally, in still other cases, we find an imperfect nesting. For example, if we were interested in studying Americans who teach sociology, we could use the membership of the American Sociological Association, which has a high but partial overlap with our target. It's worth keeping this relation between UOMs and UOAs in mind *whenever* we are letting one thing "stand for another" in our research, especially when we are measuring something indirectly. Many of our problems start before we even get to the stage of analysis, and can be solved by thinking through these issues, and coming up with a research design.

Front-Loading versus Back-Loading

There are two types, or at least two poles, of approaches to research design. They define a continuum stretching from one pole to the other. On

---

2. Now technically, this relation of "nesting" also holds for where our UOA is the individual but our UOM is an individual-at-some-particular-time. We almost always ignore this complication or, if we're a bit cleverer, assume that the UOM is a random draw from a set that constitutes the UOA, but as we'll see in future chapters, this isn't always right.

one side, we have the "stitch-in-timers."[3] Here we have "front-loaded" our work. We have a clear research design. We give up flexibility and can move much more quickly. This can be *too* fast if the world suddenly throws up a curve in front of you.

At the other pole (I guess they are the "niners"), we have back-loaded our work. It takes almost no time for us to get right into our research. We just have to toss off some proposal to our teacher or to the Institutional Review Board (IRB), and one subway ride later, we're in the field. Waiting. Wandering. Hoping for something to strike. All the time we saved not having a clear research design comes back in a karma backlash now. So as you can see, it isn't that either polar solution is perfect. Chances are that you should push yourself more toward the first pole than the second, but if you've got your arms clenched tight around the first pole, maybe you need to pry yourself away a bit.

In general, students are best off with a design that has a combination of rigor and flexibility: rigor in constructing a data set—being very clear as to what is in and what is out, being up front about your coding and all that—but flexibility in terms of analyses—if you are guided by a *substantive* question, and not a fetishized methodology, you can change your tactics, rethink your design, in response to how the results evolve. You can develop ad hoc branches of your work to focus on deciding between particular interpretations before you resume your main investigations. This isn't what we generally teach in methods classes, but *this*, as the pragmatists insisted, is the *real* scientific method—not the "one-shot" hypothesis tests that we will teach you. Never feel guilty for working hard to learn from your data. That's what it's all about—answering questions we have about the world.

TAKEAWAYS

- You should be willing to defend your terms as either real or useful mental devices, and know which is which.
- You should have a sense of what terms refer to things that you think have sufficient mojo that they can drive what you're interested in. These things had better be the sort of thing you're willing to defend as real.
- Don't be afraid of thinking about measurement—if you don't have any, it isn't a good sign.

3. From the old adage, "a stitch in time saves nine." It means, I only figured out as an adult having to mend my clothes, that if you stitch up your clothes when they first start to come apart, you only need to do a single stitch. Put it off, and you have nine times as much work to do. It's not about a rip in the fabric of space-time, as I had always assumed.

If you were going to read more....

I think you'd do well to look at Arthur Stinchcombe's *Constructing Social Theories*. It's one particular view, but a clear one, and I think you'll learn more from a clear view you disagree with than a muddled one that sounds just right.

* 2 *

How to Formulate
a Question

*Ask a stupid question, and you will get a stupid answer. And a stupid paper or
dissertation. The best questions are real questions.*

....

Why Are There Questions?

What Is a Question?

All the arguments of this book are premised on an assumption, one that
I hold to be true, which is that sociological research succeeds, sometimes,
at answering questions we might have about the world. But we can't do
good research unless we ask good questions. So in this chapter, I want to
focus on how we can get started with good questions.

I am serious about this—a question is something you don't know the
answer to. It's fine to have a hunch, a guess, even a hypothesis. And it's
certainly fine to have a theory in the sense of an orienting set of views,
or a vocabulary, or whatever. But if you are unwilling to ask a question of
the world, and have the world tell you something you didn't expect, don't
waste your time, or ours, pretending to do research.

And questions, like other things, are what they are. In this case, they
are "interrogative utterances"—things we say that are used to get others
to respond informatively to us. And we say them in a particular language.
Questions accordingly may be classified by how they start. Thus there are
"What" questions—pure descriptions. In its earliest days, ethnography
considered such questions acceptable. What do the Nuer in the Sudan
do all day? There are also "How" questions—these are about processes.
Given that something has happened, or that one thing tends to cause another, how does it work? Then there are "Did" questions. So perhaps there
is some theory that says this or that should have happened. Well.... did
it? Finally, there are "Why" questions. Many sociologists think these are
the only kind that matter. I disagree, but it's fine if you want to focus on

Why questions. We'll look at types of Why questions more closely later. But what I think we all should agree on is that you can't answer something that isn't really a question.

What Are Not Questions?

Students often start with things that they claim are questions, but that really aren't. Sometimes the students know what they want to talk about, and they know what *words* they'd like to use to talk about it with. That isn't the worst thing in the world, and enlightenment can result from vocabulary. But that doesn't make it sociological research. Others have "a thing" that they want to do, and they think that having a "research project" is basically a license to "do their thing" all over this subject. It could be that their thing is to go around and criticize every other person who's ever lived for being a fascist. It could be that their thing is to show that whatever is, had to be that way, and is just. It could be that their thing is to blow your mind with how weird things were once or are somewhere else, or how weird things are here, or how *normal* things that *seem* to be weird really are.

So a very simple test to see if you really have a question is actually to try to *ask* it. Does it start with who, what, where, how, when, or why? When you say it out loud, does it come out with a raised pitch at the end? If not, you have a problem. Now there's nothing necessarily wrong with *also* having some big agenda, whether theoretical, personal, or political. So you can *want* to show that the increased burden of the twentieth regulatory environment for producers of consumer durables actually led to increased economic growth or that the increase in incarceration caused more crime than it averted. But the way you are going to do this is to do research, and this is work that answers a question. No question, no research; no research, no methods.

Some things pass this first test but don't turn out to be real research questions, because we can answer the question without doing *any* research. The reason for this is usually that the question is too open-ended. Often, we have a question of the form "How do things like *X* happen?..." and a minute's thought leads us to realize that the proper answer is always, "All sorts of ways." Time to respecify.

If you don't have a question, don't pretend that you do by trying to rephrase your statement as a question. This is not *Jeopardy*, where you learn to state your answer as a question.[1] I know what's coming next when a

1. OK, there is one exception to this. It might be that you know (say, from your previous life as a Navy SEAL) that such and such happens, but most people in sociology don't know this. And they'd think it was interesting and important if you convinced them of it. That means that if you're going to talk to others, there must be some for whom it still is an open question. It may not be a question to you, but it is to them. In that

student says his question is: "How should we understand *X*?" The answer is going to be that we should understand *X* using the ideas that he currently has. That isn't a question. It's a slap on.

Slapping a theory on your observations is sometimes referred to as "applying" a theory. A classic of this type of sociology is Kai Erikson's (1966) wonderful *Wayward Puritans*, in which he applied theories of the social construction of deviance to the witch trials in colonial Massachusetts. As he said, he could have chosen lots of different places and times for this demonstration; he just was interested in this one. Frankly, I'm not too sure where the glory is here. If you have a theory, and you're allowed to scour all human history for an example, surely you should be able to find at least one that fits. (Further, as John Goldthorpe [2007, 1:24, 1:26] in particular has emphasized, if a claim can be tested in the present, that's probably the best place to test it because, rather than rely on the relics that history has unpredictably handed down to us, we can create our own data.)

Anyway, Erikson used Salem witchcraft as opposed to (say) the communist scare to illustrate his idea that deviance is a collective construct, because *we* don't believe in witches. So it freaks us out to read about the witchcraft accusers and witchcraft suspects all agreeing on the fundamental outlines of the phenomena—and witches literally dying when, had they made a few statements that seem obvious to us, they could have gotten off. And so we realize that it may indeed be true that we are also engaged in collectively defined punishments that aren't necessary. But I suspect that Erikson wouldn't have used as an example of his theory the French resistance to the Nazis because he'd assume there was a real threat. Something's got to be wrong with that way of connecting research and theory, if the persuasiveness fundamentally depends on our nonsociological prejudices (defensible though these may be).

And so, as a PS, Erikson was probably wrong about Salem. At the time he did this work, it seemed like the right way to go, but his approach wasn't able to push him beyond his preconceptions to learn something different. "There is nothing like a theory," wrote George Meredith (1909, 99), "for blinding the wise."

How to Generate a Question

There are various patented fail-safe procedures for generating a question; like hiccup cures, they always work well enough for the recommender,

---

case, it's OK to pose a question and answer it. But don't fool yourself into thinking you "know" things that you don't. Sociology is mostly the science of checking things that other people are wrongly sure about.

and usually well enough for some, but not all, recipients. I'm not going to spend a lot of time giving you my advice, but I will say that if you come up with a question about some *x*, and you are basically in total ignorance of the state of the literature in the relevant field *X*, you are really stacking the odds against you. An ounce of prevention is worth a pound of cure.

And also, if you think you need to find a conceptual place where no one else has done any work, you're making a big mistake. Don't be afraid of sowing your seed where other people are growing things. There's often a reason why no one is off in that *other* area. It's fallow ground.

And conversely, going with the group can make a lot more sense than you might think. Students tend to be a bit overly concerned with professional stuff like getting a job or a good grade or whatever. I say "overly concerned" not because it isn't important (or because *I* already have a job) but because you can't really be directly concerned with such professional goals. These need to be the consequence of you doing the good research, so better to be concerned with *that*. But anyway, students worry about losing this race... while they often do everything in their power to ensure that they do.

> **Go with the group. This is a recipe for excellence, not mediocrity.**

Because to the extent that this *is* a race, it is a race in which you get to choose where to start. And what direction to face. If you position yourself toward the front—you know where the field is, where it is going, which questions are considered important, and which not—then you make it extremely likely that you can stay in that race. If you decide to start out in the woods, facing opposite everyone else, then run as fast as you might, the odds are definitely against you.

Don't get me wrong. I'm one of the people who started in the woods. I like the woods, and I like people who like the woods.[2] If you want to hang out in the woods with me, that's great, pull up a toadstool. But don't think you can have it both ways. If you want something from other people, you better be prepared to give them something in return.

---

2. I am not kidding. My dissertation opened with the epigraph I took from the notebooks of the great Dadaist Hugo Ball: "A task that everyone else shudders at, no one wants to take on, and no one thinks is possible, or even necessary—that could very well be a task for me" (Ball [1920–21] 1996, 84). I didn't complain when almost none of that work ever made it to the presses. (OK, maybe I did. I don't remember.)

How to Check Your Questions

I'm sure you'll agree with me when I say that the way you ask your question predisposes how you look for answers and hence what answers you find. But chances are, you've learned that this is inherent to social investigation; it has something to do with "all observations being theory laden" and other ideas that you can use to fuel your fatalism. I mean something very different and, I think, much more useful. I'm talking about a way that questions *can* shape your answers—but don't need to, if you are careful.

Here's a famous example used by military historians. In a typical battle, we have one winner and one loser (though sometimes there are two losers and no winners). Take the Battle of Waterloo in 1815, where the French armies under Napoleon were decisively defeated by the British under Wellington. Historians are very interested in explaining why it happened this way, and looking at the role of the respective commanders.

But the people who frame the question "Why did Napoleon lose the Battle of Waterloo?" tend to come up with answers having to do with the French army—the way Napoleon organized or commanded it. In contrast, the people who frame the question "Why did Wellington win the Battle of Waterloo?" tend to come up with answers having to do with the British army! Yet since Napoleon only lost because Wellington won, and vice versa, the answer to the question, "Why did Napoleon lose?" has got to be the same as the answer to the question "Why did Wellington win?" Yet if you ask someone the question, how you phrase it will affect what factors they think of (indeed, I've run little experiments on students and found just this!).

So what can you do? Well, the first thing is, if you have a question where you *can* reverse polarity, you *should*. That is, suppose you are wondering why members of group X choose/favor/believe/do A—for example, why right-wing conservatives oppose environmental protection laws. If there's some Y that approximates the opposite of X ($\sim X$), try asking why members of Y don't choose/favor/believe/do A—for example, why left-wing liberals don't oppose them. And if there's a B that's a credible $\sim A$, even better to ask both "Why do X choose A?" *and* "Why do Y choose B?" Because there's a really good chance that if your answer to "Why do Y choose B?" is that "it's just obviously good/right/smart" then you can be pretty sure that your answer to "Why do X choose A?" is—no matter how disguised—going to be of the form "they're bad/wrong/stupid." And as we'll see later, this indicates something missing in the way you're framing your question.

This isn't a fail-safe procedure. Not all groups have an antigroup, and even when they do, the processes that lead them to do what *they* do might turn out to be completely independent of those of their nemeses. But you might be surprised at how often this works. Social things are, lots of the time, … social. That means that they are "reciprocally defined and relational," and all that other stuff you learned in theory class. You pull one group of people out of that context to ask them a question, and chances are that question will be a bad one. This is so important that we'll come back to it in a few ways throughout the book. But now, let's get back to this issue of formulating a proper question.

Theories and Questions

What We Are Taught and Why Not to Do This

Many of us are taught to do sociology in the following way. Step one: think of theory. Step two: choose data in which theory can be tested. Step three: derive implications of theory. Step four: test implications in data. Step five: reject or don't reject theory. Thank God this isn't how science really works.

The problem with this, as I'll discuss in chapter 9, is that it doesn't really matter if the world agrees with your theory… so long as there are any other theories that it agrees with just as well. And if there aren't any other theories that the world agrees with, so what if the world agrees with your theories? It could be dumb luck. You want to learn about the world, not test your own stupid theories. Further, the theory-testing logic is strong only when we *reject* theories. But failing to reject your own theory doesn't prove it's right, and you can always fail to reject a theory by doing a crappy job. So theory testing is just not something you should do with your own theories.

The only time straightforward theory testing makes sense is when there's a theory that is very strong in its implications and that's widely believed, and you think it's wrong. Because if theory *A* says "people always do this," then can you disprove it by showing that one time people don't. But as a rule, don't test theories you don't want to disprove. Adjudicating between theories—showing one beats out the other—is something different, but it's a rare day that you can really do this (as opposed to just pretending you did). Theories are like zombies. You have to get them just right to kill 'em dead. Otherwise, they come right on back.

Let Me Construct a Theoretical Framework

So there's nothing so wonderful about making a new theory. We're trying to *kill* them, not make new ones. But the worst thing about making and testing your own theory comes from the making, not the testing, part.

Thinking that you should start by testing your theory can encourage you to spend your time constructing a theoretical framework. But if you devote a fair amount of time to developing your own theory *before* you test it, you've invested a lot in it. You *want* it to be true. There's nothing wrong with scientific investment, and it's certainly unavoidable, but we want that investment to be in things that have gotten a bit more off the ground. We don't want to fall in love with a horse we've never seen run. And I've seen smart people who are so afraid of learning that their elaborately constructed theoretical framework is wrong or useless that they won't let themselves do good work.

Sometimes students will convince themselves that even if they haven't proven or even supported their theory, they should get points for just having developed one in the first place. Like you're doing the rest of us some sort of favor, in that now we have yet another wild idea to test. Nuh-uh. We've each got our own ideas. To steal a line from my colleague Ross Stolzenberg, the supply of novel ideas definitely exceeds the demand. Making theories is a bad business plan.

> **Theories are like poop. There's no shame in making some, but no one wants anyone else's.**

Establishing the Phenomenon

Let's say that you realize that you shouldn't be burning the midnight oil working on your theory. But you aren't out of the woods yet—theory can creep into your question in all sorts of nefarious ways. And what I mean by this is that even as you try to formulate a question, you turn out to have unfounded assumptions. Sometimes what you are assuming is almost definitionally true given our way of talking, and so there's really no research needed. For example, the question "I want to study how inequality is reproduced through X" can justify pretty much any trivial work. Because there will be inequality at the beginning, inequality at the end, and we can always put our thing in the middle. So you can take any old observations, and do a plausible job at stringing together this sort of story.

More generally, we should be somewhat suspicious of "how" questions. I like the idea of really trying to get a good idea of what's going on, and it seems that this often involves asking, "But *how* does X cause Y?" But then again... if no one knows how something happens, it's often a bit too much to insist that we still do know that it *does* happen. For example, you might ask, "How does the elite shape public opinion?" Some people may believe that it does, but it is unreasonable to assume that everyone must accept that this is a necessary fact. Robert Merton (1987) also made this point, which he called "establishing the phenomenon": first establish that it *is* the case; *then* explain it.

There are other ways in which our concepts can build in unjustified assumptions. For example, you may ask, "What causes racial intolerance?" Presumably you mean some form of hostility to members of different groups; the problem is that you've already assumed that you know that this hostility is a form of *intolerance*. You might be right and you might be wrong, but if you are wrong (say, much of racial hostility is simple selfishness), you may never know it. You're combining two questions in one, in a way. The point isn't that you should never use such concepts, but that you should test them first.

Of course, this is a bit a matter of dispute. As you can readily see, what gets considered a theoretical statement ("racial hostility is caused by intolerance") as opposed to a well-known fact or even obvious linkage ("years of schooling measures how much knowledge one has about school subjects") largely comes down to the number of people who believe it. Largely, but not totally. There was a time when pretty much all social sciences assumed that racial hostility was caused by intolerance, but you know what? They were probably wrong, and eventually, they were able to figure it out. To conclude, there are two criteria that a linkage should have to satisfy for you to treat it as nonproblematic. One is that *you* think it's common sense, and the other is that everybody else does too. That's what common sense is.

So now I'm going to assume that you are on the track of asking some sort of question that might have an answer. There's a good chance that it might be a "why" question. And it turns out that a lot of our ideas here need some adjusting.

"Why" Questions?

Reasons and Causes

There are two linked explanatory strategies to answering such "why" questions in social research, which I'm going to call *causal* explanation and *motivational* explanation.[3] This theoretical distinction well expresses a fork

---

3. We might also call them third-person versus first-person explanations or, following Robert Merton (1968), latent versus manifest functions or, following Jürgen Habermas (1987), system versus lifeworld approaches.

in the road for our explanations, one basically hardwired into our way of thinking. I'm going to give quick examples, and then look at the two in more detail. In a causal explanation, we tend to begin with a general relation between "variables," either attributes of persons or of social aggregates. For example, according to Durkheim ([1897] 1951), an increase in social mobility can lead to an increase in suicide rates. In a motivational explanation, we focus on individuals' reasons for their actions as an explanation. For example, some people argue that the rise of the temperance movement was actually motivated by an attempt to protect the Protestant establishment against Catholic immigrants. Sometimes the two strategies are linked—and in fact, I'll argue that the better your work, the harder it is to separate these. But as we start out, when we formulate a research design, we often make a strong distinction.

Now by "motivations," we generally mean some state of an actor's mind that preexists some act and is responsible for the occurrence of the act. We also generally assume that these motivations are accessible to someone's consciousness, even if they weren't originally conscious. So when we are interested in motivational accounts, we very frequently want to ask actors about their action, and why they did what they did. As we'll see as we go further, there are actually very good reasons to doubt the assumptions of this theory of motivation, even though it seems so commonsensical. But we're going to put that off until chapter 4, "Talking to People." For now, we'll just take for granted that we think there is a reason to believe that there are such things as motivations and that they can be used to explain social phenomena, especially social actions.

Here's the thing—you might imagine that if we are interested in motivations, we're going to tend toward methodologies that are better at uncovering subjectivity, such as in-depth interviewing, while if we are interested in causes, we're going to be more interested in techniques that gather objective data, like demography, or that focus on macro properties, like historical sociology. This is precisely 0 percent true. There is *no* relation between methods and this division. Sometimes the only way to get at causal variables is by people who have experienced them telling you about them. Sometimes the only way to get at motivations is through comparing aggregate statistics in one place to those at another.

Further, as I hinted above, it usually turns out that the better our research, the closer these two perspectives—causes and motivations—converge, to the point where it seems a toss-up which we use to describe our claim. And the reason is that the better the research, the more concrete the answer. You can start with a cool theory of one abstract variable causing another, such as "lack of regulation" causing "anomia" (a sense of normlessness), as did Durkheimians. But to go beyond something like a *number* that you are hoping can be a sign of this relation, and to really nail it down, you need to make this much more concrete. And Durkheim himself tried to, though mostly by painting a psychological portrait of what it felt like to be a person lacking enough regulation. If he had had better data, and could make this more concrete, it would have been better research. And as the description of the interiority of the actors got richer, these social "causes" would seem to dissipate into actors' motives.

> **Start with an abstract cause? See if you can make it more concrete. Start with a way of seeing or wanting? See if you can situate it.**

At the same time, if we started with motives, and really tried to situate them, we'd find ourselves reaching further and further outside the heads of the actors. So when Paul Willis (1981) wondered about the motives that led some working-class kids to act in school in such a way that they had no chance of upward mobility, he realized that you couldn't just describe their "motivations" as if they were disconnected from the real world. Their motivations were a *response* to that world, and from a particular position in that world. To understand the motivations, one had to understand all this other stuff. This is one of the reasons why (as we'll see in chapter 6) ethnographers often seem to "side" with their subjects. Many of the things that strike a naive observer as a weird choice that some group members make turns out to be pretty obvious and straightforward once you know more about the world they find themselves in.

I really want to emphasize that this isn't some theoretical perspective that I am laying on you, some doctrine that these are inherently two sides of the same coin. I'm saying that as an empirical regularity I find that better research nearly always pushes in this direction. So, if you start with an abstract causal model, "tell the story." That is, tell a concrete story, maybe about some pretend people, by which your theoretical pattern actually happens. If you get stuck, where you can't translate some abstract theoretical term into something that makes sense in terms of a "first this, then that" world, there's probably a problem somewhere. You may be right, but you will have a hard time demonstrating that you're right. That means you want a research design that doesn't prevent you from getting this more concrete information if you can.

If you start with a motivational account, don't let it be one that never gets on the other side of your actors' eyeballs. Make sure that you understand the situation(s) that they are in, and how these might be different from other people's situations. That means you want a research design that doesn't prevent you from noticing things about the situation if you can. Of course, no design can do everything. But it's easy to build in unnecessary assumptions that hold us back.

Why This and Not That

Like many sociologists, I'll fuse these "comparison questions" with one type of "why" question. The reason for this fusion is that "why" questions usually work better for us if we can put them in the form of "why do we see *X* and not *Y*?" Like: "Why was there a revolution in this country but not in that country?"

But it's very important to make sure that we haven't proposed an implausible joining of "this" and "that" as alternative realizations of a category that doesn't really make sense to anyone *but* us. Let's imagine that, for some very stupid reason, I was interested in the theoretical construct of "tented interaction," where many people gather under a tent. I could then ask, "Why do some of these turn into circuses, and others turn into religious revivals?" I think people would reasonably reply: "You've just called these the same thing, but they're different, and so there's nothing to explain." This objection logically can apply to the countries-and-revolutions issue in many cases. That is, our cases are too different for the framework to make sense. Just because we call them all "revolutions" doesn't mean they're of a single kind.

Thus, before we compare to find differences, we need to make sure that our units are, in the minds of most people, sufficiently similar that they can be seen as comparable. Otherwise the exercise is all futile. But even with comparable cases, we can ask bad questions.

What Strategy Is Best?

Two persons working differently come out with the same effect;
and of two persons working identically, one is led to his end, the other not.

MACHIAVELLI, *The Prince*

Very often, we get inspired to do a "why this and not that" question where we think we have the most natural, and most useful, outcome of all, namely, success. Given two organizations, two movements, two sides, we ask: "Why did *X* succeed while *Y* failed?" Interestingly, it turns out that this is often one of the cases in which we *shouldn't* try to force our explanation into the simple comparative form.

Let me use the case of comparative studies that try to explain organizational success. The studies (not surprisingly) find that one organization does one thing, and it leads to success, while another does something different, and meets with failure. Our assumption is that the first organization hit on the right recipe, with the implicit "counterfactual" assumption, namely, that the second would have enjoyed equal success with the same tactics.[4] Although this sort of idea is the basis for the fads that they teach in business schools, practical businesspersons often doubt that there are recipes. I suspect they're right. I want to suggest three reasons why a good counterfactual doesn't always demonstrate that we have produced a recipe.

The first is the simplest one, specifically, that in a world with a lot of chance, sometimes things work and sometimes they don't. Just because it worked here, doesn't mean it *had* to work. Some phenomena seem to be very sensitive to the surrounding conditions: for example, an innovation that works in one context doesn't take hold in another. A military strategy that worked against one enemy doesn't work against another. When we are talking about multiplayer games, there isn't necessarily any optimal strategy, as it depends on what the other fellow is going to do. And the sorts of social processes that are most associated in our minds with "failure" and "success" tend to fall into that category.

The second reason that these sorts of comparisons aren't so promising for isolating the recipe for success is that there are many cases where some path *can't* work for everyone. There's no strategy that could win for both Wellington and Napoleon. But the third, and most subtle, problem is that sometimes some strategies just aren't available for everyone. The single best rule of war was given by military theorist Carl von Clausewitz, who said, "Always be *very strong*." The funny thing about this for us is that, of course, we already know that. It's like saying "the best tactic is to win." But if we didn't know anything about military history, we might think that you're saying something smart when you said "the best tactic is to ruthlessly and speedily overwhelm the enemy and destroy his forces." Adolf Hitler said that kind of thing to his generals and thought he was a great tactician. He was extremely frustrated with his incompetent generals for not doing in Russia what he had, in Poland, demonstrated was *the* successful tactic! (That is, "to ruthlessly and speedily overwhelm the enemy and destroy his forces.") It worked great against Poland, very poorly against Russia. That's because you *can't* speedily overwhelm the Russian forces. But in some organizational studies, we basically forget this and imagine

---

4. This is called a counterfactual because it is counter to the fact. In the real world, our second organization didn't use strategy S, and failed; in the world that didn't happen, we predict, if it *had* used S (which it didn't), it would have succeeded (which it didn't).

that losers could take on winner's tactics. The reason the German offensive against Russia failed, we conclude, is that the Germans did not use the proper tactics, to ruthlessly and speedily overwhelm the enemy and destroy his forces. The analogue is that there are tactics that, for whatever reason, aren't plausibly available to certain players. Before we even come onto the analytic scene, things are already different.

> **Secret Tip: Don't be like Adolf Hitler. Tasteless, I know, but you won't forget this now.**

So the challenges are in some ways not only to reconstruct the differences between actors but also to contextualize them in terms of the situation faced by these actors. Because, very often, the thing that we think explains the success is itself caused by the success, or is a sign of the success-to-be. Our Monday morning quarterbacks say things like, "If you only did the eighty-yard pass, you would have won! If only *I* was the coach instead of that idiot!" There's often a reason people didn't take the option that seems like it leads to success. They're not all as dumb as they seem to a hasty analyst. If you ask one of these "success" questions, chances are good that what you'll find, at the end of the day, is simply... nothing succeeds like success. Right.

A last type of nonstarter question here—and I'll explain why this is a problem in more detail in our chapter on experiments—is to ask, "Does *x* cause *y*," when we know that *x* can, *sometimes*, cause *y*. So we can look around and find a case where it does. But that's doesn't mean it's the most important, most interesting, or most manipulable cause. I'd say, if you are even asking whether *x* causes *y*, take for granted that it does, sometimes, somewhere. Otherwise you'd be pretty stupid to be even thinking about it. So the null hypothesis is rejected. Not worth testing further.

Ideas and Asymmetries

Symmetry

Now as we start to move to comparative questions, I think it's vital that we ask them in a way that has as much symmetry as possible. In fact, I think—following Bruno Latour and his crew—that this is really a central principle of scientific sociology, equal to those of systematicity and fair sampling.

This principle is expressed in a number of ways. First, we generally want to make our research design one that will basically be as good at giving us a "positive" answer as it is a "negative" one. Of course, sometimes we want to be conservative, which means being asymmetric against our claim. You may be able to find a philosophy of science that denies that this is true— but I can also tell you from experience that other people become more interested in your finding when it comes from a conservative design.

And this has implications for your questions because it means that the best ones are those in which no matter what you find, your finding is interesting and important. You flip a coin, and either way, you win. This isn't valuable because you get an A+ or a publication; it's good for two other reasons. First, it means that you are going to be less tempted to put your thumb on the scales to have the evidence come out the way you want. Second, it generally means that you are oriented to something that people actually care about. You can, of course, instead make a cool, huge, weird theory all of your own, and if you find evidence for that, well, I suppose that's interesting. But if you find that the evidence *doesn't* support your pet theory, no one is particularly interested. Who really expected it would turn out to be true anyway? Important questions are those where people really want to know the answer, either way.

The U.S. Army sponsored some very strange research in which people who believed in ESP were given grants to try to push ESP powers further. The results (probably still highly classified) were very negative.[5] The army was delighted. "At least we don't have to worry about the Russians blowing up our heads by concentrating psychic powers." Either way, it seemed important to know.

Some questions in sociology are like that. Are people getting more or less religious? It's a good question. Of course, it depends on who you are talking about, and what aspects of religion you're talking about. But they're *all* important. So if your question has a real symmetry to it, in that both answers are interesting, that's a good sign.

But the principle of symmetry goes further and has implications for *how* we ask questions, and not just *which* questions we ask. In particular, the principle of symmetry can often prevent problematic questions when students are interested in analyzing *beliefs*. And since this is such a common form of question, I'm going to give it some detailed attention.

What Causes Ideas

Here we examine a family of related, and intrinsically flawed, questions that we often start with, usually of the form "Why do people X believe Y?"

5. My source here is a vague memory of an interview with Jack Sarfatti published in some street zine many years ago, unarchived and lost to history except via this memory.

This sort of question usually doesn't turn out so well, and that's because it relies on a folk theory that we have about cognition coupled with our own somewhat incoherent professional understanding of explanation. To really make this point would take a whole book, but luckily, I've already written it (*The Explanation of Social Action*). Here's the short version.

Our folk theory (A) is this: we have values and interests, things we care about, and when we encounter some particular issues, we need to translate our values into a stance. Wheels turn and grind in our head, and then a little something pops out of us like a lottery ball—a vote, an action, an opinion, an idea. Our disciplinary idea (B) is this: we explain things, even ideas, using a template of causality (though suitably smudged), whereby one thing affects another. Both A and B are wrong, but the worst results come when we put them together, switching back and forth asymmetrically.[6]

Why? Because according to A, in everyday life, to ask some people to explain their position on some issue is to ask them to justify it—to link it to overarching commitments that we all accept. But in sociology, if we set out to explain a subject's position on some issue using B, we are going to look at all the previous states of that person and seek out those that best predict his taking whatever position he has. As a result, what we tend to do is mash A and B together and produce some results that seem reasonable to us but almost certainly aren't true. That is, we imagine that people's ideas or commitments are *caused* by the justifications to which they appeal. Or we do, at any rate, if we *like* them.[7] Otherwise, we explain their beliefs differently. We're using what we can call the *Flipper* lemma (see box).

Flipper Rule 2: The *other* guy is the dipshit.

So the asymmetry comes in the idea that *their* beliefs need to be explained, because they don't really follow and aren't consistent... while *our* beliefs don't, because they aren't inconsistent... well, OK, maybe this *looks* inconsistent, but I can explain that... but, anyway, we don't want the *other* folks to explain away the inconsistencies in *their* beliefs, because when we ask, "Why do you believe this," we don't want their justifications. We want a causal explanation. We'll talk about this in chapter 9 (on inter-

---

6. Arnold Schopenhauer's ([1847] 1974) first claim to fame was hammering home this difference and refusing to allow anyone again to confuse the *ground* of an idea with its *cause*.

7. Here again I point you to Charles Kurzman's (1991) wonderful work.

pretation), because even if you get the idea that you shouldn't *set out* to compare "smart beliefs" to "stupid beliefs," you might find yourself doing exactly that. For now, we're going to return to the issue of asymmetry in our questions.

Constructing Constructions

Here I want to briefly open that can of worms that is often loosely called "construction" or "social construction." I'm actually on the side of those who think that this "construction" is, in most cases, the right way to go—the more scientific one—namely, to be always willing to unpack the concepts that people and analysts are using. It can be done well, and done seriously, but is often done poorly, and foolishly. And that happens when it is done asymmetrically. (This is a point that has been emphasized by one of the most farsighted people in this camp, Bruno Latour [2004].) It's basically a form of the division of ideas into good (i.e., mine) and bad (i.e., yours).

If we are trying to explain why some people were mobilized in an anti-crime campaign, and we said, "They were upset at the dramatic increase in crime in their neighborhood," a good sociologist will stop us right there. "Really? Are we sure there *was* an increase? How did they learn about this? Where did these ideas come from?" Just because people thought there was an increase in crime, and acted accordingly, doesn't mean there really was. Instead, there may have been a change in how, say, media outlets are reporting: what stories they follow, where they place them in the paper or broadcast, and so on.

Now here's the thing. Even if it turns out that there *was* an increase in crime, if you want to be technically correct, you could still say, "It wasn't that the increase in crime motivated the actions, it was their *belief* in the increase in crime." That's pretty much always going to be true for people. So you can always change X to "people's belief in X." If you want to do that, however, you need to do it everywhere—that is, in all cases, focus on the beliefs and where they came from. Otherwise you can get away with implying that some people are wrong and others right, just by asymmetrically using the language of construction whenever you wanted to imply (without really demonstrating) that these beliefs are wrong. Because our beliefs are transparent when they are correct, drawing attention to them *as beliefs* implies that they aren't.

Yet sociologists often use this language of construction when they are too lazy to find out the real story. So they'll say that something like "the media constructed X as Y"... which tends to imply that X wasn't *really* Y, but they'll then counterpose this to other statements, which aren't tarred by the casual brush of social constructionism. Clearly, that's not cool, and it's not good science.

How can you avoid this? First, retain symmetry. Don't imply that *some* things you heard (especially those that those *other* dipshits believe) are constructed, while you don't turn that skepticism on the other side as well. Second, if it matters whether or not the beliefs are valid, you're going to need to put in the legwork into tracking down what happened. Don't just assume that because the other guy actually *is* a dipshit, he can't be saying something true, something inconvenient for your point.

Final Problems with Questions

Broad Questions

If we come up with a bad question, sometimes we don't know it until we start trying to select our case for investigation (which we turn to in chapter 3). Because one way that we sometimes realize that we have a poorly formulated question is that we can't find a good site. It isn't that our question is too narrow, and we're wondering, "Where am I going to find acrobats with physics PhDs in the military, anyway?" On the contrary, it's that our question is too broad. When a question has a large set of answers, possibly a near-infinite one, all of which are different but equally valid, that's a good indication that we don't have a real question. So for an analogue, consider the question: "How do living things gather the energy they need for metabolic functions, and what do they do with it?" That doesn't guide a research project, it defines a science.

Now it isn't unusual for us to begin with a question that is too broad. It's no problem if you can limit your question as you interact with others, either by reading work done in this area, or by clarifying your thoughts through dialogue. But you don't want to try to narrow it down simply by jumping into a site where you believe you're likely to see a lot of whatever you're interested in, and let your observations shape your thinking and help you formulate a clearer question.

This last tactic can lead you to limit your thinking in ways that you won't understand—because you lack the comparison to know what you're *not* seeing. Imagine that you *were* wondering how living things gather the energy they need for metabolic functions. And so you think to yourself, "Hmm... gather energy... that's basically eating. What eats a lot? Probably a whale! So I should study whales!" And then you come back and say that "things gather energy by straining krill through baleen." You can have a nice debate with the other graduate student who studied great white sharks, which also eat a lot. She, of course, rejects your theory, saying that, actually, living things rip up flesh in big mouthfuls. Perhaps you can settle this only when you have a random sample of all the things in the sea and add proper controls.

Of course, I'm being silly. But it's worth really pondering—if there is a range of cases that are appropriate to your question, is there any reason to think that we can learn *anything* from one particular site? If so, where is that site? Can we get to it? If the answer isn't yes to all of these, maybe you need to rethink your question. We'll return to the issue of how to deal with site-dependent questions in chapter 3, as we think through sampling and choice of a site. But you can avoid some of the problems in selecting a site if you select a proper question.

Holding Too Many Cards

The last thing I'll say about getting started is this: think of playing gin rummy. You have 9♠, 10♣, J♣, 2♦, 2♥, 4♦, and 6♠. You've got some good cards, some potential, but you're going to have to put something down if you're going to come up with a winning combination. Any of your fledgling patterns *can* work out... but they can't *all* work out.

So, too, I see students who have a theoretical question they are interested in. And a site they are interested in. And a method they want to use. But often, they don't all go together. One simply can't use *that* method to answer *that* question at *this* site. Even further, often students have a question that mixes their interest in a particular causal factor and a particular outcome. They really, really want to have the answer to "What is the cause of Y?" be "X," and so they have a research design that can't find the cause of Y unless it's X. Chances are, they're not going to be that lucky. They're going to need to put some cards down and pick some new ones up.

Now if you think, "But I *can't* separate my theory and my method," then this is either very good news or very bad news. The good news is that you're working in a subfield that is one of the few areas that is really working according to a true scientific logic, in which a strong and well-accepted theory is guiding further explorations in a cumulative fashion. The bad news is that you're clearly not in sociology, and so you wasted your money on the wrong kind of book. Am I joking? I'm not sure. I'd have a very hard time making a case for any such subfields in sociology except probably conversation analysis, and I really doubt you're in one.

So this point has another implication—you want to avoid what I'll call "unit construction" in your question. In the old days, your motorcycle had an engine, a primary chain, and a gearbox. Three separate things, three separate kinds of oil to check, and so on. Now they are almost all unit construction—one closed case. Something goes wrong with one part, the whole thing has to come out. I admit that when it works, there's a lot to be preferred here. But when it doesn't, it's nice to have the separability. You need to work on coming up with results that will be understood as significant by those who *don't* share your theoretical orientation. Indeed, you and your nemesis should basically agree as to the value that your findings (would) have (though your nemesis can say you did it all wrong and so you don't have these findings). If you haven't yet figured out how to break up your unit, don't go any further until you do. My bet is, you don't have a real question yet.

TAKEAWAYS

- Don't pretend you are asking a question if you aren't willing to learn something new.
- You should have a question that doesn't have an answer built in.
- Any theory of science that encourages you to privilege the way you want to label your observations or think about things is not your friend.

> ### If you were going to read more...
> You'll see I refer to Bruno Latour a lot. Some of his writing is a tad self-indulgent, I know, but if you are serious about wanting to be a social scientist, this is where you start.

* 3 *
How Do You Choose a Site?

Rule: The problem of sampling on the dependent variable is bigger and deeper than you think, and this remains true even when you take this rule into account.[1]

Idea of Sampling

OK, so you have your question and a basic research design, which probably involves some sort of comparison. But you need a place to start. You need to choose a site (or set of sites). Within this site(s), you may well do additional sampling, and we'll get to that later in the chapter. But the choice of site also involves some sampling issues. So I'm going to start by introducing issues of sampling here, and then consider some common problems in choice of site.

Now, at least when I was in graduate school, lots of us thought sampling talk was for squares. Strictly for the survey research types. If you were going to be an ethnographer, a historical sociologist, or whatever, you didn't have to use this logic.

Dead wrong. This is the core of sociology. Listen up. It could save your life.

Why Sample?

Just like a theory usually has many implications, so a question usually has many ways in which it can be answered, and in particular, there are many places where it could be answered—whether by "place" we mean a physical setting or a particular data set. You're always going to be choosing a subset of all the things you *could* study. Sampling is about having this be scientifically defensible. Sampling is indeed about inference, but it isn't necessarily inference the way sociologists normally discuss this—making inferences to, say, the U.S. population.

1. Yes, I stole this from someone else, but I don't remember who.

Let me review the conventional language used in sociology. The *universe* is the set of instances to which you'd like to be able to generalize or infer. Classic example: all American adults. But it's hard to figure out how to sample from the universe, so we construct a somewhat narrower *population* that we know how to approach. For example, we could use all telephone numbers. Or all noninstitutionalized civilians between nineteen and sixty-five dwelling in the United States on January 1, 2014. We pick some of the members of the population, and this is our *sample*.

But guess what? Even if you want to study just a single person, you probably really want to talk about this person as a whole—your universe is all his acts and thoughts, say. But usually, you can't show up at 11:30 P.M. So your population might be this person's actions and statements at work, weekdays, 9 A.M.—5 P.M. From here, you might sample—drop by at certain times and spy out on what he's doing. If you suspect that you shouldn't infer what he will say or do at 11:30 Friday night from what he says or does at 9:30 A.M. Tuesday, you're starting to think through your logic of sampling.

Sampling and Sites

You will need to be choosing a site (or sites) and people (or documents, or what have you) within your sites, and the same principles here hold for both. It isn't the case that any site is as good as another. What is key is to search for a *fair* site, not a "representative" one.

Most of us understand that no single site, or pair of sites, is likely to be representative (though, for the United States, Muncie, Indiana, turns out to be as close as you can get). For this reason, some single-site workers (like ethnographers) cringingly confess that they are unable to generalize at all. Poppycock! To take a wonderful metaphor from Matthew Desmond (2014, 573; also see Orne and Bell 2015, 59), "Just as the mechanic who cut his teeth under the hood of a 1967 Mustang will not know everything about the inner workings of a 2007 Volvo sedan but will know something about it, owing to generalities of automechanics, so too will the ethnographer who studies eviction in Milwaukee, deforestation in the Amazon, or immigration along the Texas-Mexico border be able to generate findings about each of these dynamic processes that are simultaneously informed by and transcendent of the particular locales in which they were discovered." Damn straight.

Not convinced? Let's say that we're interested in the effects of income on political beliefs. We've been studying the Midwest, say. We've been finding that richer people are more conservative. Then someone says that our work stinks, because the Midwest isn't representative. He's got a national sample, and his numbers are different from ours.... in his, we don't see that relation at all! There isn't actually an effect. We are *wrong*.

Actually, *he* is wrong. Why? Think of it this way. Either there is meaningful difference within some unit (say, the nation), or there isn't. First, imagine that there isn't. Every place, every subset, will give the same results. Then certainly there isn't anything wrong with any particular site.

So let's imagine that there *is* heterogeneity—the relation is one way in some subsets of the population (e.g., regions, religious groups, ethnicities), and the opposite in other subsets. In our case, there is heterogeneity by region. But that means that when we find a relation in the Midwest, we are right... if only for the Midwest. Of course, it's true that we don't have a representative sample. But if there is heterogeneity, why would you *want* one?

Well, you might if you were interested in predicting an outcome, say— even if you had no idea why the data were one way as opposed to another. But that's rarely what drives sociological interest. We want to have some understanding of the dynamics involved. That requires exploring the heterogeneity, not averaging it away.

There's another reason, not quite as easy to defend but certainly not silly, why you might want a representative sample in the face of "heterogeneity." And that's when even though there's some difference across subsets, there's not that much. So the relation between income and political beliefs tends to be one way pretty much most places, but a few places are different. So we can dock our overall relationship a few points because of the unusual places and still describe the "mostly" of the phenomenon.

But if that's true, then chances are good that your site is pretty close to the average... so long as you've picked a fair site. If you decided that you were interested in Hollywood actors, for example, you might find a different relation between income and party, but people would be scratching their heads, and thinking, don't we all know lots of Hollywood actors who are rich but very liberal? That seems like you're choosing an *unfair* place for your investigation.

Our challenger suddenly perks up. "I know why it's important to have representative data! Because only with them, can we *test* whether there is any heterogeneity! No matter what, I can model the differences with my representative data, and so I win!" But there are a near infinite number of different groups within which there might be heterogeneity. He can't test them all. Not, that is, unless he knows in advance where to look. And he might—if other people like you have carried out just the sorts of studies that we were talking about, the value of which he didn't see at first. Now he does.

In sum, we definitely want to be able to make claims that are transposable across site and across research design. That's what theory is. But the way we do this is by learning what is going on at some places, at some times, trying to extrapolate, and adding to our stock of knowledge. What you want is a site that isn't predisposed to mislead you into overly confident inference. That's what a fair site is, and that's all you need. Guess what—the vast majority of sociological research that students set out to do fails here, and fails miserably.

Discrepant Cases

Now there is one particular kind of case selection that doesn't have to be fair, and this is the "discrepant case." This works out quite well when both of the following two things are true:

1. There is some theory that is widely held in sociology and believed to be consequential.
2. This theory not only predicts that there are no cases of a certain type, but runs into deep trouble if this prediction is falsified.

There are actually very few theories of this type—perhaps one appears every decade. But when they do, we all have to admit that the normal issues of error, inference, and sampling don't apply. If you're testing the hypothesis that there are no red marbles in a bag, and your sample includes one, you don't do all the statistical tests. It's that simple: if you have a red marble, you know there are some, and any theory that claims there aren't is just wrong.

The problem is that most sociological theories don't have that strong a claim. They are more like theories that say "every marble in the bag is blue, mostly," or "all marbles in the bag are blue, and by marble I mean a stone or glass sphere less than one inch in diameter of blue coloring." If this is what we're dealing with, a single red marble doesn't make front page.

And here's the nasty trick that social theorists often play on students. They often make theories that sound no-red-marble-y, and when you talk about them in class, everyone feels like they are saying that there aren't any red marbles. After all, the theory is called the blue marble theory! But if you go around trying to get some traction with the red marble you found, it turns out that nowhere in print was there ever a strong statement denying that you could find a red marble. So after all that hard work, you've got nothing. Functionalists accept that some things don't work out for the best, Marxists accept that some workers are overpaid and happy, and so on. The mark of a naïf in social science is gunning against theories that you only hear in class, and not bothering to read the small print in the written work. That written work usually has something like this at the bottom: "* The high-flown rhetoric above in no way constitutes a guarantee that identical phenomena will be found in all cases. Consult your local data for information on the precise conditions in your topic."

So if you are looking for a discrepant case that will bring down some big claim, make sure you have that claim in unqualified form, in writing, by someone that sociologists take seriously. Otherwise, it probably isn't such a great idea to pursue a discrepant case, even if it seems to be a really important one. Because the theoretical significance of discrepant cases also isn't necessarily proportional to their substantive significance. Certain chance mutations can be very consequential, but they aren't more likely to get at the core phenomena of interest than are any other mutations. Weird stuff happens sometimes, but as Spencer-Brown (1957) said, science is based on the stuff that happens over and over again, when you want it.

Further, there can be a powerful rhetorical advantage in taking an unusual case . . . if you want to show something more "usual." That's especially true if the case is widely understood as a substantively important one. For example, David Gibson (2012) showed that how speakers use various conditional constructs—and whether they finish their turns—affects the way a group envisions its future. Ho-hum, many non-microsociologists might say. But the case he has is the deliberation of the executive committee during the Cuban missile crisis. If things had gone differently, chances are good you wouldn't be reading this, because your parents would be crispy toast.

Finally, as I'll emphasize later, it can be that if you trace out the connections of your case, discrepant or not, to the wider environment, its very particularity is revealing of general principles. So maybe if you just took one gang, and really looked at the context, you'd learn an incredible amount about social life, even if not about all "gangs."

A discrepant case *can* work. But I'm going to try to scare you away from them. Our real problem is that most of us *are* doing discrepant cases, and we just don't know it. Why? We'll get the answer when we turn to the more general issues of how we select a "regular" case, which is what most of us will do. And then you'll be glad I made you read about sampling and selectivity.

Cases of Cases

Insiders and Outsiders

First, let's review what we read in the chapter 2 (32–33)—sometimes the way that you realize your question wasn't a good question is that you are having trouble finding a site. Usually, if we feel there are many, many different places that we can ask our question, all equally good, our question is just too broad. And when we have our pick of a range of cases, we almost always pick poorly.

The biggest mistake you can make as a student when choosing a site to investigate is to decide just to study where you're working, or living, or praying, anyway. If we talked about the fifty thousand problems with this, we'd never get to anything else. I'm going to emphasize only the most flagrant ones. Number one: I cite one of the rules that some Dennis Hopper character gave (he was playing a TV guru in the movie *Search and Destroy*): "Just because it happened to you doesn't mean it's interesting." Get it? You already know *you* like stamp collecting. Your threshold of interest is therefore certainly lower than that of your readers.[2]

> ## "Just because it happened to you doesn't mean it's interesting."

A second problem is that if you study something close to you, as many will tell you, you may actually miss a lot of what is most important. Why? It just seems "obvious" or "necessary" that group members do this or that, which means that large chunks of possible questions fall away for you. A third problem is that, especially for a short project, you may still be more oriented as a "stakeholder" than an observer. You would basically rather do bad sociology and report the party line than betray the trust of your buddies and discount their way of talking about things. Going somewhere new, in contrast, is likely to provoke insights—and sometimes, the further an outsider you are, up to and including initial dislike and resentment— the better your findings.

But let me bring up another problem with the insider study that has to do with your training. If you study a group that you're a member of, chances are you aren't going to actually learn your trade very well. All the sorts of things that you learn when you have to figure out how to (1) get access to a new site, (2) understand what others are doing that seems strange, (3) negotiate difficult interactions, and, most importantly, (4) learn from people who aren't like you, you're never going to get to do. Your second project (if there is one)—what do you plan for that? Study your uncles? You gonna keep this up, all the way to the ethnography of your retirement community?

---

2. In particular, a warning to bicyclists: *never* write on anything that has to do with bicycles. Ever.

Re-Search and Me-search

And this brings us to an issue that troubles everyone: whether we can criticize a student's project for being too close to home. Here the term bandied about is "me-search." That's when whatever you're interested in is so bound up with yourself and your own search that it is unlikely to work as a sociological contribution.

Now this rightly raises a lot of worrisome flags for students. Most important, we have learned to understand that what is called "universal" is really just one more form of localism (or, at least, it turns out to be this most of the time). That is, if you are Vietnamese and study Vietnam, why is *that* any more "studying yourself" than if you were an American studying America? How come *that* isn't me-search? Foreign sociologists gnash their teeth over the provincialism of American sociologists. (Or at least there was a time in which this was true; now it's often the opposite, that there's a premium on non-U.S. sites.)

I don't deny that some people may assume me-search when the statuses of the researcher and the target population align. Sometimes they are wrong, and you can get pissed at them for thinking you're doing me-search when you're not. Just because your subjects share an ancestry with you doesn't mean that you're doing me-search. Absolutely right. But then again, don't use righteous indignation to ignore what might be an important lesson: left to yourself, you're predisposed to not recognize me-search when it *is* present, just like some of your teachers may be predisposed to misrecognize it *as* present when it's not. But if it is there, you won't be able to hear this—when they say, "I don't think that's interesting," your feelings will be hurt. You don't want to be in a place in which you confuse reasonable criticism with insult.

Let's consider three different dimensions of a topic. The first is what most folks will call *identity*—stuff like where we are from, and all the things we'd check off on a survey about ourselves. The second is what we can call *ideology*—the social or political causes we might think are important, interesting, or whatever. And the third we'll call *issues*, meaning something we are trying to work out in our own lives, for whatever reason— something big like "who am I?" or something small like "finally beating the Guinness book of world records longest jump rope session."

> **Identity**
> **+ Ideology**
> **+ Issues**
> **Total Bust**

It's usually *issues* that are most problematic, but it's not always as visible as the other two. And it's when they are all coming together—that your study plan combines your identity, issues, and ideology, that folks are rightly suspicious—that whatever you're doing isn't for the benefit of sociology as a field, but for you. That's getting back to the choice of site. It can be true that the best place to study stratification is in world record rope jump studios. But no one will believe you. Most important, if your thesis can be interpreted as a move in a field in which you are a player, aligned with some against others, they're rightly concerned that you don't have the self-control to avoid letting your thumb rest conveniently on the scales.

Are there exceptions, where me-search has worked well? Sure. But they're not as common as the disaster stories, and most of the successes involved people who branched out to study identities other than their own. That is, they kept the issue but varied the identity. Finally, look at these people's second projects before you decide whether their first was really so great. Sometimes we think that someone is a great sociologist just because she's the first person to struggle onto the land of academia and bring reports from somewhere else. That's an important contribution—but it doesn't always make her a good sociologist.

So now let's assume that you are going to look around for something other than your own existing group or whatever to study. How do you choose that site?

Bad Sites

Tragically, it is not uncommon for the answer to be "convenience." Convenience sampling is when you choose data to study that are easy *to get*, and/or at a site that is easy to *get to*. This is, as you might expect, not very powerful rhetorically. Sounds like you're lazy, doesn't it? Further, and I'll harp on this continually, whatever it is about this site (say) that made it easy for you to get to may well be related to the theoretical questions you're interested in. For example, if you want to study how undergraduate-age men view gender relations, you could interview members of a discussion group on gender relations you know of. Well, the reason these guys are available is because they're concerned with gender relations, which might make them atypical. Not "unrepresentative," but probably unfair for your question.

Unfortunately, some convenient sites may be fair but still a poor choice. If you are interested in organizational failures, and you happen to have a friend who works in an erotic bakery in Vogeltown, just outside of Wellington, New Zealand, you might think that it would make sense to do your ethnography there. Now if you actually had randomly picked a country, and then opened up the yellow pages and put your finger down, and this was what came up, then some people might find this relatively interesting, and be willing to continue reading your results. But otherwise, there's no intrinsic interest in the site. Absolutely, an erotic bakery is just as much an organization as a hospital. And Vogeltown is just as valid a place as is Chicago or New York City. And it is true that some processes are nearly universal, so we can go anywhere to study them.

But if you really can go anywhere, why not go to a place that people care about? Usually people, even professional sociologists, care more about big things like life and death or politics, gratifying things like food, entertainment, and sex, than they do about theory—even their own theories, usually, but certainly yours—and *way* more than about *your* life or hobbies or friends. That's why, if you are interested in organizations, it makes sense to study (say) a major hospital in Chicago, even though it's not intrinsically theoretically privileged over the bakery. That way, when someone asks you at the end of your job talk, "So what?" you get to say, "And this is why when you go to get your appendix out, there is a one in ten chance you will wake up dead, at least if you are in the United States." If, conversely, you put your desire to spend time with your friend in Vogeltown first, and choose to study the erotic bakery, you have to conclude: "And this is why when you go to get a penis cake for a bachelorette party, there is a one in ten chance it will be misshapen, at least if you are in New Zealand." Scientifically, the two are equally significant, but in terms of getting people to care, to invest in you, and to listen to you, the first is much better. And I think there's nothing for us to be ashamed of in that. We want a social science that can help people with the things they care about, and while sometimes making that science requires strategic attention to things we don't care about, that doesn't happen as often as we pretend.

So a casual approach to your choice of site has its problems. But there's a deeper problem than your pet project not being of interest to others. There's a very good chance that the place you want to pick as your site is precisely the worst one. Here we'll introduce...

The Anthropic Principle

In physics, the anthropic principle is a cute idea, coined by Brandon Carter, as an answer to the question of why the physical constants of the universe (things like the charge of an electron, or the gravitational constant) are what they are, and not something else. The answer is that if they weren't, we wouldn't be asking this question, because there couldn't be any intel-

ligent life. It's a nice—and often smart—way of reversing a question, trying to back up and see what we can tell about our own position in some
distribution of possible worlds.

In many cases there is something similar that happens in sociological
research. If you are planning on studying, say, a radically democratic social movement that has no organizers and no rules, and you wonder why
movement X has no organizers and no rules, the answer might really be
that, because if it wasn't this way, you wouldn't be studying it.

> ## It's like that because, if it wasn't,
> ## you wouldn't be studying it.

Now in sociology, we're familiar with the problem of sampling on the
dependent variable. The idea here is that if we're interested in what causes
something else (e.g., what causes people to be drug addicts?), we can't
start with drug addicts and see what they all have in common (e.g., they
all drank milk as kids). Instead, we have go forward, starting with a fair
sample and watching some become drug addicts and others not.

Well, to some degree, the anthropic principle is an extension of this
problem of sampling on the dependent variable. But I mean something
even more radical: if your interests lead you to a site, there's a very good
chance—I think it's more likely than not—that you're finding the worst
possible place to do your study.

To explain this, let me use an example of a classic organizational ethnography, one that came from a University of Chicago dissertation, albeit
many years ago. This is Charles Bosk's *Forgive and Remember* ([1979] 2003).
Bosk was interested in questions about the professions. The conventional
idea of what makes a profession a profession (as opposed to it being just
any old job) is that professionals have a privileged position of trust; the
client being served can trust the professional to look after the client's interests, and not the professional's own. Professions get the right to police
themselves, on the assumption that they care more about their colleagues'
proper behavior than does anyone else. Some people thought that this
was giving the so-called professionals basically a blank check that they
didn't deserve.

So Bosk chose to study doctors, who had often been criticized for a lack
of professional control. Within this set, he chose surgeons, who have a
great deal of autonomy and whose errors are clear and unambiguously attached to their action—*you* were the guy with the knife, and it's *your* fault
that the lung is lying on the floor ([1979] 2003, 28–29).

And so he chose to study a large, prestigious teaching hospital that he called Pacific Hospital. (We'll return to this aspect of his work later, in chapter 6.) And here he chose two surgery rotations, where attending physicians worked with residents and interns, who are advanced medical students. Was this a "representative" site? There's no such thing. Still, he initially claimed that this was a perfect miniature for the profession as a whole ([1979] 2003, 184; this was corrected in his later edition, xvi).

In any case, his conclusions were that, in fact, doctors do instill moral guidelines and do all the sorts of important ethical things that you'd want professionals to do. We see this, he argued, when surgeon professors respond to the errors made by their underlings. They focus more on "moral" errors made by their students that indicate a lack of care and responsibility, and they go easier on those who have just made technical errors. In fact, Bosk uncovered a new kind of error, the "quasi-normative," which differed across the attending physicians. This was when the attending physician knew that the rule he was enforcing wasn't uniformly shared, but considered it a moral imperative that the underlings do things *this* way on *his* rotation.

So here's the funny thing—you read Bosk's work now, and you notice (in large part thanks to his own additions) that rather than the research demonstrating that physicians could be trusted to police each other, all the evidence is that they have no intentions of doing anything like that: Bosk reports the doctors saying that if they knew about an incompetent colleague, their response would be to do exactly nothing. All the supposed self-discipline was bosses yelling at underlings. As Bosk later realized (xviii), a training situation isn't the best place to examine self-policing.

In other words, it is just as if there was a controversy over the cleanliness of food preparation in most restaurants, and you went off to an elite culinary institute. Surgeons at a high-prestige teaching hospital are probably the single worst case you could pick. So why did he go there? He was interested in professionals' authority. He let that pull him toward where there was the most of it, like a rat being guided into a trap by the wafting scent of cheese. Thus he ended up in a place where professionals had an unusual amount of control. So much so, that (as we'll see later), he himself lost his own analytic independence. Only with years of distance was he able to realize what had happened (and we'll return to this when we consider interpretation in chapter 9).

Sociological Foci

That was a nice case, but there are more subtle problems, problems that are so common to sociologists that we don't even recognize them *as* problems.

Let's take one of the best ethnographies ever, William Whyte's ([1943] 1981) *Streetcorner Society*. Whyte was interested in slums, which were (at the time—this was back in the 1930s) said to be "disorganized" communities. He wanted to prove they weren't (and he succeeded).

So he studied a slum in Boston. But how to get access? Well, Whyte had a few failures, and then he contacted a settlement house—a place where social workers are based. They hooked him up with the leader of an informal organization, a gang. He hung out with them, and then, using them as a base, was able to study other organizations, informal, criminal, and formal.

Sounds good, right? That's what sociologists assume—that society is made up of groups. We are, we think, inside a structure of social organization. And so on. But this means that his approach cuts out of his study all those who are more peripheral or those who don't hang out a lot. In fact, by the nature of his design, namely, to look at group life, he's going to end up with social organization. If there's any of it there, that's where he'll be. He only looked at a tiny slice of life, but used that to make his conclusions, which were, not surprisingly... that there was a lot of organization.

How would you *find* disorganization? Sociology isn't going to be able to say how organized slums are if they only know how to study the organized parts. This isn't saying the work is worthless or that it's hopeless, but this is again a lesson on the expanded idea of sampling on the dependent variable—whatever brings you to this site is likely to be related to what makes this a bad site for your claims.

We can call this the seek-and-ye-shall-find problem. It's such a devilish problem because it appears to us as the solution to a different problem, a practical problem, of getting access. The problem isn't that Whyte overgeneralized or that he didn't determine the scope of his claims. Certainly, he can't know from his one site how general it is. But what he could have done was realize that he was trying to engage a question about the degree of organization in a community by studying only the organized aspects. Only a theory that says that there are *no* such aspects can be tested this way. One that says that "slums are way less organized than middle-class communities" can't so be tested. Maybe he was, in a way, dealing with a discourse that emphasized the first form of the question (no organization). But he was smart enough to have gone the next step, and push it to the second (how much and what kinds of organization are there?).

> **Seek and ye shall find—and therefore get your ass lost.**

Strength of Influence

We saw Whyte allowing his interests to give him a biased view of the community, but it's a typical and generic one—we overstate organization because our techniques take us there. There's a very similar formal problem when it comes to studying influence. You're interested in, say, how new laws get passed. You take a sample of laws and try to trace where the ideas come from. It turns out that they all were born in some shady think tank run by elites. "Holy smokes!" you think. The country is totally in the hands of these ideological experts! Rush to the presses!

But you sampled only on successful outcomes. Of course the initiators look strong. But if you were to start with all the ideas they have, all the laws they are trying to get put in place, you might find that they have a really low success rate. This is a general phenomenon—when we go *backward* from *successes*, influence relations seem a lot stronger than when we go *forward* from *attempts*.

The same thing was uncovered in the sociology of new religious movements. Looking from the perspective of those who joined, the groups seemed frighteningly powerful, leading recruits to cut off ties with others, adopt radical practices, sacrifice their own interests, and so on. It seemed reasonable to go around warning people not to listen to anyone wearing a robe who wasn't a Supreme Court justice.

But, as Long and Hadden (1983) argued, if you looked from the perspective of all the people the group was *trying* to recruit, they looked remarkably weak. Most people ignored them or dropped by for a lunch and never came back.

> **Processes that look strong going backward look weak going forward.**

The implication is that how you sample can affect your conclusions... but in very predictable ways. Anticipating these allows you to adjust a sample so that you don't confuse the patterning of your sampling with the patterning in the world. Let me give a few other common examples.

State and Trait, Stock and Flow, Ceiling and Floor

In American cities in the 1980s, the writing classes found themselves wondering where all these homeless people had suddenly come from. Some said that it was a result of deinstitutionalization (mental hospitals releasing inmates instead of keeping them indefinitely). Others said that it had to do with high rents and poor social safety nets. So researchers began studying the homeless, and although the results were different in different cities and so on, in many places, researchers were surprised to find, first of all, that the homeless weren't a distinct subpopulation. In psychometric language, homelessness wasn't a (time invariant) *trait* that characterized some people and not others, but was a *state* that people could pass in and out of.

What's the first sampling implication? That when you try to grab a sample of the current homeless, their probability of entering your sample is proportional to the length of time they are homeless, all other things being equal. We're not wrong, but we're implicitly taking the homeless-day as our unit for sampling, not the homeless-spell, and certainly not the people-who-have-experienced-homelessness. We miss a lot of the short-term homeless.

What's the second implication? We can consider this a stock-and-flow problem. At any time, there is a stock of homeless people. This stock may be relatively constant in size, but even so, there is change, as some people enter and others leave. What does that mean? It means that depending on where you watch this process from, it looks very different.

So once people realized that homelessness was a state, and they saw people moving *out* of homelessness, some in effect thought, "perhaps homeless isn't so bad—because people seem to transition out of home-lessness all the time." But that should raise an immediate question—if I see people transitioning out, yet there is still a stock, where are they coming from? Sampling on the homeless means you'll see people transitioning to housing. But if you were to sample on those in unstable housing situations and saw them transitioning into homelessness, presumably all that optimism would be replaced by its inverse.

Further, you can see an increase in the stock over time, even if there isn't an increase in the flow. Fearon and Laitin (2003) considered arguments about why there was an increase in the number of civil wars over time. Most of those arguments had to do with period effects: something *new* is happening. They argued that in fact, there had been no change in the number of new civil wars that were breaking out. It's just that the old ones hadn't all been settled.

The final implication has to with what we call *floor* and *ceiling* effects. Sometimes we're looking at some phenomenon (say, social status) that exists in a relatively restricted range (if only by definition, because you can't be ranked higher than first). There's nowhere to go lower than the floor; nowhere to go higher than the ceiling. We know how to do statistical adjustments to deal with this, but it has more general implications.

If your sample is near the ceiling, you're going to see a lot of downward movement. If you don't like the people at the ceiling (e.g., the superrich), that's going to seem good news. If you do like them, it's bad news. If your sample is near the floor, you're going to see upward movement. Occasionally at the floor or ceiling there's almost no movement. But that doesn't mean there isn't plenty of movement in the middle.

In sum, there are characteristics of our site that can lead us to be predisposed to certain types of conclusions—and we need to avoid confusing these with answers to the questions that we might have started with.

Who Steps Up

The seek-and-ye-shall-find problem arises again when we start looking for particular people to talk with. Once again, the problem is a problem because it seems like a solution to a worse problem (you have no one to interview). You are so happy when, as a frustrated and anxious field-worker, suddenly your work starts moving forward, and you don't want to look a gift horse in the mouth—to question the motives of your new informant or second-guess your new insight—but you need to. Because you are basically replicating the process of choosing a site, and choosing what to study, and you need to think through the logic of your sampling now, even if you didn't before.

The most insidious form of the seek-and-ye-shall-find problem occurs when we go to study hard-to-reach populations. In Japan, there's supposedly an epidemic of *hikkomori*—young people about thirty, jobless, friendless, who live at home and never leave their rooms—their mom slips food under the door. They sit on the bed, playing computer games, reading manga and listening to J-pop CDs. How could anyone let their life sink to such a low? (Though, come to think of it, I don't know why reading *Sayonara, Zetsubou-Sensei* and listening to Judy and Mary is so much worse than reading the *American Sociological Review*... and listening to lectures on methodology.)

This might be where we think the good ethnography will shine. By studying and talking to such folks, you will be able to figure out their motivations—or at least, get a sense of how the world looks through their eyes. But there is a pretty obvious problem in finding retreatists. If they've done it well, you won't find them. That means that you can imagine that your sample is likely to be biased away from what you are looking for (the more retreating they are, the less likely to talk to you). And more generally, it often turns out that when we look for the subjects who are best at articulating what is special, distinctive, and sociological about the phenomenon... we've got exactly the wrong people.

Huh? Well, suppose you find a group called *Hikkomori* for an Imaginary Tomorrow that has an online presence and a mission statement that says "Japanese society has been built on conformity, overwork and self-sacrifice, but it no longer even rewards those who enter the machine with a minimal standard of living. Therefore, we opt out entirely." Perfect! You think. Just the people you want to study. And so you reach the core members and find that they can give a cogent explanation of their way of life. You write it up, get a book contract, and want to go back to get a few more quotations... and you find that they guy who used to be the head blogger for this group is now a vice president at Bear Stearns! And all the others are also employed. What's up? It's a more general problem: the people who are best at giving a cogent, sociology-paper-ready exposition of some idea usually—not always, but I think usually—have more in common with sociologists and other middle-class service workers than they do with other group members.

> **Morpheus to Neo: You thought you were looking for me, but *I* was looking for *you*.**

That's why you "found" them—*they* found *you*. That's why you quote *them* as opposed to the other few folks you managed to meet up with. That's why your work went so smoothly. Why you were done ahead of anyone else in your writing group. And why your work is all wrong.

An Analytic Space

What can we do? Here, we can take a tip from Peter Blau, who had a great project to compare public and private bureaucracies in terms of their bureaucratic rigidity (Blau 1955). The problem was that he couldn't get permission from any private bureaucracy to do the study. He realized that if you are interested in the rigidity of groups, you might not be able to study the rigid ones, because they aren't flexible enough to allow you to study them.

What Blau did, therefore, was to construct an analytic space in which he could imagine situating possible sites. In his case, there was only a single dimension (degree of rigidity), but often we can come up with a number of plausible dimensions that might structure the space of possible sites. Now in most cases, we won't really know exactly where a potential site sits, and we only have guesses as to what the important dimensions are. However, just trying to think this through can do wonders for us.

It's related to what Duneier (2011) has called "inconvenience sampling"—thinking about all the people you *aren't* talking to, the things you *aren't* watching, and imagining that they are called to the witness stand to testify *against* your argument. You wonder, what is at the opposite end of this space from the case I was thinking of using? Could that be a better case? Which case is fairer for the claims I'm hoping to make?

It's important that we don't confuse this *analytic* space with a *thematic* one. The latter is when we think about the substantive variation and use conventional understandings to array sites—for example, if we have a question about organizations, we might array them as economic, religious, educational, social, or community. That's a thematic organization. But if our question was about the formation of factions, our analytic space might have dimensions having to do with size, leadership, turnover, and decision-making procedures.

This is the heart of "thinking through methods" in action. We don't just let stuff happen, even when—no, *especially* when—it seems to be "good." We question it all, worrying about everything that looks too good, never friending that Nigerian prince.

The Average Class

And this gets to an issue that is easiest to see when we are interested in more than one site, but has implications even when we are choosing a single one. Sociologists are often interested in groups and tend to sample from groups. But that can be misleading if you switch to talking about people.

I'm going to introduce this in a form you won't forget, the paradox of the average class size. Most universities boast something like "the average class size is under eighteen!" And yet, students scratch their heads, because many of them have *never* had a class under eighteen. This doesn't sound at all right. The reason is that the average class size is not the same as the average size of a student's classes. Why? Imagine there are five classes, with 15, 15, 20, 50, and 200 students. The median class size is twenty. The total number of "student class seats" contributed by these five classes is three hundred. Of these three hundred, only fifty are in classes with twenty students or fewer. The vast majority of students (in this case) don't get these small classes.

In general, when we choose by groups, we are weighting groups equally. A group with ten members is one group, just as is a group with a thousand members. That means, in a way, we are giving disproportionate attention to individuals who like smaller groups. That isn't a problem so long as you understand it. Maybe you don't want to talk about people; you want to talk about groups. Or about small groups. But "most people" are usually somewhere else—they're over in that one, huge group, the one you *don't* want to study.

Only One?

I've been talking about choosing "a" site. But I don't think you should—choose only one, that is. Let me use the example of an ethnographic investigation, although there are analogues for other methods, especially historical. I think you should always start with two sites, sometimes three. Now some people advocate a comparison across sites as the only way to establish a causal relation between (*a*) something that differs across the sites and (*b*) some outcome. But the idea that your two cases will only vary in two things, one the cause of the other, is so implausible that it isn't worth doing for *that* reason.

So why should you have multiple cases? First, comparison *is* important—your cases may vary on one of those analytic dimensions you are interested in. That may affect what you see. Am I backtracking, and saying you *are* establishing causality? Of course not. You don't study a small business and a big business to *prove* that business size affects employment policy. No one needs to have this demonstrated. It's that you want to get a sense of the variety in the phenomenon you are studying. We'll call this the patterned heterogeneity—the way in which there are differences, but differences that have some sort of order or logic to them. If each of your cases can establish what's going on in its own region of this analytic space (and most of us assume this is so, which is why we allow field research), then having more than one case, taken from different areas of this space, tells us about how the heterogeneity is patterned.

But you can also find that this sort of comparison, even if only implicit, sharpens your insight and helps you find things that you would have overlooked. For example, in an awesome comparative ethnography, Chantelle Marlor (2011) apprenticed herself to two groups of experts who deal with the same sort of clams. One set consisted of contaminant biologists at a university, and the other, Kwakiutl Indian professional clam diggers. Things that might seem obvious to someone schooled in a Western tradition (such as that the head scientist doesn't himself visit the beach but only goes over the data) suddenly jumped out as theoretically central once she compared to the diggers—and got their opinion (one informant was outraged that a scientist would make claims about an area he had not personally visited based on work he had not personally done: "he is just cheating!"). The comparison highlighted the importance of interpersonal trust in the Western tradition.

And even when it isn't a matter of sharpening your insight, having multiple sites offers insurance against one of them going south. More often than you might think, a site turns out to be boring. Or it collapses. Or you get kicked out. Nice to have your foot in another door. And now let's talk about just that—what you do to get your foot in that door and hopefully have the door opened all the way.

Getting Access

Getting Introduced

Once you have a site, you need to get access. This is more familiarly a problem for ethnographers or observers, but those trying to get proprietary data, or those having to do interviews with expert informants, usually face similar problems. I will use the modal case of trying to get access to a group, and make a few comparisons to other types of cases.

How does one even start? Strangely, there's a rather good rule of thumb, and it is this: for *formal* groups, even if you first require the permission of a top administrator (which you usually will), your entry into the group you will study needs to be bottom up. If the plant foreman introduces you ("Listen up, meatheads! This guy's from the university and he's gonna study y'all, so you help him out, ya hear?"), it's a long, hard slog against the suspicion and resentment others might feel toward you. That can even be true when you think that you've got a group in which everyone has an intrinsic motivation to participate (e.g., you're studying a social movement whose goals you're sympathetic to).

If you are studying an *informal* group, however, you want to proceed relatively top down. That doesn't mean that you need to do what William Whyte did and enter into a close collaboration with the leader. But if your entrée comes because you befriend "Dumb Jim," it can be hard to shake that stigma, and folks are less likely to want to introduce you around to others. You aren't always some prize, but more often than you might think, you're of enough interest that, like a good YouTube video, you can be used by someone to reach out to someone else. Don't assume you're immune to the social dynamics of your site just because you have taken social psychology! In her kindergarten ethnography, Barrie Thorne (1993) wonderfully reported how difficult it was on her to get cornered by an unpopular kid who had no one to talk to. It wasn't just that it made it harder to observe the others—she found herself thinking, "Marcy, don't drag me down with you!"

OK, but how do you reach the informal leaders? Most sociologists are going to use brokers of some sort—someone who stands between them and their target subjects. William Whyte ([1943] 1981) used the social workers at the settlement house. Martín Sánchez Jankowski (1991), in his mammoth study of street gangs, talked to community leaders who interacted with gangs and asked them to make the introduction. Importantly, he emphasized that the broker didn't have to vouch for him, just introduce him. From then on, he had a short amount of time to convince them. That's a nice way to proceed—to use social contacts but without holding yourself hostage to them unless you absolutely have to.

Trust and Explaining Who You Are

Back in the days in which ethnographers fetishized the membrane supposedly separating the insiders from the outsiders, they talked about this problem of entry in terms of gaining the "trust" of the subjects. But access doesn't mean the end of distrust (as we'll see in chapter 5, when we recount Duneier's wonderful story in *Sidewalk* of some of his informants caught on tape discussing their theories of him). A person who, in an expansive moment, may call you her blood sister, can spitefully run you down as a treacherous worm the next day. That's the way it goes. In some cases, yes, you need to convince your subjects you're not a cop or management spy. But more important than trust is usually habituation. Primatologists slowly get the monkeys to get used to them. Each day, they come a little closer. The monkeys sometimes cautiously come over to see if a lens cap is edible. The primatologist, what with her strange clothes and equipment, is, at first, interesting and maybe scary. But after a while the monkeys get used to her. We humans do the same thing. We habituate to the researcher.

There is something trustlike about this—they figure that you've been normal every day so far, so you probably will be normal in the future—but it's basically about omission of thought about you, not your elevation to some status (like "true brother"). If you stick around, they still may think you're a jerk. But they'll think, well, he's *our* jerk.

So getting access isn't about getting "inside" a social boundary so much as being minimally acceptable, nonirritating, and (very possibly) an aid to someone else's project. We'll talk more about getting along with folks in ways that are more specific to ethnography, but for many types of research, sociologists fumble at the very first stage: explaining what they are doing.

What Am I Doing?

Many of us think (wrongly) that if we say what we're interested in, then our subjects will understand what we're driving at, and so we'll "contaminate" them and compromise our research. But it doesn't seem to be the case that you really compromise your research by simply letting people know what it's about. I'll return to this below as the "Becker principle." But those who are afraid of this contamination think differently. To prevent that, they'll lie to their subjects or, at least, tell them something uselessly vague. The lying-to-them technique, where you say you're interested in one thing, as a smokescreen for your real interest, runs into some serious problems. At the very least, the subjects will waste their time (and yours) trying to help you on what you said you were interested in. Often, it will seem strange that you're asking then about something different. They may think you're incompetent, confused, or duplicitous. (And I think they'll be right.)

The "be so vague they can't figure out what you're interested in" tactic also has real practical drawbacks. First, they'll have to *interpret* it (as in, "What did she mean when she said, 'life these days?'"). Chances are that their interpretations will be different from yours. And then, when they realize that you didn't mean what *they* meant, they'll either feel embarrassed and stupid or they'll assume you lied to them (and I think they're right). If you say you're studying "this town" and you're actually studying them, you're lying. They thought they were your hosts and informants, not research subjects.

Most students seem to agree with me on this, but they often go overboard in giving detailed explanations. This frequently backfires because most people don't understand the debates in sociology and your explanations quickly get boring; they don't really care as much as you might think about your own ideas. A nice lesson is found in Peter Moskos's (2009, 12–13) ethnography of police, *Cop in the Hood*: "When questioned, I tried to explain my research goals as clearly as possible, a task made difficult by the fact that I really had no clear research goals."

Remember: telling them what you're interested in isn't the same thing as telling them your angle. Coming up with a good way of explaining what you are doing is important, because it's usually in response to failed attempts—often overly general—that students suddenly find themselves blurting out their "hypotheses" (or prejudices, or hang-ups, or the like). Now, it's true that if you give people your own hypothesis, you're contaminating them. If you really try to explain it, you end up saying not just what you are studying, but what your whole current theory is. They often try to "help" by showing you what they think you want to hear—unless your hypothesis is dismissive of their autonomy, in which case they may freeze you out.

Imagine that we can arrange all possible topics in a space, and you can indicate those you'll study with a circle. The important thing is be honest in a way that correctly lays out a radius that includes all the things you're interested in. But that radius you give can be, and should be, considerably bigger than the minimum necessary to do that. You want this expansive radius not because you're afraid a smaller one will guide them or make them self-conscious (which it probably will), but because it's doubtful that you'll actually stay in that area. You'll need to go outside. At the same time, you don't want to be misleading, by indicating a range "over there" where you won't actually be.

So, for example, let's say you're interested in domestic abuse among recent immigrants who live in an ethnic enclave in a city. If your gut feeling is that it's wrong to say "I'm planning on studying domestic abuse in ethnic enclaves," you're right, and it's not just that these terms may not make sense to your respondents. Even saying "I'm studying wife beating here" is bad. It's going to put you in an adversarial position to some people you need to talk to, before you even get a chance to sit down with them. But it's just as bad to try to distract them, saying something like "I'm studying this town." What do you say? "I'm studying family life among immigrants, how things change when they come here." That's true, and in fact truer than the narrow version you might tell your adviser, because if you're at all a decent sociologist, you'll need to go outside your narrower initial interest.

Further, one of the great things about giving a wide sense of your actual range of interest is that many of your informants will actively figure out things to bring to your attention. You need to think this through— theorize their processes—but it's a lot better if they have a broad orientation when they do this as opposed to a narrow one. By stating that she was interested in the process of "uncoupling," Diane Vaughan (1990, 8) found people all over brightening up and offering to participate. Granted, that's a topic that brings out people's desire to tell their story more than many other topics would, but still, you're more likely to get that positive response with a clear, general, and accurate explanation than with an indirect one or a false one. So by getting a sense of what you're interested in, folks will connect you with others and bring relevant material to your attention—but it won't be as selectively marshaled as if you told them your hypothesis or your "line."

If you can't figure out something that hits it just right, an all-purpose one is "I'm interested in how [firemen, female ninjas, single fathers, whoever you are studying] deal with the regular problems that arise in [fighting fires, assassinating superheroes, getting by, whatever]." If this isn't true about your study, it probably should be.

Provisional Fieldwork

Very often, students find it nearly impossible to start a pilot project; this is especially true for those who are doing a class assignment that could turn into a bigger project, but isn't itself going to be a full-length observational study. It's one thing to say, "I want to write a book about you," and another thing to say: "I want to observe you for a two-page exercise." If you are embarrassed to say this, here are two things that are often true; if either is true for you, you can use one of these.

1. "I was always sort of interested in checking out _____; but I never quite got around to it. Then I got this stupid assignment to participate in some group for a stupid class, so I figured, this would be the perfect time to finally get off my butt." Here you build rapport and indicate that the end of the assignment isn't necessarily the end of the contact; further, they treat you like they would any novice.
2. "Our teachers really want us to get out in the world, and see what is really going on with _____." Now your imposition doesn't seem like an exercise that doesn't matter, and more about really learning something important from folks.

In general, one of the best ways to get people to like you enough to talk to you is to make them experts. I don't mean some wide-eyed phony-baloney, "Oh my gosh, you are so strong and smart" nonsense, but to (correctly) let them know that you want to learn from them. And that learning about them is itself an important thing for you, maybe for others.

As a student, this might strike you as disingenuous. You think, "the professor doesn't actually 'want us to get out in the world, and see what is *really* going on with _____,' he wants us to write a paper or get a publication." But you know what? Speaking at least for myself, I *do* want you to get a sense of what the hell is going on with other folks. That's what sociology is all about. There should be an honest answer to these questions that satisfies your respondents. And, as I'll defend in more detail later, if there isn't, you should do something else.

> **Leave the lying to the experts:
> I hope you're not good at it.**

We'll return to this in chapter 6, but no reason not to introduce it here. It's a simple principle: don't lie. You're probably not very good at it. Leave it to the experts: businessmen, politicians, and administrators.

Now that we have a site, we're going to go on to the next part—how to choose whom or what to study.

Sampling

Applicability of the Logic

So if you are smart, you've been reading this bearing in mind that this stuff about selecting a case isn't only applicable to choosing a group for an ethnography project—it also applies to choosing a historical focus, for example. And so the things that I'm going to say about sampling also are of wide applicability. Although I will stick with the more familiar case of choosing individuals within a site, we always sample. Of the many possible observations, we choose only a few. And how we do this can make the difference between success and failure later on. I've decided to put the section on sampling documents in the chapter about using documents (because some of the ways this plays out is particular to documents), though the basic issues are the same.

Types of Samples

Now fortunately enough, those who have really sweated about sampling of their site often get to coast through at least the first stage of the process of choosing individuals *in* a site. That's because they are studying a small group—which group they decide to pick is a major headache, but once they've decided, they know they're going to try to study everyone. Of course, that's only true when a group has a clear boundary, and most don't. But when a group does, the researcher may indeed get a pass from "sampling your population" class. But remember, the same issues of sampling will arise again, when you have to deal with the fact that you are only observing some people at some times. But we'll push that to the side for now and focus on cases where we can't study everyone in our site. So whom do we talk to?

In some cases, there's no question about whom to interview. If one is studying the Los Angeles Police Department's response to the Rodney King–related riots, one will want to interview the people who made the decisions (and then perhaps also some of the other police). The issue of interviewing the major players in some case is often confused with the issue of getting informants as opposed to getting subjects. I'm going to talk more about that when we get to "interpreting," but let me just say this. There are times when we are studying a relatively rare population. We might go to a high school and be interested in students who have returned to school after becoming parents. There might be only a few. We'll want to interview all of them. In this way, it's just like the question of interviewing the bigwigs who made the LA decision. We want them, specifically, not because they're intrinsically trustworthy as interpreters but because there were very few of them.

But other times we are interested in a large population, and we can't interview all of them. So we have to sample. How do we do this? Certainly, it's great if you can actually do what is sometimes called a random sample, but is usually, at best, a "probability sample." This means that you accept that not everyone in our population has exactly the same probability of ending up in the sample, but you're pretty sure we know what each's probability *was*—and who you didn't get. (The reason we don't usually have simple random samples is that people can say no.)

Further, we often need to conduct what is called a stratified sample, in which randomness of different kinds enters at different points. So, for example, in a national sample we might first choose counties randomly (though we would usually weight the probability of choosing any one by its adult population), and then within counties, we might choose towns randomly (ditto), and then within the town chosen, we'd choose blocks randomly (ditto), and then within blocks, choose houses randomly. With a lot of good statistics and the gift of multiplication, we can still figure out the probability of anyone entering our sample, though if we stopped right here with choosing our houses randomly, we'd be in trouble.

Because when you really start taking sampling seriously, you find that it is an extremely conceptually difficult—and perhaps even exciting— methodological challenge. For example, some households have more adults living in them than do others. If you first pick a household randomly, and then pick an adult within the household (which we do when we choose a block randomly and then go to houses and try to interview someone), then a person from a bigger family is less likely to get picked than a person from a smaller family. Because there's only one person in a one-person family—she's going to get chosen. But if there are four people, each one only has a one-fourth possibility of being chosen. That's a big difference. But the more people there are, the more likely *someone* is to be home. So this goes the opposite way—this leads single-person families to be undercounted (Gellman and Little 1998).

Although most of us aren't going to construct a random sample like this, it's good practice to think these issues through, because they have analogues in all sorts of other research. Hanging out on the corner means you're more likely to see people who have a place to go (as they go by) but more likely to talk to those who don't (as they will hang around and talk to you). At any time, if you visit an organization, you're more likely to encounter long-tenure employees and less likely to meet those who leave more quickly. The census finds more long marriages than short ones. And so on.

The takeaway, then, is that the particularities of our procedures lead us to end up with predictably twisted sets of persons in our collecting bag. It isn't a problem so long as we think through the logic of what we're doing.

The Patterning of Your Data

Given that a probability sample is probably out of the question for you, how can you still gather a fair sample, and, even better, one that gives you maximum power to learn important things about your site? The key is to think through how you are finding your respondents, so that you can tell the difference between patterns *in* your data and the pattern *of* your search procedure—that you keep in mind the difference between the universe you'd like to be talking about, the population from which you are trying to sample, and your actual sample. You need to know everything you can about the process whereby some members of the population end up in your sample and others don't. You don't want to confuse *that* patterning with the patterning that you are claiming to have found in the world.

So how can you understand how you've constructed our sample? Let's think about some of the ways in which sociologists work. One way is to collect what we call a snowball sample. Here you start with perhaps one subject, get her to recommend some other people you can interview, and then you get them to recommend some other people, and so on and so on.

The advantages of this method are clearly that it is cheap, and in many cases, you can get better rapport if each new informant knows that she has been referred to you by a friend. The disadvantages are bigger. They are, first, that we're usually staying within a social circle. By definition, we can never break out. (That is, unless the whole world is one big happy circle of friends, and it just might be at that. We still don't know.) And the second problem is that we tend to have what might be called correlated errors— even within the particular circle, whatever makes this person unusual is likely to characterize the next generation too.[3] And third, we tend to go to more and more central people over time. Although it sounds crazy, it is

---

3. There's been a big push by a creative mathematical sociologist, Douglas Heckathorn, to demonstrate that, in many cases, we don't have to worry about this. He says that what he euphemistically calls "respondent driven sampling" (which is snowballing with an incentive for respondents, who get cash for every lead they provide that materializes) leads to distributions of people on important characteristics that are independent of the seed. This isn't true. The math requires that you make assumptions that we know are hugely not appropriate. We often have to use respondent referrals to get to small and hard-to-reach populations, and there are ways of making this better or worse (e.g., see Coxon 1995), but don't fool yourself into forgetting that referral processes are suspect for a very good reason.

completely true that, as Scott Feld (1991) brilliantly puts it, "your friends have more friends than you do." You won't believe me, so draw out a social network of folks who have different numbers of friends. Notice that the average person's friends have more friends than the average person—popular people (not you, sorry) have lots of friends, by definition, which means that their less popular friends (this is you) all have a popular friend. Which means that if you start somewhere in this graph, choose a link randomly, and repeat, you're going to tend to "walk" toward the most popular people. And the most agreeable people. And the most helpful people.

There *is* a time when a snowball can actually be better at getting to a range of cases. That's when your alternative is to repeatedly "reseed" your sample by using your own social networks. In many cases, rather than asking thirty people that you know, you're better off asking, say, three people you know, and then let each of them initiate a chain. Each chain is going somewhere funky, but at least, they have a chance of moving away from *you*. But other than this, snowball samples go to a place in social space in which particular kinds of people tend to be found, and that isn't good.

So it's for good reason that we tend to put snowball sampling (cheap, convenient, flawed) on one extreme of a continuum, on the other end of which we find probability sampling (expensive, difficult, valid). We almost always would prefer to move further to the second pole, if there were no other concerns about cost, time, and so forth. Students regularly say, "Since that second pole is obviously impossible, I did the other kind"—as if there was nothing in the middle. No! What we can do is push ourselves as far as we can toward that second pole, while theorizing the forms of selectivity that are still present. Most obviously, even when we can't rely on a formula for achieving representative samples, we can be driven by a principle of good faith. This tells us, first, to seek out cases that are different from the ones that we used to generate our idea. So when Helen Ebaugh (1988) talked to lots of ex-nuns and got an idea of what it means to leave an important status, she didn't stop here. Why? In part because it was me-search (she was an ex-nun). So she knew she had to get outside this group. If she just compared ex-priests, she wouldn't necessarily be leaving her position in this analytic space, and so she went and studied very different role exits (such as ex-spies).

Second, the principle of good faith tells us to look at comparison cases. When we don't know exactly what our claim might be, we sometimes just want to get outside our prototypical case. If we are studying delinquents in a neighborhood, we probably should talk to some nondelinquents. When we have a clear theoretical claim, this is sometimes called theoretical sampling and is more likely to involve sampling on different values of a proposed *cause*. If we think we're saying that girls have more hierarchical relations when they're in same-sex groups, we're probably going to compare to girls in mixed-sex groups. The clearer our theoretical claim, the more comparisons we may want to be able to make. (For example, do girls in same-sex groups have the same sort of relations as do boys in same-sex groups?) Sometimes it can be difficult for us to figure out which category is the one that really carries the story. We can make a comparison of Republicans to Democrats and have a story that really is about Republicans. But if we now compare Republicans to independents, we find they're the same, while both vary from Democrats. Maybe our story should be about Democrats.

Another sort of accessory comparison we do is an attempt to split away things that are empirically lumped. In *Suicide*, Durkheim ([1897] 1951) presents an exemplar. He wants to compare adults with and without children, as well as the married to the unmarried. The problem is that most people with children are married, and vice versa. So Durkheim looked at widowers with children, as well as married people who hadn't had children. And he knew that the former were likely to be older than most, and the latter, younger than most, so he tried, as best as he could, to make balanced comparisons. When we choose individuals, we often choose judiciously so that, in the future, we'll be able to make at least some of the comparisons we expect we'll want to do. If we don't consciously plan this out, we're likely to "stock up" on one type of person, often the prototypical cases in our mind. Yet without the comparisons, we often can't make a strong claim.

One way to get variation is to introduce some sort of randomness. This can be a good idea even when we have no comparative project and are targeting a particular category of respondent (e.g., Southern Baptists in the non-South). Even if we can't afford to do a truly random sample, we can still attempt to gather a semirandom sample. For example, sometimes sociologists will go to a typical place—a grocery store parking lot, say—and see who they can find to talk to. That might seem pretty lame, and it can be hard to get people to agree to talk, but it has advantages over starting out with a single, heavily selected group (like a church). In other cases, we construct what is sometimes called a purposive sample. Here we are actually going out and looking for people who fit into predetermined categories. The difference between this and theoretical sampling is that we aren't necessarily clear on why we need this sort of variation. We just want to cover the board as best we can so as to minimize our losses. If you're interested in how people think about money, you might not want to finish up and realize you'd only talked to young, college-educated, European American women. There might not be any reason to expect that how they think about money is any different from anyone else, but why take the chance that you're wrong?

Finally, sometimes we purposefully choose to sample from a different population than the one in which we generated our ideas. For example, one sociologist of culture, Jo Ellen Shivley (1992), was interested in how Native Americans interpreted Western movies in which Indians were generally the bad guys. She wanted to hear both how American Indians and non-Indians saw the same films, so she asked the same questions of both. Even more, it seems that she first developed her hypothesis of an oppositional reading from her experience on college campuses. So she made sure to do her main work with non-college-educated people. And in fact, they had very different reactions.

Here's a takeaway and a more general conclusion: use of a strategic sample puts a lot of power in the hands of the researcher; that can be used for good or for evil—for being conservative (making it harder to establish your claim) or sloppy (making it easier). The nice thing about a probability sample is that you usually don't need to know about the axes of important variation in the population. A strategic sample requires that you do. If you can make a guess, then you can do a better job of being conservative... but you have to want to.

Getting Participation

Now that we've chosen our site and our people, how do we get them to participate? Here I'm going to switch and use in-depth interviewing as the model case because this is where this task is often most difficult. Outside of an ethnographic context, in-depth interviewing may (unless it is a snowball sample) require a new "entry" process for contact with each subject. The researcher (that's you) has to start cold each time, which is emotionally draining for you as well as usually having a low success rate. You're asking folks for a major time commitment, and unlike a participant observation study, you aren't around as "part of the group." Still, getting participation from regular folks is often easier than might be thought, since people (at least, most Americans) tend to like to talk about themselves.

The precise way in which one gets participation of course depends on who is being interviewed. But there are still a few general things that can be said. First, there are two types of motivation, and a reasonable (though not ironclad) rule for how to get people to participate. The two types of motivation are extrinsic and intrinsic.

Intrinsic motivation is when the potential interviewee actually has a motivation to be involved with the research. This is not a major problem when it's generic intrinsic motivation, like just wanting to talk to anyone about anything, which is often true of people "marooned at home" (Weiss 1995, 33). But more often, we latch onto people's interest in a particular topic.

This kind of motivation makes the researcher's job a hundred times easier, and so we usually sigh with relief when someone says, "What a great idea! I think that's absolutely of highest importance, and you bet I'll help!" For that reason, we're often far less skeptical of relying on intrinsic motivation than we should be. As always, a solution to one problem brings a new problem with it.

There are two problems with intrinsic motivation. The first is the more serious, and it is that the people who end up in our sample are different from those who we don't talk to, and often they're different in a way that makes them the worst people for us to use. A classic example is the sex study carried out by the Januses (Janus and Janus 1993). They left flyers advertising their studies all over—in doctors' offices, in cafés, and so on—and they had a huge response. So they said, we know it wasn't purely random, but our study was so big, it has to be basically right. Well, once Laumann et al. (1994) finally did a serious probability sample study of sexual behavior, it turned out that the Januses had inflated the proportion of senior women having weekly sex by 1,200 percent—that's quite a margin of error! Because the people who got into the sample got there precisely because of their intrinsic motivation, people not interested in sex never got into the Januses' sampling frame.

However, sometimes you find that almost everyone you talk to is really interested in the topic and wants to tell their story. In this case, you don't really need to worry about the selectivity in terms of determining who enters the sample. However, there is still reason for caution if you find that they have strong intrinsic motives to participate. First, unless you are absolutely sure you understand why the people want to talk, you risk being used as a go-between: they want to use you as a vehicle to get their story out to someone else, and that may not be the information *you* want. Second, even if there is no such deliberate scheme, you may find that once the interview has begun, your respondents are still highly motivated, and they are highly motivated to take the interview somewhere far away from where you need it to go, which can be very hard on you. You may *never* be able to get it to be where you need it. And finally, if respondents are heavily emotionally involved in some issue, they may require similar emotional investment from you (i.e., react with betrayal if you don't "take sides").[4] Or, more likely, they may assume that there is some emotional investment

4. I've emphasized the importance of getting both sides of a difference whenever possible. But there can be times when an issue so polarizes the sides, and they are so visible to one another, that being with one will lead the other to refuse to work with you. What then? As Cherry, Ellis, and DeSoucey (2011) suggest, divide and conquer—team up with a partner researcher.

from you and feel hurt when they find it isn't. (In chapter 6 we'll look at some ways to defuse this.)

The other option is extrinsic motivation. There are usually two kinds at our disposal. The first is *money*. You might think you have none, but there are people with less. Still, only for some relatively hard up can money be a motivation in itself, and even then, I frankly think it's a bad idea. "I'll give you some mo-ney" establishes a relation of mutual exploitation. We may offer money to respondents as part of a good-will gesture, to show that we understand that their time is valuable and wish we could compensate them for it, but we probably won't be able to really use cash alone to sway them. Yes, there are exceptions, either for people who are very hard up or for people who are used to being highly sought after as research subjects. And there's a possible exception with students, who are used to being bought and sold like chattel, and—as far as I can see—don't resent it as much as they should.

The second kind of extrinsic motivation is *science*. Unlike social science graduate students, most Americans really believe in the value of social science, at least on some level. If researchers communicate that this research is potentially of great importance, and that it will be noticed by lots of people, and that each contacted person's participation is important because we all know how important it is to get a scientific sample, then people may be willing to participate to help out science.

The only problem is that when people are too impressed with the importance of science, they may try to give you what they think you want, because

1. they want to help science
2. you are doing the science
3. ergo: they should help you.

In general, probably a bit of scientific motivation and a bit of intrinsic motivation is best. In fact, one of the first French sociologists, Frédéric Le Play ([1862] 1982, 63, 173–74), seems to have hit on the key principles in his studies of the European worker. He had found that people were more likely than one might imagine to agree to be studied, because they enjoyed talking about their family histories, local customs, and whatnot. He suggested that the researcher get access by emphasizing the altruistic nature of the work and calling out for the subject to reciprocate with an equally altruistic sacrifice of his time, though also offering to compensate the subject for this loss. When the interview started, the researcher should begin with memories that the subject would enjoy recounting, which would set a positive tone and make the subject more likely to put up with the boring questions later. This is a pretty good rule of thumb.

Of course, getting participation, like getting access, isn't always a one-time affair. Even someone who has agreed to do an interview may never be there when you call, may break appointments, and so on. But sometimes this works to your advantage—the person who refused to participate when asked the first time may change his mind when he learns about who else is participating. Here's a nice example. In his study of gangs, Jankowski (1991) found that many gang leaders were far more willing to have him study them than he imagined. That's because they themselves would like to know how gangs work in other places.

But now, let us say, you have your participants. What are you going to ask them? That's the subject of the next chapter.

TAKEAWAYS

- When you ask "why am I here," the answer can't be, I like it here, I was already here anyway, or it was easy to get to.
- You aren't scientifically "compromising" to choose a site your readers will find interesting or important. You're showing that your science matters.
- You can't let people come to you. You have to go to them.
- Explain your purposes in ways that are honest but allow you to be totally reoriented by what you learn.
- When things are going well—you have lots of people wanting to participate, and they seem enthusiastic—be afraid; be very afraid.

If you were going to read more...

I think you'd do well to read whatever stupid methods or stats book you stuffed under the short table leg. That stuff on sampling is applicable to you, whoever you are.

* 4 *

Talking to People

You are not in the middle of a gab fest. You are an instrument, like it or not, setting tasks for your subjects to complete. If you do not adequately theorize this process, you will have no idea what you are doing or what you have done.

We've talked about getting to the people, but now it's time to start talking to them. I'll often focus on when we use interviews alone as a method, though they are often also used in combination with other ways of gathering data. Further, I'll be concentrating on more in-depth interviews, as opposed to survey interviews, since that's what you're more likely to do. But because the same problems are found in all sorts of interviewing, I'll be emphasizing the commonalities across them. In fact—and this rubs lots of students the wrong way—I think the best way to become a great in-depth interviewer is to understand survey interviews first.

The reason is that "just talking" doesn't cut the mustard as a scientific strategy for data gathering—not because everything has be standardized to be scientific but because you've really got to think through what you're doing. A conversation is a social interaction—involving at least two people—and you can't take one-half of it and treat it as if it were something that can be examined on its own. If you've started cheering, "That's right! It's all deeply social and deeply contextual and we can't take some sciencey approach to all this," get ready for a big disappointment. The problem with the contextual nature of the interview is that we can't take what it produces as if it were just some dump of what is in the interviewees' heads. Rather, these products are a response to specific tasks that we give respondents, and we have to have a clear and accurate theory of this interactive process.[1] A great interviewer *can*, I admit, often walk into an

1. Here see Hyman (1954, 18, 80). Yes, sixty years ago, there was a more profound understanding of the social phenomenology of the interview than you will get taught in class today.

interaction without a script and leave with good data. But a good (though not great) one won't even try. And bad ones walk in and walk out and never know that they stink. Here, we're trying to go from poor to good, not poor to bad.

Paul Lazarsfeld, one of the founders of modern survey analysis, used to say, "If you want to know something about people, why don't you ask them?" I like that sentiment. But it implies that this is all very simple. And that's dead wrong.

What Are Interviews Good For?

Getting at How People Think?

One common idea in sociology is that in-depth interviews can't give you objective data on behavior, but they're great for learning "how people think." Huh? First, while you certainly get to hear the words of your subjects, and integrate their (expressed) point of view with your own, why is that the same thing as "how they think"? It actually takes a lot of work to go from "this is how they talk in this particular situation" to "this is how they think." It isn't impossible, but it requires more skill and care than you might guess.

Rather than saying that interviews are great at getting at how people really think, I'd say interviews are good for getting at practically anything, so long as that thing, or part of that thing, travels through human minds. Good, but not perfect. And you certainly can use them to find out what people have done.[2] You can use interviews to learn about what life used to be like for some people—but their memories are imperfect. You can use interviews to learn about biological states like health—though people's way of describing things can differ from doctors' (look at where they point when they talk about their "stomach"). You can use interviews to learn about social networks—except that people don't always distinguish between who they *want* to be friends with and who they *are* friends with. You can use interviews to learn about people's complex thoughts on all sorts

---

2. Recently, Colin Jerolmack and Shamus Khan (2014) tried to draw attention to some of the problems with interviewing (or, as we might say, *bad* interviewing), but they cast this in terms of the "attitude-behavior problem," a way of thinking that pushes us to looking for *the* verbal answer and *the* actual action, and then looking for a "correlation" between the two. I'm going to just hope that none of you are doing research that could even be used to compute such a correlation (here see Dean and Whyte 1958). Certainly, anyone who asks "what would you do if..." and runs off to write up the results isn't competent, but if you think no matter how hard you try, you can't get people to tell you things like whether they ever had braces or what they did last night you are insane.

of interesting matters, like religion and politics—except that people's thoughts are tangled, and depending how you ask them to walk through this tangle, you get all sorts of results. And you can use interviews to get at what people generally *do*—only they forget, compress, omit, and tend to squeeze their memories into meaningful forms like narratives.

Control

There's often an assumption that if you can talk, you can do interviews, especially if you're a "people person." But some people persons are charming partly because of what they themselves add to the conversation. If you really like talking, you might have a hard time listening. You can have good rapport on an emotional level without having the ability to actually retain what someone else has said.

Most important, as I'll emphasize, you need self-control—the capacity to hold back as opposed to jumping in and making statements of your own. You have to be able to draw people out, without confirming some responses as good or right or in any way selectively assenting (which does not forbid a generic, background affirmation). And this requires suppressing many of the nonverbal or semiverbal cues that we normally unwittingly give as someone talks.

This is crucial, because saying "OK" can suggest that you consider the answer basically done and you want them to shut up. You might think: "But I *always* say 'yeah,' or 'mmm-hmm'—this doesn't mean anything!" But chances are you don't always say it. You do it at certain times. And bad interviewers steer their respondents into saying certain things without ever knowing that they have done this.

We're going to call this the Clever Hans syndrome. Wilhelm von Osten, in the early years of the twentieth century, had a horse that could do addition and more. Von Osten would put out big cards (for example) on which were written "3" and "4," and ask Hans to add the numbers. Hans would then indicate his answer by stamping: "stamp... stamp... stamp... stamp... stamp... stamp... stamp!" and then stop. People were blown away by this. But then some clever skeptic tried to get Hans to do it without the owner being present. And Hans couldn't. Why? Because once the problem was set for Hans, von Osten would get tense; Hans would start stamping, and whenever Hans got up to the right number, the owner would unconsciously relax. What Hans had done was learn to stamp until the owner relaxed. Von Osten hadn't figured that out, because Hans's answers were *right*.

Something very similar can happen with interviewing. The researcher stops the respondent whenever the respondent says something that the researcher thinks is a good answer but waits for more whenever the respondent says something unsatisfactory. This can in effect be a form of putting answers in people's mouths. They will learn, consciously or not, what to do. I'm not exaggerating. Debriefed interviewees who dealt with bad interviewers often report being acutely aware of when their answer "wasn't enough" for the interviewer, when their answers "disappointed" the interviewer, and when they tried to "go on" and come up with something that would get the reward of "okeydokey." The interviewer can walk away sure that it was a fabulous interview. As Bruno Latour (2005, 125) says, we have to proceed extremely delicately when trying to learn about human beings. "You can never stifle the voice of non-humans, but you can do it to humans."

> ## Take a tip from Jane: Exert yourself!
> ## (from *Sense and Sensibility*)

How do you avoid this? Exert yourself! Maintain control over your pie hole. That doesn't mean you can be silent. You will need to make affirmative noises ("mmm-hmmm" or "uh-huh") for most respondents. Some respondents will pause and wait for you to make such a noise to confirm that you are following. The key is not to make such noises only when you like the answer you have been given so far. Are you worried that if you attempt to monitor yourself, you'll simply make it *more* likely that you'll screw up? That the "cognitive load" is just too much? Very possibly you're right. You can't fix this by thinking about it. You have to make it habit. Which means... practice, practice, practice.

Lying

This brings us to the key lesson about lying that I'll emphasize a few times: most of the time, if interviewees lie, it's because we made them do it. And it usually indicates a bad relation between researcher and subjects.[3] Still, it is true that if you ask people something, they don't always tell the truth. But I think it's important to make a big distinction between what I'll mean by "lying," which is the statement of a positive fact (such as, "I have a degree in engineering") from "concealing," which is a common

---

3. "Social anthropology might be defined as the study of the lies that natives tell to anthropologists, especially anthropologists who work with people like the Tauade" (Hallpike 1977, 33). Hallpike and the Tauade did not get along very well.

conversational move that in everyday life is often considered a morally acceptable disinclination to expose private matters. In some cases, you provoke concealment because you've gone too far and asked something you shouldn't have in the setting. If you ask someone point-blank, "Did you just fart?" don't call her a liar for saying no. Furthermore, there are also cultures in which saying an abrupt no is considered somewhat rude. What might strike an interviewer as evasion is often considered a way of breaking the news gently to you (e.g., that they do not agree with your understanding of something).

Sometimes respondents will seem to deny the truth because they are concentrating on the truth of a metatask. For example, artistic creators will often correctly indicate their relative position in their field by emphasizing their commitment to "purity." Vanina Leschziner (2015) found that many elite chefs would insist that they never read cookbooks by others, and when she asked them about the shelf full of them, they would insist that they only looked at the pictures. Yet later, they might criticize the approach taken by a competitor to turning restaurant recipes into cookbook ones. Similarly, some musicians will insist that they only play for themselves, and they do not care if the audience likes it, or even if there is an audience at all (yeah, right…). I think you best understand these sorts of concealing as them thinking, "the only way I can communicate my position in the 'high-devotion-to-purity' area of my field to this outsider is to conceal this fact that the interviewer would misunderstand."

You can also force denial from someone if you box them into a logical corner. You've forced them to say things that will produce a logical contradiction, unless they deny some matter of fact. They will, because you've given them no out. That's your fault, not theirs.

> **"Mind your own business" isn't a lie,
> even when it's pronounced "no."**

So remember, "no" sometimes means "it's none of your business." And *that's* often a very true answer. Finally, just like people will sometimes say no when they mean "I'm not telling you," so they sometimes say yes to mean "sure, if you want the world to be that way." It means you have not exerted yourself.

What about actual fabrication? There are some people who are creative enough not to just stop with concealment but to make up an alternative fictionalized history. If you're asking Exxon executives responsible for the decisions regarding the treatment of the Valdez crisis about their actions, your respondents may be flat out-and-out lying. Because they've known this question was coming and they were prepared for it. But most people aren't good at making up things on the fly. Of course, that doesn't mean that they never will make things up.

In a delightfully nontrivial number of cases, informants may lie about things for the fun of it. This is especially likely to be the case if you are doing ethnographic interviews either with people who are all physically together when you go up to talk to them (and trying to see who will crack up first, saying that their priest's name is Bigus Dickus) or when you're going to be around for a while so that they can witness the hilarity of their pranks (like convincing you that the local drug dealer is a college student doing a study just like you). The Nuer people of South Sudan in Evans-Pritchard's (1940) account loved to lie about their lineages, perhaps because it was so easy, since it all happened in the past. They would go on for hours, day after day, giving him names with funny double entendres, while Evans-Pritchard took careful notes, and then the next week, someone would meet him and say, "So all that stuff we told you last week, did you believe it?" And when he'd say yes, they'd roar with laughter.

In fact, ethnographers are more, not less, likely to get most kinds of misleading information than are in-depth interviewers. We think that because the ethnographer is "there" and can "check" there is less room for fabrication. Maybe there's a little bit less room for it, but there's a lot more reason for it. And that's because it can really matter what they tell you. And not just for the entertainment of getting to watch you make an ass of yourself. What someone tells you may get to their friend or to their enemy; they may need to keep you on their side, and so on. A randomly chosen respondent from an interview-based study might indeed want to impress you a little bit, but certainly it's not going to make much of a difference in her life what you think (also see Hyman 1954, 35). Any desirability bias is likely to be outweighed by the enjoyment people seem to get from spewing the truth (or, more accurately, what feels like the truth at the time that they are talking to you).

When people do lie in an interview, we tend to assume only one version of why they are doing so, namely, that they are motivated by selfish reasons: for example, they want to look better than they are, defend actions, use you as a sounding board for self-pity. But in fact, they may be guided by altruistic reasons—to defend someone else's reputation, even if they privately condemn that person's actions. They may want to change or preserve their relation to you.

And worst of all, they may tell you what they think you want to hear, because they like you and are trying to "help" out. They may even invent stories that are more exciting than the truth for you, to make your project more successful. It sounds funny, but sometimes they really basically think that you're there for good stories, and they're not doing anything wrong by taking a good story and making it better. And probably, the more you like your respondent, the more likely she is to be adjusting her reports, however unconsciously, to what she thinks you want. Contrary to our gut feeling, groups can't change what they do that much in response to the presence of an ethnographer. It's too hard. But a single person's conversation is exactly what we expect to be very sensitive.

To recap: for most of the things you are interested in, though anyone can clam up, only the truly sociopathic or deeply funny can spin stories from whole cloth. If someone says she has "three children: Iphigenia age eight, Cindy age four, and Little Leekie age one," chances are very good she does. The more information people can give you, the more likely it is true.

> **If your brain is your third favorite organ (eyes and ears come first), your gut is your last.**

Do not use your gut feeling to determine when people are lying. That's mostly going to get what we're going to call the like-like factors: whether this person is *like* you and whether she *likes* you. Every bit of social psychology tells us that your subjective sense of "being sure" about a person is not a good guide. Further, as Hyman (1954, 37, 45) found (and I've seen in student exercises), there's a very weak association between whether the interviewer thinks that there was rapport in an interview and what the interviewee thinks—it's the latter that counts (and you only have access to the former). Finally, don't listen to any phony pop psychology about how to tell when people are lying. If you need to determine truthfulness, do what Desmond did in *Evicted* and Duneier did in *Sidewalk*: old-fashioned detective work. Fact check.

What Is Truth?

Most difficult, however, is the more common case in which the answer is truthful in a sense, but not the way you wanted it. You may ask for a statement of fact, but get a statement of valuation back: "Do you mind having Hmong move in as neighbors?" "Oh no." Maybe this person actually does mind, but means, "I know I shouldn't, and I'm trying to be better about it, but...." Or you mean to get an informal answer, but you prompt a formal reply: "Who is most important around here?" "Well, Sampson is the executive manager," even though everyone knows that if Dougie the letter carrier doesn't like what you're doing, it doesn't get done.

And most complex, sometimes you are asking about a *cause* ("what caused you to drop out of high school?") and instead you are getting an *account* ("how can I demonstrate that my action was that of a plausible and responsible adult?"). All the evidence strongly suggests that people aren't telling you the former, if only because they can't. We don't store our memories that way. This issue is so fundamental for interviewing that we'll devote a section to it below. Here I want to stick with the issue of when people's responses aren't quite the truth the way we, the interviewers, were thinking of it.

We often incorrectly imagine that when we are accepted into a group, we get the "real" story. But it can be precisely the opposite. The young man who may frankly discuss sexual dysfunction and fear with a clinician may give you, as the "accepted" researcher, the same braggadocious stories that he gives his other friends. The key isn't that insiders know the *truth*, but that different settings allow for and provoke different types of talk. The good researcher bears this in mind. The bad one tries hard to forget it.

Finally, informants will contradict each other. Victor Turner (1970, 133) reports one informant giving him a clear and beautiful interpretation of plant symbolism that no one else had been able to explain. Meanwhile, Kasonda, Turner's African assistant, "was whispering to me, 'He is just lying.'" Turner wasn't sure who to believe, as each would denigrate the other and insist that the other was manipulating. One or both of them could indeed have been a sneaking snake. But it also might just be . . . they disagree. That's the thing about the social world—sometimes there isn't just one right thing, one group culture, one "meaning" of this or that. What does it mean to *you*?

Theory of Interviewing

Questions and Tasks

Before I go into how one constructs an interview of a certain type, I'm going to lay out a theory of interviewing—a way of thinking about what's going on. The essence of the theory is this: the interview is a set of tasks, strung together so that it feels like a conversation. Each time you ask a question, you are setting a task for the interviewee. When you correctly understand the nature of the task as the respondent interprets it, you can understand the response. Otherwise, you can't.

I'm sure some of you are saying to yourselves, "ugh, what a creep. There's no way that's true. The whole reason I want to do interviewing is to get away from that dehumanizing approach to sociology. Interviewing is all about the establishment of intersubjectivity, a reciprocal engagement of minds, and not some sort of poking-frogs-with-electrical-probes science." I say, bullshit. If that's your attitude, you're starting down the road we'll have to revisit in the chapter on ethics. Why? Because you're making it impossible to theorize the process whereby your data are being jointly produced. You won't actually write the truth: that your "method" was "I chatted with him for a while and had a great time, recorded it, and then later I chose certain parts to string together to support a claim I wanted to make." Instead, you'll say "Stanley (not his real name) insisted that the neighborhood's decline was due to immigration. 'It all started when the [——] moved in,' he recollects...." In other words, you'll still go ahead and interpret your data as if they were responses to tasks—in this case, "summarize all the factors that you might think were responsible for the change in your neighborhood, and choose one as the leading cause"—that almost certainly weren't the actual task you had set. And that's why "Stanley" will feel like you misunderstood or manipulated him.

So no excuses for not thinking through the various tasks you are setting the respondent—and understanding that they are often nested. For one, the interview as a whole has task-like aspects. Frequently, the general task the respondent begins with is "acquit yourself well in this interview"—to put your "best foot forward," in the famous words of Riecken (1962). But then within this meta-metatask, there can be the metatask "communicate your *self* accurately."

Generally, the higher-level tasks will trump the lower-level ones. Given a choice of acquitting oneself well or communicating one's position, most will choose the former. Given a choice of communicating one's true position or giving a literal answer to a question, most will choose the former. Make sure that you don't give people a forced choice between two tasks, because you'll have a puzzle interpreting your data. If you deliberately give such a face-off, it usually indicates a fundamentally disrespectful attitude to at least someone, like your questions are more like "tricks." Most of the time, however, we don't understand that we are actually doing this—and respondents' tendencies to focus on higher-level tasks can actually help us. They will sometimes override a task with a variant that they think will better allow them to complete the metatask that they correctly understand is more important to you. For example, they may "misinterpret" questions in a way that allows them to do what they correctly understand you want them to do. Sometimes they will collaborate with you to turn bad questions into plausible tasks.

A good example here is found in some 1950s' and 1960s' "measures" of prejudice. Americans were asked whether they agreed with statements like

"Many Negroes spend their money on fancy cars instead of saving" and "Jews have more money than the rest of us." Here's the thing: given that there are millions and millions of African Americans, of course "many" do pretty much anything you can think of, and the only reasonable answer, if you interpret the question literally, is yes. And Jews, in fact, did have higher incomes than most other groups. The only informed answer is yes. And yet, when the results came in, they certainly seemed to work well as a measure of prejudice. Why? Because the respondents understood the true task, which was "we're going to run a flag (racism) up the pole. You salute if you like it." And they saluted smartly.

In this case, respondents saved the research by correctly focusing on the task of self-presentation and not the words of the question. But they may do this in other cases where we don't realize it. That's probably the case where we give them cognitively daunting tasks like hypothetical actions ("imagine this situation. What would you do?"). Your respondents probably have never imagined this before, but now, without taking more than ten seconds to make this real, they need to answer. So they are likely to first try to figure out: (1) What message about myself am I trying to communicate? And then (2) how can I answer to best imply this about myself? What the respondents have not done is what we often assume they have, namely, imagine this world.

For one example, let me take the classic work in political psychology, *The Authoritarian Personality* by Theodor Adorno et al. (1950). They concluded that there was an authoritarian personality that was very different from a liberal personality. Part of their evidence came from their psychological interpretation of answers to questions like this: "What are some desires you find hard to control?" Authoritarians tended to say things like "punch someone in the face." Anti-authoritarians (good guys, a.k.a. liberals), in contrast, gave answers like this: "To lash out at those people who voice an attitude of racial discrimination or an attitude of a dishonest intellect" and "Telling people about fallacies in our economic system." The researchers coded these responses as indicative of the great psychological health of the anti-authoritarians (1950, 554–57). Clearly, liberals didn't have bad desires like wanting to smash someone's head in with a rock. But what was happening was that these respondents weren't actually describing desires they had—they understood what the political bent of the researchers was, and those who agreed tried to demonstrate their agreement, probably to be "helpful."

Now in sociology, we're very attentive to one form of this, which we call desirability bias. However, we almost always mean by this impression management—the deliberate attempt to present a certain type of front—which doesn't get us very far. First, it simply isn't true that desirability bias and impression management are one and the same. Don't take it person-ally, but not everyone thinks you're so great that they're going to go out of their way to win your approval. If people are going to try to manage their impression in such a way that researchers don't see what they're doing— which is a pretty hard thing to do well for those of us who aren't used to it—there are all sorts of goals they might have other than just having re-searchers like them.

Further, some forms of desirability bias have ecological validity. That is, there's desirability bias in the world. We bend to what other people (es-pecially those with guns) want us to do. It isn't clear to me why the "true" answers are ones that would only have any relation to what a person would do if she were locked in an underground box with no windows. Finally, when there is positive impression management, we often misinterpret it. We often say something like, "Well, this at least shows what the person values." If you ask your respondent, "Do you think we should forgive crim-inals who are honestly sorry?" and she says yes, but doesn't really think we should, it means (so we hypothesize) that at least she recognizes that mercifulness has a compelling value claim over her.

Maybe. But that doesn't follow if it's really a form of desirability bias (as opposed to, say, a dual preference structure, where there are things that we value, and then other things that we value valuing, though we don't value them). In the desirability bias case, all it means is that the respon-dent thinks that *you* value this ... or at least, that you value it in *others*. Of course, if she isn't trying to win your approval but, instead, communicate her contempt for you, she might disagree with anything that she thinks you value in others.

Here we're getting to stronger ground, and more general ground than the conventional sociological interpretation. It's less about bias than about theorizing. Respondents will use *their* theory of *your* theory of *them* to communicate what they want to communicate, and most of the time, this is what you want them to communicate—which is to say, what you and she both will consider the "truth." How will you get out of the "but did you know I knew that you knew I knew?" kind of circle? Two ways. First, most people are doing this not through a conscious calculus but by in-stinct. So in a way, they're not really in that circle in the first place. Rather, the two of you are talking, and if, through your early communications, you can establish your genial blandness, you don't get heavily "theorized" any more than do other people. Second, if you write good questions there won't be a difference between the truth they want to communicate and the literal response to what you have asked. So once again, we find that we need to theorize the tasks we are setting interviewees, and we need to have a plausible cognitive model connecting their responses to these tasks.

Tasks and Minds

Whose Hang-up Is This Anyway?

When we think about the tasks we give respondents, we're going to recognize early on that we can't attribute characteristics of the tasks we give people to the people themselves, can we? But we often do. Here's an extreme example. Bob Altemeyer (1981, 233–34) asked student subjects to give sentences to various hypothetical offenders, and then asked them: "How bad (repulsive, disgusting) do you consider the criminal in this case to be?" He found that the more right-wing students tend to see the criminal as badder than did left-wingers. But he went on to argue, "What is striking here is the tendency to see 'common lawbreakers' almost as a lower form of life ('repulsive, disgusting')," as if the quoted words were those of those of the respondents, and not his own.

Sounds crazy, right? But we do the same thing when we ask respondents to distinguish two classes (say, people you look up to and those you don't) and then say that "Americans divide the world into two classes." They do indeed—if we ask them to. Our data don't tell us about the static organization of others' minds—they tell us about a potentiality that others have that can be used to accomplish certain tasks in certain environments. But that's fine, since that's what a mind is—it's a set of potentialities, and not a cluster of statements, and our questions are tasks that can, if properly designed, evoke these potentials.

Making Opinions

For this reason, people don't necessarily have ready-made opinions. Instead, they often have an inchoate mass of ideas; the question you ask creates a task that requires the respondent to marshal her faculties and thoughts. How we ask a question can greatly shape this process (and I'll get back to this when we discuss survey data), but this very lability offers us a great opportunity for watching people unfold their ideas.

In many cases, the issues people are most interested in are those that they are least likely to have clear opinions about. One student in my methods class participated as an interview subject for a class exercise; she was fortunate enough to be interviewed by someone who shared her own research question. So she was getting questions on an issue that occupied her theoretical attention most of the time. She was surprised to find she had no clear and definitive answers to give about what she thought.

That's because we are often ambivalent about what we care most about. If you ask questions in the wrong way, you can erase the traces of that ambivalence. In-depth interviewing, however, is the ideal place to put this ambivalence front and center. In fact, one of the reasons people like being interviewed by researchers who are not being their advocates or therapists is that it gives them the chance to mull over things that might be important to them but to which they never give sustained attention (Weiss 1995, 122). If you're patient, and allow them, they will hesitantly move out in one direction, come to a place they don't like, backtrack, and try again. It's really fascinating to see the fragile sugar sculpture that a human mind can unfurl if asked interesting questions. Unless you *want* to smash that into dust.

> **Minds are things we use to make beliefs;**
> **they aren't bags we store them in.**

It's a somewhat stupid analogy, but in quantum physics, there's an idea that some particles are in a sort of probability distribution, until you measure them. The measurement causes a "collapse of the wave function," which previously was a continuous probability distribution, into a single point, where the thing now "is." I think something very similar happens each time we ask someone to take a stand. All the ambiguity can vanish, and, if we are crude about it, we can make it impossible for the person to re-create those other ideas and ambiguities for us. But a good, gentle, and slow interview can preserve these more delicate cognitive structures. The way to do it is to avoid making people take a stand, or simplify, until you've really gotten a lot of the more subtle, potentially complex and contradictory, bits of their thought out.

Further, when there *are* things that people have thought through and rehearsed clearly—what often turns out to be (seemingly) the best data for a sociologist—you may very well be getting something that is in flux. This story or opinion is so clear because it's currently the subject of a lot of cognitive work. We'll follow Harrison White (1995) and call this "Bayesian updating." The basic idea, taken from statistics, is that we often have more than one model of the world, and we are continually revising our probability of each of these models.

> **If you make your questions like hammers,**
> **you will smash people's heads.**

One area in which this has been well studied by sociologists is in the process of relationship breakups. There can be a time in which one partner is alternating between two models of the world. One is "we are definitely in love but we have these serious problems" and the other is "this was always a mistake and this person is basically not worthy of me." People can, if we catch them at the right time, leap vertiginously from one to the other (see Swidler 2001). When we catch them right after or at the breakup time, then, as Diane Vaughan (1990, 29) found, we get a very clear and crisp narrative... one that might weaken and allow for more ambiguities over the years.[4]

In sum, when we give someone a task, we can either be implicitly asking for a simplification—present only a single model of the world and shore it up selectively—or getting the data that allow for a more complex, and probably more accurate, understanding. One way to do this is to try to avoid forcing a "collapse" of reality. Sometimes we're going to get a collapse no matter what we do. But it's important to remember that even this may well be a state that someone is passing through.

Accepting Accounts

A well-known problem in interviewing is that if we ask people "why" questions, we're likely to get "accounts," not data on a causal relation—that is, people are *justifying* their behavior. Since this is so well known, you might imagine that we're by now immune to treating these as data on occurrences. But there is something about the method of in-depth conversation that makes us likely to accept people's self-presentation as fact. Good interviews require rapport, and a normal conversational flow, and that implies a successful socioemotional bond, even of a very weak sort. But in a conversation between nice, polite people who like one another, it is socially impolite for one to doubt the word of the other. And how could you? All you have to go on, much of the time, is what the respondent has told you. And what he says about one thing supports what he says about another, and this confirmation seems to convince you merely through repetition.

And just like we are all better actors than we know, people are better at distracting and tricking interviewers than they really know. They use the same conversational tactics we all use when we want to maintain a self-presentation. They let you be the one to fill in a piece of information by implying it, or arguing against it—which makes it seem a matter of fact, one you can safely take for granted. People introduce irrelevant evidence—

---

4. And one of the great things about her work is her interviewing the same people a number of times and, thus, being able to see changes in the narrative interpretation of the "same" history (Vaughan 1990, 202).

irrelevant to the research question, that is—which often serves to "up the emotional stakes" in making it harder for the researcher to probe further. Indeed, convincing people to see as relevant what we see as relevant is pretty much what bringing people to side with you is all about.

It's harder than you might think to maintain your perspective without getting enlisted in someone's side, because on the fly, we're not good at determining where facts end and interpretations begin. And we push this line back and forth depending on the rapport we have with respondents. We'll return to this issue in chapter 9, when we have to deal with how to interpret our data. At this stage, you can make life easy on yourself by not asking questions that provoke accounts that you'll later be tempted to misinterpret.

Accounts are data for studying accounts... not necessarily anything else. These aren't lies, but they are retrospective stories that make a course of action defensible. They don't necessarily have a clear relation to what most of us imagine is a "motivation," namely, the combination of a set of defined goals or general values, a set of feelings about different options, and a process of deliberation. Most of the time, people aren't making choices in the way our folk theory suggests, and even if they were, there's little reason to hope that humans are particularly good at storing away this information. With the passage of time, people's memories tend to settle into an account, and the more often they talk about it, they firmer the account may become.

Further, there are certain genres of accounts that are well understood as narrative forms. Many westerners assume that for every major life decision (school, marriage, career), they should have a such an account. So even if they haven't rehearsed it, many can formulate a decent one on the fly if we ask them a question like why they joined or left a relationship, a group, or a movement.

A well-studied example is religious conversion. At first, sociologists asked converts *why* they joined the group, and they got narratives that tended to have a typical structure (was unhappy, looking for more, amazing coincidence brings me to the group, the teachings make sense, join, fulfilled, stay). But then some ethnographers started hanging around with novices or those who were in the process of being recruited. They found few cases that seemed to fit the narrative—in fact, many seemed to be brought in just because a friend was participating, without looking for or wanting anything in the way of new religious commitments. But it turns out that one of the things that adherents get when they join the group is the shared narrative of why they are there. So someone who started attending just because her roommate did and said it was fun, and that they were having good food, but who ends up a convert, will later say that she was always looking for something more in her life, and the group filled that empty spot. She isn't lying, but like most of us, she got her identification of the problem when she got a solution (this is a principle we'll pay more attention to in chapter 8—solutions bring problems with them).

Narrative forms bring their own content.

There's another principle here, one that I'll treat more fully in chapter 8 (202–6), which is that certain narrative forms bring their own content with them. That doesn't mean you should dismiss the content as a fabrication. Just because you realize that you have elicited a "horror story" (a conventional narrative form in which the respondent accentuates the magnitude of an injury) doesn't mean that the things you are hearing aren't true. But you do need to understand that the process of the selection of elements has to do with this form and that you might have heard something different had you elicited a different narrative form. Not understanding when you have provoked reliance on a conventional form isn't quite you making up the data, but it comes close.

Explaining Belief

In chapter 2 (29–31), I explained why you should never set out to "explain" your subjects' beliefs. Feel free to go back and review that section if you need to be convinced again. Let me pick up where we left off. So when we ask people about their beliefs, we often think we're getting at the "causes" or "roots" of the belief. Instead, people are attempting to *justify* their beliefs—especially by linking them to more general values. Of course, sometimes we think we can get around this by cutting to the chase and trying to learn about people's values. That should be interesting, we think, and won't have this problem of justification, because values justify themselves.

The problem is that it turns out that when we ask people decontextualized questions about preferences, opinions, or ideas, these almost always are used by respondents to communicate their theories of themselves. This is important information, and for this reason, the responses can have predictive capacity when it comes to behavior (Vaisey 2009). But it's easy for us to confuse their attempt to work out their sense of self in terms of abstractions (on the one hand) with their internal cognitive organization (on the other).

This is especially difficult when it comes to issues where there is, for most sociologists, a "right" answer. I'll return to this below, but respondents often quickly size up whether they want to make a bond with the questioner, and if they do, then they are pro- all the "good" things. They're not lying—they actually are for these things. The cool thing about decontextualized choices is that you can value everything. Because almost everyone actually does want to live in a safe neighborhood with great schools, no unemployment, low taxes, and liberty and justice for all. That's not the practical issue that actors usually face in real life—the issue is what cards they have in their hands, which ones they are willing to give up, and what they can plausibly get in exchange.

For this reason, sociologists often look at concrete zero-sum decisions, where people must make trade-offs, and so where a lot of fighting and yelling and hence data happens. The problem here is that we're wrong to think that the ideas that people appeal to in the fight explain their position, any more than you'd say that World War II was caused by the presence of tanks. These ideas aren't *why* they're fighting; they're what they're fighting *with*. Often you can predict pretty well who is going to be on which side of one of these decisions. They line up according to social characteristics, according to their habits of previous sides they took, or according to pocketbook interests. You don't need to listen to a word they say to put them on a side. Of course, if you ask *them* "why" they are on this side as opposed to that, you'll get them busy deploying their arguments. It's not that this isn't interesting (OK, actually I admit usually it isn't, but it might be, sometimes); it's just that if you are looking to this to explain why they are on the side they are, you are almost certainly moving toward an asymmetric interpretation, for reasons we'll get to in chapter 9 (we'll call it the "rebbitzen principle").

The Fundamental Attribution Error

So it's hard to get people to help us with an investigation of the causes of their beliefs—they're going to be giving us the justifications of their beliefs—but it's also tricky to use interviews to get at causality in general because this is an issue that is also closely bound up with accounting. There's no magic cure for this, but sociologists and social psychologists have uncovered some generalities that help guide us when it comes to sorting through conflicting claims. Most importantly, attribution theory—a branch of social psychology that focuses on how regular people decide why folks do what they do—has found that when we think about why *other* people do what they do, it's because of the kind of people they are (see Kelley 1973; Jones and Harris 1967). So if you see someone else yelling at his kid for dropping an ice-cream cone on the dog, you think, "Boy, that is some crabby guy—he must be a pretty bad father."

But when we think about why *we* do the things we do, we tend to stress the situation we are in. So if my kid drops an ice-cream cone all over the dog, and I yell at him, it's because we're running incredibly late, he promised he wouldn't make a mess if I got him the ice-cream cone, and he also said he would take care of the dog, which he doesn't, and now I am going to have to clean this disgusting mess up off the dog, which will make us late for the play we are going to. Does knowing all this let sociologists get at the true story? No, not necessarily, not usually. But it will help us organize the differences in the data that we get from our subjects, which is what we should be doing as sociologists.

And an awareness of this tendency helps us start off on the right foot. Early Chicago studies very often focused on the *problems* that people of a certain type (hobos, doctors, whoever) had in going about their daily routines and getting their "jobs" done. That came from the influence of the pragmatist philosophy of action on their work. Yet it also led to far better data than other researchers were getting. Why? Because of the fundamental attribution processes and our tendency to view our own actions as reasonable responses to problems. By starting with problems, the researcher implicitly locates himself in the mind of the interviewee and is automatically getting things from "inside." It's a lot easier for people to divulge information that could, in one light, be seen as indicative of malfeasance if it comes as an (implicitly necessary or excusable) response to a problem.

For example, if you were interviewing a precinct captain of a political party, and you asked, "So do people ever buy votes—well, maybe not even buy, but just give some sort of special consideration...?" chances are that, unless you've already established a particular relation—or your informant has a particular ax to grind—you're going to get the same answer you would get if you were deposing him before a trial. The set is you-versus-him. Whereas if you started from "So, tell me about what your job is?" and then go, after a while, to "What are the big problems here that you encounter?" and then, "Whew! That does sound tough! What can you do about *that*?" you might get the same person offering that, indeed, he has worked out a brilliant solution to the problem, which involves something very close to vote buying!

In sum, we want to use the interview as a way of getting data—and not jarring people into giving us accounts. This requires really planning what we're doing. Yet if the interview isn't going to be boring, grueling, degrading, or invasive, it has to do this as part of a conversation. How can we make that happen?

Overall Structure

The Semistructured Interview

Interview formats range on a continuum from totally structured to totally unstructured. At the structured end, we have interviewers reading a prepared script and often requiring that the subject choose from prefabricated answers. We'll look at the structured end of this continuum when we discuss surveys at the end of the chapter. Even if you aren't doing a "survey," you may be pushed to more structure if, say, you are interviewing hotshots who require a list of questions in advance before they will approve the interview, or if you are dealing with such sensitive information (e.g., asking prisoners about trading weapons in prison) that an IRB requires seeing your questions and warns against deviation. But if you can, you'll want to avoid that sort of interview, and for good reason: it is hard to keep it from feeling boring, grueling, degrading, or invasive. And short. Since your respondents are likely to feel imposed on, they're less likely to help you by correcting false impressions, rewording poorly phrased questions, and anticipating what you will need (see Weiss 1995, 13).

The other polar position, the totally unstructured, is usually worse, generally because you can easily walk away not knowing it was bad. That's because you can feel like you had a great experience and that there's tons of great data—without ever having "thought things through." So we're going to focus here on trying to get as much control over what you're doing as possible, without losing a decent human feeling. There are, of course, exceptions: interviews you do as part of an ethnography may need to be totally unstructured, as they happen in unpredictable circumstances. You also can't necessarily be as "controlled" with people who you've already established a different sort of relationship with. But most of the time, you'll want to sit in between these polar cases of all structure and no structure.

This leads to what is called a semistructured interview. Like a structured interview, there is a protocol sheet describing key questions that must be asked and a general order to the questioning to be pursued, but like an unstructured interview, you let people deviate from this order, pursue their ideas with further nonstandardized questions, and generally answer things out of order.

How can you have clearly defined tasks for respondents without it seeming like an inquisition? The easiest way is variety. If you have a set of different types of tasks, you can find that respondents get repeatedly reenergized. Answering questions is not usually fun; having a conversation can be fun, but easily spins into a joint hallucination between you and the interviewee. But having different "nuggets" that you can ask in any order, and weave together with small talk and general questions, can allow for both control and spontaneity. Creativity regarding the tasks you give makes an interview fun for respondents, alleviates tedium, and gets at data from different angles. For example, the nuggets may be:

1. a life history narrative
2. vignettes—hypothetical questions where you lay out a scene and ask them to comment, predict, or decide what they would do
3. open-ended or projective questions (like, "What is the most important thing that ever happened to you?")
4. "games," like sorting cards into piles or drawing maps of one's day, and so on
5. social data (like age, income, sexual orientation, race, ethnicity, marital status, etc.)—the "usual suspects" for sociology.

Of course, there are some topics that are so serious that this sort of variation would seem inappropriate. In these, you are more likely to have success by at least planning to follow the simple "U-curve" format. You start somewhat superficially, slowly get to deeper and more difficult material, and have a planned retreat where you will slowly return to more superficial issues without any abrupt change. Still... be prepared for curves!

> **It's the incompetent police detective who always starts by saying, "Gather up the usual suspects."**

When it comes to the more objectifying "social data," it's best if you are able to fill this in as it naturally emerges during the interview as opposed to explicitly asking it; and then, at the end, ask about anything remaining that you haven't learned. The idea here is that if you are going to objectify your respondent and piss him off, you only do this as you are concluding, after you've gotten your best data. But do bear in mind that if you are relying on a snowball-type sample, you may be less likely to get other interviews if you leave a bad taste in someone's mouth. Work very hard to try to get all these questions answered during the interview, and if you can't, it's worth asking yourself if you really need this information anyway.

> **Bad Interviewers**
> **Blame**
> **Bad Interviews**
> **On**
> **Bad Interviewees**

Finally, you may find that although you planned a semistructured interview, with some respondents, it becomes totally unstructured, while with others, it's completely structured. Some variation is unavoidable, but too much disparity can arise if you haven't really planned how to set up the relationship you're going to strive for in the interview, leaving it up to the interviewee to make this call. Further, watch out for a tendency to dump all the negative feelings about a bad interview (one where you feel like you are pulling teeth and staying very close to a formal schedule) onto the respondent (who becomes a "bad subject"). It isn't just that it's an example of being unwilling to think through what is really happening (and preferring to "account" for it)—it's that you'll have a tendency to dismiss data from this person, when this could be key to getting at the variation in the world that should be your real story.

Relationship

The interview is an interaction. Usually, it is up to you to define the general tone of this interaction, and the sort of relationship that connects you and the respondent. This sets the context in which your answers need to be interpreted. There are different overall types of relationships that interviewers can have. Some are very formal.

Others attempt to draw out their respondents by appearing like a sort of gullible "respectful student" who is impressed at how much the respondent knows about things. In particular, female interviewers find this tempting with male respondents; men often seem to like showing off how much they know. Many interviewers using this approach first seem to get a lot of data, but later realize that they've actually set up a pathological dynamic and need to back off. So being a respectful student is good, but not *too* respectful. The key, as everyone will tell you, is that an "outsider"—someone unfamiliar with some particular sphere of life—can be a better interviewer than an "insider" precisely because people assume that they need to instruct the interviewer in details that they'd assume an insider would know. So the interviewer who tries to show how cool he or she is by "being right there" with the respondent can be far worse than the naive one.

Others adopt a more probing, even challenging, role. This doesn't mean they think of themselves as enemies of the respondent, just that they will politely push back on things that the respondent says that don't seem to fit other things they've said. There are risks in that—the researcher may browbeat a respondent into accepting his or her line—but these risks are just as great when the interviewer is being understanding and sympathetic but just gets it wrong. That is, the interviewer says, "Are you saying *X*?" and the respondent is too polite to hurt the interviewer's feelings (precisely because the interviewer is being so nice) by admitting that the interviewer isn't really following. Weiss (1995, 74) suggests saying, if necessary, something like, "Is this *exactly* right?" to make it easier for your respondent to correct you.

Sometimes a real challenge *is* acceptable (for a great example, see Pinderhughes [1997], 170). But more often, instead of challenge, interviewers and interviewees collaborate to produce good answers. What is essential is that, as Weiss (1995) emphasized, you can push on an answer without impugning someone's integrity. If a respondent's answer doesn't fit the other ones this respondent has given, you can "be confused" and ask the person to explain more. Since all of us have inconsistent ideas, you can always find inconsistencies if you direct the inquiry to that space of their heads. So there isn't anything momentous in finding inconsistencies, and it shouldn't seem weird to talk about them. Nor do you need to avoid them. It's possible to find such a wrinkle "interesting" or even "fascinating," while still treating it as completely normal and unproblematic. If you need to push but are worried about injuring rapport, you can put your challenge in someone else's mouth. "It seems to me, conservatives might say...." or "I suspect a lot of white folks might say...." You never want to put yourself up against the interviewee (as in saying "I would have thought...").

This must, however, always be done in the form of questions, not reactions. If you are resisting what you are hearing (finding yourself regularly beginning responses with "But..."), you're implying that you won't allow your interviewee to say things that disconfirm your expectation. That's a deal breaker.

Don't Be Self-Indulgent

One additional caution regarding the relation you establish. You should be incredibly skeptical of any urge toward self-disclosure in an interview. There are people who have adopted such formats as, in principle, morally righteous because they see these as more egalitarian. Whether these interviews are more egalitarian—whatever that even means—than others and whether that's a good thing, I don't know. But I am pretty sure that they are very different from other sorts of interviews, and different in ways that beginning researchers may not fully understand.

In a standard interview, the interviewer tries to recede somewhat into the background and make the speaker feel unself-conscious and accepted. This approach is taken to facilitate clarity and willingness on the part of the speaker to express herself, and rightly so, I think.

If you take some opportunity to shift attention to yourself, even if you are doing so to bond with your interviewee, you are fundamentally changing your conversational role. In particular, you are giving off a cue that you need to be "handled." You have feelings and opinions of your own. The sphere of freedom in which the other can move without concern shrinks. It is rude for anyone to hurt a conversation partner's feelings or contradict him or her. Now, you may have said nothing beyond, "Oh, that happened to me too. Isn't that terrible?" But you are still reminding your interviewee that you are a personality and you are bringing the interview closer to a less productive conversation where your interviewee will have to think things through before speaking to make sure that what she is about to say is something that you will be OK hearing, or, even worse, she'll shift into a mode of interaction where she won't even think this— she'll just do it.

I know it's hard. If you had some major and unsettling experience as a child, and you have a respondent tearfully recounting his own similar experience, of course you will want to let him know that happened to you, too, so he won't feel so alone. And there may be settings in which you need to do this (such as an ethnographic context where it's likely to come out sooner or later). But try to avoid this if you possibly can. And don't think, "These warnings don't apply to me, because I'm going to be talking to a very select group of people, who are already going to think a lot like me. I don't need to act like it's some random sample of any old people." Because that's the kind of bad thinking that makes itself true in your data—you'll never get to learn whether they really do see things the same as you do.

Questions

Writing Questions

I'm now going to go through and discuss some particularities of the sorts of questions you should and shouldn't ask. I'm going to go into a fair amount of detail here because I find that most of the methods books that students read don't do this, and I see so many students starting off on terrible projects because of flawed questions. The basic principle here is that your informants won't lie unless you make them. And we often do just that.

And it's for this reason that I think it is 100 percent unacceptable for you not to write out a full interview schedule before you jump in. Of course, you can deviate from it—you'll have to—and of course, you can change it based on your results. But you need to start with this, just like you were doing a survey, because unless you are so good that you are not reading this book, you cannot trust yourself to improvise questions.

> ## Bad questions lead you to rely on the like-likes.

Your precise words matter. A lot. People may take a question literally when you aren't thinking about the literal meaning of your words, or they may pick up on an implication, when you weren't thinking about it. So make sure that there is no disjunction between the connotations and the denotations of your words!

When I listen to student interviews, or look at their interview schedules, I almost always find that they are incredibly optimistic about everything falling right into their laps. For information that probably requires ten questions to get, a student will have a single question. That's basically the interviewer assuming that he'll only be getting good data from one type of respondent (the like-like, almost certainly). And then that type will be interpreted as the "general." Here's an example. First I'm going to show a typical unfolding of a poor interview schedule, and then how to rewrite poor questions in such a way that you'll be a good interviewer (see fig. 4.1).

Now I'm going to show how a question similar to that last, poorly asked one, should be written, if you wanted to actually get data, as opposed to only getting consent to your own theory (see fig. 4.2).

By first getting the respondent to correctly orient to a specific time and place, and giving her time to start having her memories become concrete, you get her in a mental place where she's more likely to have actual memories in response to your question. If you start tugging on enough different strings, each of which run off into tangles of memories, you're more likely to get your interviewee to produce an actual, concrete memory, as opposed to answering off the top of her head, based on her theory of society, her theory of herself, or her theory of what you want to hear. The art of doing this—of constructing tasks that guide the respondent to a place where she can produce the data you want—is the art of writing questions.

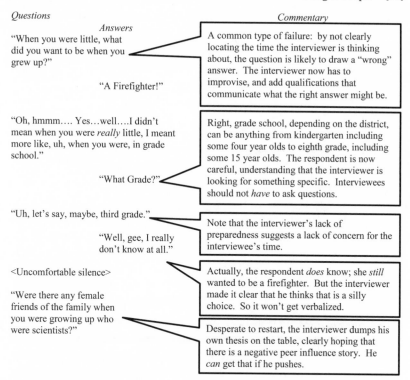

FIGURE 4.1. Example of a poor interview schedule

General Principles of Question Writing

Don't Ask Your Question

Before getting to general principles of question writing, actually, let's just dispose of the single, biggest error, which is to ask the respondent to answer your theoretical question. An example of this can be found in figure 4.1, with an interviewer interested in role model and peer effects on career choice. So he asks some woman if she would have been a scientist if she had had role models. What could be wrong with this? First, that's saying, do my work for me. Second, it's saying "make up lies." People can't answer these types of questions—not because they don't know enough but because such questions are really about another world we don't live in (the one where she had a scientist aunt). In general, if one person could answer the question, we wouldn't need to ask lots of people.

Further, leave the lawyering to the lawyers. When you're really intent on your own hypothesis you may be tempted to construct a set of questions

Student's Proposed Questions   *A Better Schedule*

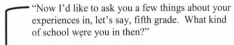

"Now I'd like to ask you a few things about your experiences in, let's say, fifth grade. What kind of school were you in then?"

"Were there any particularly memorable teachers that stand out for you?"

"What classes did you really enjoy?" "Tell me about that."

"And when you were in school, did you and your female friends think of science as something you were interested in?"

"What classes did you hate?" "Tell me about that."

"And in college, were there lots of women who seemed interested in science?

"You didn't mention science classes. Did you have a general science class? Do you remember this?"

"Can you remember the teacher?"

And so on....

FIGURE 4.2. How to expand a bad question

all narrowly focused on just the point you want to make—like a lawyer just wanting the little bits he can use to string together his case. Respondents can sense this and they hate it. Asking for specifics is one thing, but communicating that you only want one part of their answer is disrespectful. Finally, if you do this, you can easily miss what's going on, because you're so intent on this one thing, that if something else is the real story, you'd never know. You need to back up and look at the big picture.

Instead, what you should be after is getting at the data that are most likely to allow you to answer your question, *and* to figure out if you asked the wrong question to begin with. You need to go broadly into things so that you can find out if you missed something. To do that, you need to craft your questions like the instruments they are. Only when you are very good will you be able to do this on the fly.

Clarity

So let's think as if we were writing out each and every question. There is a continuum from more directed to more open questions. At one extreme are questions intended to extract a particular piece of information. And sometimes we know the range of possible answers. In such a case, everything can be written out like a survey. As a good survey question writer will know, questions that might seem equivalent but "less formal" are often worse than their more precisely worded cousins. You might think that "what state were you born in?" doesn't sound like part of normal conversation, and want to substitute "So, what state do you come from?" But the latter one can have multiple true answers depending on how one interprets it. I'm not saying it's better to be wooden than to be ambiguous, but I am saying that you need to be neither. It's all about clarity.

And for this reason, it's important that our questions be as simple as possible. That means they need to be relatively short. And we want each to have a distinct idea. Almost everyone should be able to understand what the questions mean and this meaning should be the same for all persons. That implies, most obviously, avoiding "double-barreled" questions, those that evoke more than one belief or attitude at a time. For example, we ask people to agree or disagree: "In America, every person has the same opportunity to study hard and get ahead." Suppose I think that every person has the opportunity to study hard, but not to get ahead? What do I say? Suppose I think that every person has the opportunity to study hard, and also to get ahead, but that studying hard doesn't lead to getting ahead? Too confusing. Simplify.

Every negation used makes the sentence harder to understand and increases the likelihood that you'll lose people. Complex branching structures, or conditionals, are even harder. If you need to give someone a conditional, break it up. So a question like "If you were going to move to another state sometime in the next year, what would guide your choice of neighborhood?" is a disaster. While your respondent is still trying to get a handle on this alternate world, *and* figure out what the point of the question is, you demand the specifics. Break it up: "I'm interested in how people choose neighborhoods to live in. Let's say you were going to move out of state, say, in the next year. So your kids are basically at the ages they are now. What would you be looking for in a neighborhood?"

It's one of those stitch-in-time issues. You can rush into interviews with poorly thought-out questions, and then get into interpretive nightmares (see chapter 9!), or think through what you are doing now, and have the interpretation run smoothly later.

Specificity and Plausible Tasks

It's important that you avoid posing tasks that are really too ambitious for the respondent to complete accurately. That means that you shouldn't ask respondents to generalize beyond their real abilities. Don't ask them to tell you, for example, what they "usually do" when they have disagreements in their friendships. Ask them about a particular person, or a particular fight—the most recent, for example. "Usual" is a key for people to switch into their normative self-understanding—you are what you "usually" do— and so when asked about this, their response has a lot to do with what they think they want to be (e.g., "I usually try to communicate with them about the real problem"). Of course, everyone can be a good person who just happened, last time, to slam the door, unplug the phone, pretend he didn't know her.

For instance, when people are asked how often they attend church, a bit fewer than half usually say that they go every week (or did in the 1980s; Hadaway, Marler, and Chaves 1993). But if you ask them to walk through what they did every minute of last Sunday—or if you actually run around Sunday morning and try to count who is sitting in the pews—you'll get maybe half this many. That's because when they answer the question about attendance, they aren't taking into account all the times they wanted to or planned to go to church but just didn't. Since it's not their fault that Susie was sick and they didn't go, or there was too much to do in the house, it doesn't really count against them, and so someone who went twice in the last month feels truthful in saying he or she went weekly.

Even if interviewees wanted to do the hard work of figuring out how to answer this sort of "usually" question—and let's hope that they intuit what particular summary statistic we are thinking of!—it's a difficult cognitive task. A seemingly simple question like "How often do you do the dinner dishes?" requires that respondents retrieve, aggregate, and carry out mathematical operations on dozens of events that have probably not been deliberately committed to memory. If, however, you ask, "What did you have for dinner last night? After dinner, what did you do? Who did the dishes?" you are likely to get a good answer.[5] You might get an exceptional answer (this is the only time in the year this guy has done the dishes), but since you're asking more than one person, you probably won't get led astray and report a self-concept as fact.

Of course, sometimes you do want self-concept. We might, to give one example, ask them what they think it means to be a man, or what it means to be a woman. In such cases, it can help to also ask for specific instances, but we don't want to miss out on learning that people have big ideas that aren't the same as what they do.

And there's one other qualification to the principle of specificity: we can easily demand information from people that they are extremely unlikely to possess. Asking a forty-year-old "Why did you choose to take the Shakespeare class in tenth-grade English" is like asking, "So where were you at 8:20 P.M. on Thursday, June 25, 1964?"

---

5. I should note that Tourangeau et al. (2000) find that some general time questions are more accurate than the "most recent" type questions; but still, start with Schaeffer (1991) and Gaskell et al. (1994).

People will do far better if you ask them about recent things. A question that begins "was there ever a time..." will get you the same sort of answers that your third-grade teacher got from similar assignments: garbage. Even if you want to ask about the past, start with the present, start with something concrete, and walk backward.

Finally, as I tried to show above, by breaking a cognitive task up into stages, you make things easy on your respondent. If you ask, "Did any female science teachers ever reach out to you?" there's a good chance your respondent will feel pressure to answer before she could possibly remember anything. But if you first get her to walk through her science teachers, focus on the female ones, and ask whether any of these reached out, your respondent has time to dust off those memories.

What People Don't Know

So people don't always know exactly what happened when. And most sociologists intuitively understand that. But there are other things they don't know that we often ask them about. We ask them what other people thought. Of course, they don't actually know, but they'll usually answer nonetheless, if only to be polite. We ask them why other people did the things they did. And our respondents don't know, but they'll answer that, too. We ask them what they would have done in such-and-such a situation. And they don't know, but they'll answer. We ask them if things would have been different had some factor been present or absent. And they don't know, but they'll answer.

Sometimes we don't want to know these facts; all we really want to discover is how our respondent talks about things. But more of the time than we admit, we *do* want the facts, even though we have little disclaimers to the contrary. If so, there are definitely ways we can ask questions so that we're getting better information. For example, if our respondent reports being fired, and we ask "Why did they fire you?" we are making two mistakes. First, using "why" is likely to provoke accounting, remember? Second, this question is about a motivation to which the respondent has no access. So this is most likely to provoke the respondent into giving a self-based account to communicate her theory of herself, for example, "I was more competent than anyone in the office, and they felt threatened by me."

> **If you don't make your interviewee lie, chances are she won't. So lead her not into temptation.**

Whereas if you were to simply ask, "And did they give a reason?" you are focusing on something concrete to which the respondent had access. And then you might get the answer "They *said* I kept showing up to work obviously drunk, which was total bullshit."

People don't know what's in others' heads. But they also often don't know what was in their own head a while ago. Even for something really momentous (like: "How did you feel at your wedding?"). This is especially true if you are asking about a state that involved uncertainty or error on their part—and making decisions very often does. Once people learn the right thing, they no longer hold onto all the different ideas they had that turned out to be wrong. They purge those from their minds like a computer losing a memory cache when it is turned off. When you ask them about it, and they recreate the situation, they're likely to refresh their memories with what they would have thought then if they knew then what they know now. They're not lying when they seem to insist that they always had it right; they just haven't stored their false beliefs.

Remember that, when a respondent recounts a situation to you, he'll be likely to add in many inferences, things like other people's mental states, their motivations, their emotions. There's no reason to think he's wrong, but these are still his *theory* of the event. If data on *his* theory is crucial for *your* theory, then by all means. But if you need the facts... you'll need to take another approach.

Prompts

Now even if we write out questions, we're not going to read a script, and we need to adapt on the fly. The virtue of writing your questions out beforehand isn't to take away your capacity to improvise, it's to equip you with good conversational chunks that, when you *do* need to improvise, are likely to be what comes out of your mouth as opposed to poorly chosen ones. Think of it like practicing the scales for a jazz musician. On stage, she won't be playing scales, but if she doesn't practice, what she does play is going to be a tad rough.

For this reason, you should have a good bag of ready prompts. By "prompts," we mean short responses, from the more context specific—like: "Was that the last time you talked?"—to the more general—like: "And how did you feel about that?" to the totally vague "anything else?" You want your use of prompts planned, as opposed to blurted attempts at disaster relief. Carelessly written interview schedules often involve sets of chunks in which a poorly phrased question yields confusion, and then a prompt redirects, the old one-two, over and over again. Why? I think it's because beginners often want to start by asking something general and underspecified, hoping not to put too much in the question, so that they can see how the respondents think about things in their own terms.

Avoid the old one-two.

But they are ready with clarifying prompts if there is a failure to communicate. Say you ask: "Do you think American democracy is working or not working these days?" And then the person can't seem to come up with an answer so you helpfully add, "By 'working,' I mean really helping empower all citizens." What you've done is give a signal that your words don't mean what they say, and that there is possibly always lurking behind them the *right* understanding. Now the respondent is oriented to you more as a tricky examiner. If you try to ad-lib prompts, you may realize that they were less "neutral" than you thought only when you're going over your transcripts. It's like looking at film contact sheets and seeing a thumb print on every one. That thumb print is often your preconceptions, pushed onto every respondent's brain.

Pretesting

In other words, you should never have to explain a question. How do we avoid these problems? We "pretest." That means that we ask our questions of people for the express purpose of learning about our questions: how they are interpreted and whether they are confusing, ambiguous, or insulting. Good pretesting brings to light bad assumptions that you didn't realize you were making. Not everyone who is twenty has actually had sex; not all who have had sex have ever gone on a date; and so on. You should try to purge your questions of assumptions before pretesting, of course, but sometimes we don't know which ones are going to be a problem and which aren't.

Usually, you first start pretesting on yourself. You read your questions out loud and see if you can answer them. Then you try them on a friend or classmate, and ask for opinions. Then you try on someone else who isn't a sociologist. After you give the interview, you don't just ask how it went as a whole, but go back over your interview schedule with your respondent. "When I asked you about getting in trouble in school, what were you thinking about?" Push your pretest subjects to give you bad news. They're likely to err on the side of being polite. And of course, pretesting on a restricted type of person isn't going to be as good as pretesting on a wider range.

For this reason, you might want to start out, even before pretesting, by gathering up ideas from test subjects. A great technique, and one that is underutilized by students, is to begin with a focus group. You collect four to eight different people who could be subjects and have an open conversation about the topic. As they bounce their ideas off one another, they free up all sorts of interesting possibilities and give you some sense of the range of people out there. You can raise your own hunches and see whether the members react with affirmation, confusion, scorn, or anger. People who would be bullied by you in a one-on-one might, in a group, let you know your assumptions are off.

Then, on this basis, you're in a much stronger position to begin crafting an interview schedule, which you then revise after further pretests. When you do these pretests, you need to record yourself. If you have never listened to yourself interview someone, you have no right to go out and perform any interviews. You may cringe in horror when you hear yourself, not just because no one likes to hear their recorded voice, nor even because you hear yourself make mistakes, but because you may sound like Moon Unit Zappa on a bad hair day. Too bad. Get better. Do it again, and record yourself again. It's easy to assume that because you now "know" that you say "Wow! Bogus" at one-minute intervals, you've stopped doing it. Maybe you have. Time to check.

Hey, you! Yes, you, the guy who thinks he's such a great, natural interviewer that you don't need to write out your questions in advance and, in fact, see this whole chapter as for the mental midgets. Videotape your interviews and give them to your professor. Stop writing yourself your own letter of recommendation. If you're not a naturally good interviewer, you will never know through introspection. Let someone see what you actually do.

Some More Particular Issues

OK, now I imagine that you accept that you need to at least think seriously about taking control of your interviewing process. I'm going to start off with a few things *not* to do. Sorry it sounds so negative, but better you hear it from me now than from your critics later.

1. Avoid Response Set

I've emphasized the importance of not just asking your own theoretical question to your respondents. Unfortunately, sometimes even when we realize that we shouldn't do this, we basically do. And we do this when we ask a series of questions about ideas that are all worded in the same direction. No survey writer now would do this, but in-depth interviewers still sometimes do.

The first problem is that it turns out that some people tend to say yes to everything. When Theodor Adorno and his pals (1950) went fishing for fascists in the U.S. population using a scale of (what they thought were) pro-fascist beliefs, they were pretty excited that so many folks who seemed like nice old ladies on the outside turned out to be fascists on the inside. They weren't. They were just agreeing politely with someone who seemed pretty insistent.

But even more, many people can get a sense of when you're basically asking, "Do you agree with *me*?" Then they have to decide whether they want to affiliate with you or disaffiliate. You've given them a task that overrides the "communicate my thoughts" task—it's the task of "befriend me or reject me."

2. Don't Contaminate

OK, so you get that you shouldn't just have all the questions worded in terms of your opinions. But your questions can still communicate clearly to your respondents what the "right" answer is. If you ask, "To what extent are you concerned with materialism in today's society?" if you get *any* variation, it will just be based on whether people see what you're about or not, and whether they like you. What you've done is contaminate the interview beyond repair by using terms that are both vague and loaded. The real problem with such contamination is that those who do it often think they're the best interviewers because they're getting such good, deep, theoretically compelling material! Woody Allen used to tell a joke about hitting it off with a woman at a party; making eye contact from across the room, walking over, he smiles, she smiles; he winks, she winks; he makes a kiss face, she makes a kiss face. Emboldened, he takes off his shirt, she takes off her shirt, and . . . he realizes he's been looking in a mirror. It's not very funny. But neither is doing crappy interviewing, thinking your data are great because they aren't data at all—just your own preconceptions, dutifully parroted by your respondents.

3. Avoid Buzzwords

Even when you yourself don't have a clear idea what's going to contaminate the interview, you still can contaminate it accidentally if you rely on buzzwords. But (don't get mad), often in sociology, some of our core concerns turn on terms that we think of as being "theoretical" but enter the wider world as loaded buzzwords that imply only a few possibly acceptable responses. Words like "diversity," "tolerance," "gentrification," or "patriotism" have no place in an interview, unless you're asking what these words mean to respondents. (And the answer is usually, not much.)

4. Don't Force Choice

Here I'm arguing that we should write questions for in-depth interviews, just like we write them for surveys. But there's one important way we shouldn't copy surveys, and this is by giving people forced-choice questions. This sometimes seems a nice way of helping interviewees have a clearer task and helps orient them to the way in which you're thinking about the question. But the great thing about in-depth interviews is that we shouldn't need to do this. Avoid it whenever possible, because when you say *"A or B"* you make it hard for people who think *C* to let you know.

5. Beware the Overly Open

To get away from this problem you may want to start with very open-ended questions. Sometimes, being *too* vague ("tell me about yourself") can be a disaster, and one that can bias a whole interview. Why? In a nutshell, not all respondents are equally comfortable seizing this sort of invitation. While personality matters most here, still, the like-likes are more likely to give you data. And a respondent who feels like she has failed to give a good answer to a task that seems unstructured, or who has demonstrated she has little to say, may withdraw and avoid elaboration for the rest of the interview. You can be specific without constraining your respondents' options.

6. Don't Ask Why

You probably have gotten this by now, but in case you haven't, here's the rule of thumb. Rephrase "why" questions as "how" or "what" questions whenever you can. A classic example comes from Howard Becker, who realized that "why" questions tend to provoke accounting and thin data. His example (1998, 58) is occupational choice. If you ask, "Why did you becomes a doctor" someone answers, "to help people." But if you ask, "How did you end up being a doctor?" they say, "I was trying to be a physical chemist, but the physical classes were always full, so when I graduated with a lot of organic chemistry, I couldn't get into a good physical chem program, so I went to med school instead, with my strong org background."

7. Triangulate

To summarize: the conclusions that we take away from an interview might well depend on what kind of questions we ask. This implies not just that we should ask good questions, but that we might get a better sense of what is going on if we ask about the same thing different ways. For example, if you ask someone, "What do you think is the meaning of masculinity?" you might get an interesting answer such as: "Confidence and taking care of others—putting others above your own pride and basically maintaining peace and order." But let's say that you also give that same person a vignette, "Ralph is at a party when Mark carelessly knocks into him and spills Ralph's drink on his new suit. What should Ralph do?" The same respondent says, "Bash him in the face," which implies a somewhat different view. And then you ask, "What did you have for dinner last night?" and the guy says, "Quiche lorraine," and when you then ask, "Who cooked it?" he says "I did and did all the dishes afterward." This gives us a more rounded sense of what this person is about. Any one of those things by itself, and we'd have only a partial sense.

> **If it's worth asking about in the first place, it's worth getting it right.**

Now, with some good questions written, and some pretesting, you are ready to do interviews. What next? Let's do a walk through.

Conversation

Getting Ready

So you're set to do an interview. Getting ready means getting your recorder ready.[6] Don't assume that your respondents will balk at this; usually, people are fine with it if you ask nicely. Do take good care of any recordings—don't leave them lying about. But don't trust your memory. Other people won't. Try to record *all* your interviews. Whether you transcribe all, some, or none is a different story. But record. And this means have *two* recorders, by which I mean dedicated recording machines—not

---

6. I think the Smartpen system is great for those who want to take notes, too. This can help you avoid transcribing the whole interview. And no, I don't get kickbacks from them.

your phone. You want something that is clearly divorced from your personal life, and you want two for when one turns out to have no battery charge.

Will people be awkward and self-conscious because of the presence of the recorder? Sure they will. For a while. But folks get habituated to this, just like they do to your presence. Will they refrain from bringing up certain topics? Certainly less than you would guess, because it's too hard, especially in an ethnographic field setting, for respondents to keep track of what they are and aren't supposed to talk about in front of whom (Milroy 1987, 61). Duneier (2000, 338) calls this the Becker principle—"that most social processes have a structure that comes close to insuring that a certain set of situations will arise over time."

Then, arrive. Get there early. And if your looks make a statement, don't ignore it. I'm not saying you should do anything in particular, and certainly under the Constitution you have the right to wear your Butthole Surfers T-shirt anywhere you want. And I don't deny that there are some good interviewers who somehow get their interviewees to see right past their pink Mohawk very fast. But you don't control who gets over that or not. So focus on what you are doing and what your goals are, not how cool you look. I'm not saying dress to fit in—this isn't Halloween—but think about whether you are distracting people.[7]

Finally, if you are doing a home interview, resist the impulse to let your eyes wander when you are visible to your respondent (see Hyman 1954, 51). That extra detail that you might be able to use to "contextualize" (stereotype?) your respondent doesn't make up for the distaste you are likely to inspire. The exceptions are photographs or other things made to be displayed to guests. These can in fact be used to start an informal chat.

Starting It

Often, we expect that people will be reticent to talk to a researcher, who, after all, is just taking up their time and giving them nothing in return. Surprisingly often, though, people are quite happy to spend lots and lots of time doing just that. There are a number of reasons for this: generally, people like to talk about themselves, and they find the attention flattering. Most of the time, the world makes it pretty clear that it doesn't care a tinker's cuss about what we think; it's pretty cool when suddenly, someone *does*. Further, once people get the sense that maybe, for you, their opin-

---

7. And if you are, sadly, cursed with the presence of hair on your head, make sure it is tidily fixed in a motionless form. You most definitely do not want to be adjusting your hair or touching your head during an interview.

ions count, they may suspect that they can help put a spin on your story, if this is a relevant consideration. Further, they may want access to you to check their own ideas, or at least use you as a neutral sounding board to work their ideas out. Most importantly, as you will recall from chapter 3, they often want to *help*.

Still, it can be hard to get people to talk the way you want. This is especially true as your sample diverges from middle-class Americans and Europeans (although now the experience of interacting with nongovernmental organizations has accustomed many people the world over to social science standards). But those who aren't acclimated may be suspicious of the kind of information you are asking about; they may believe that there has got to be someone with more information than they, and that's who anyone with a brain would be talking to. Further, if you communicate that you are actually interested in *their* day-to-day take on things (as opposed to correct information), this may strike them as unlikely. Presumably, this is part of your job, and you are trying to make some money out of this. But they've known all this stuff for years, and it hasn't helped them any, so how could it help you (Glazier 1993)? And if it does help you, how are you going to help them in return (see Weinreb 2006, 1020)?

You might not be prepared for such challenges, because first-worlders have mainly been socialized into the idea that good people always give information to others when asked. But we would never *work* for someone for free just because they asked us. There are other cultures in which these assumptions are reversed. An adult will go to great lengths to help another through work, but one adult never quizzes another.

Be ready to explain truthfully why you are doing what you are doing. Strangely enough, in some cases, you may find that people trust you more and like you more if you explain how this will help *you* in a straightforward, materialistic way ("once I get my degree, I get a job that pays much more money") than if you try to explain why it will improve the world. The theories that your subjects come up with to fill the gap you leave may be a lot less helpful for your research than a straightforward pocketbook explanation (see, e.g., Goffman 2014, 219, 221).

Opening Gambits

OK, you've got your subject ready to talk—how to start? In an in-depth interview, you often want to begin with questions that do three things: first, they demonstrate your sincere interest in the subject as a person; second, they allow you to learn the most important things about this person that would be awkward to have to ask about directly; and third, they give you the opportunity to judge the person's interactional style. For example, does she pause for a long time before continuing her thought (so you need to know not to jump in)? Does she have an accent that will take you a while to become familiar with? Does she have weird gestures that at first freak you out and that you need to habituate to? Having become accustomed to someone's interactional style early on, when you get to the more crucial data, you're more in control of how you are conducting the interview.

A great way to accomplish these goals is to ask some sort of general life history question. As I've said, avoid ones that are overly open-ended, because some folks will have a hard time getting oriented. A totally open task, such as "Tell me a little bit about yourself," can fail miserably for the shy, but so can a more specific one. If your opening gambit permits a short answer that doesn't naturally unfold, it can be worse than nothing. "So, you're in demolition! What's that all about?" "Breaking stuff." So craft your opening questions such that it's hard to give short answers to them, but so that, at the same time, one can feel like one has given a successful answer.

It can help to ask questions about the respondent's current situation, which will seem relatively natural, even though a complete answer will tend to require the respondent to bring in all sorts of different elements that you can then use to orient the rest of the interview. While people can give very short and contained answers to questions about the past, they tend to be chattier about the current situation. And then they've established a precedent of openness.

You want questions that will have answers that tend to unfold. Where people come from is often a good one. As people explain when they moved, and why, they'll tell you all sorts of useful things you might not have wanted to ask (their parents' occupation, their level of schooling, their prison record, and so on). A usually safe beginning question is therefore, "So, were you born around here?" If the answer is no, then you get the "moving" story. If the answer is yes, you ask, if they're old, "Have things really changed a lot?" (because you can be pretty sure they have). Or if they're not old but not too young, you ask, "How have things changed?" And if they're young: "Plan on staying around here?"

When you are doing in situ ethnographic or organizational interviews, you don't always have that much time. You might have a few minutes to chat with one person before he disappears. So how can you get something more efficiently? Here's one brilliant trick I take from Becker (1998), who says he got it from Everett Hughes. And this is to ask a harmless indirect question that requires the explication of the sensitive information, namely, "are things here better or worse than they used to be?" (Or you may need to come up with a variation that suits the circumstance.) The key is that most people won't lie because they can't lie—it's too hard to come up with a definite but false answer. Interactionally, it's rude not to reply, and few of us have the foresight to have fabricated answers ready. So unless the question is aggressive enough that the respondent will realize that he can decline to answer, he will say *something*.

Keeping It Going

Some students imagine that in order to avoid "biasing" the respondent, they can't have similar questions next to one another, and so they try to mix them up randomly. This drives respondents insane. It's true you don't want to have obvious context effects (such as following "Do you support the death penalty?" with "What are your feelings about abortion?"—which might show how *you* are linking the two). But for better or worse, the interview is going to need to have the overall structure and feeling of a conversation that has continuity.

And so a lot of your work comes in the form of you picking up and keeping the conversation going. That involves paying attention to what Weiss (1995, 77) calls "markers"—things in an answer that indicate something significant to the respondent that you might want to follow up on later (but don't be distracted and drop the main thread of questioning!). For example, if you are asking a question about geographical moves, and your respondent thinks these through by recounting job moves, this suggests that for her, employment is the structuring force in her life. Maybe not, though; don't assume it, but come back and feel around.

The hard work of interviewing involves having respondents develop answers further by getting them to extend a description of an incident forward or backward in time, getting them to fill in detail or to identify actors or others involved, and—to the best of their ability—getting them to regurgitate their inner states during all this (Weiss 1995, 75). In no way do you want to oppose or block where your interviewee is going. Still, sometimes you do need to break in, if only because your interviewee is going off on tangents or becoming too emotional. In either case, it can help to stop them with a request for an innocuous clarification. "I'm sorry, is this the Reggie that you met in Omaha? And can you remind me where you lived then?" This can give a respondent the time to reflect that maybe this is not where he or she wants to be going.

Responding

There are times when respondents will say things that confuse you, and you will need to ask for clarification. Sometimes you just need them to fill in some background knowledge ("Just who is this Cthulhu, anyway?") or terms ("What does it mean to say that something is 'the cat's meow?'"), and I doubt you'll have trouble with that. But sometimes people will say things that you think you do understand, and they still don't make sense. Going back and pushing on these can be scary, because you may be worried that you will come off as rude. But I am going to urge you to take the risk, because this is often where the most interesting material will be.

Let me give you an example from some fantastic work by Jocelyn Viterna (2013) on the role of women in the El Salvadoran Farabundo Martí National Liberation Front. Like Mitchell Duneier, she never doubts the words of her respondents... but she does a heck of a lot of fact checking. There have been claims by scholars that women in the camps were exposed to sexual harassment. Her women informants deny this. So she also asks men, who confirm the women's story. Did men pressure women for sex, she asks one man? "Women were never forced to have relations with anyone. And if that happened, the [People's Revolutionary Army] was very strict in that, such that many [guys] died for such things."

Presumably you see the problem. If women *never* were forced, there would be no guys to "die for such things," and yet the respondent indicates that *many* did. You might think that this "proves" that he is "lying," and triumphantly move on, knowing you can bust him later. But that's a hasty conclusion. Pushing on this can be used to get a richer understanding of what he means. It might well be that the first statement meant something more like "the standard operating procedure, which was officially recognized and treated as legitimate by almost everyone, was such that it was acknowledged that this was unacceptable." What "never" happened wasn't the act of rape, it was a kind of coercion against which a woman would have no recourse. And it might well be that the second statement meant something more like "while there really weren't that many offenses, those who did offend were invariably treated harshly, and few got away with it."

But that's just one possibility out of a huge number. My feeling is that, if it is worth asking about, it's worth getting it right, and, like Viterna did, you should take the time to really understand what your respondent is trying to tell you. Pushing on the inconsistency isn't cross-examining, it's dispelling confusion, and you should be able to do this without breaking rapport.[8]

---

8. Viterna herself provides an excellent example of how this can bring out new insights: pushing on how her informants told her *both* that young women couldn't go to Honduran refugee camps because they would be raped and killed, *and* that whenever an actual female guerilla became pregnant she was able to enter the camp without any problems, her respondents made clear their theory of the gendering of combat positions: "Young women were 'guerillas,'" said one respondent, "but a pregnant woman, she had become a 'mother'" (Viterna 2013, 171).

Adapting It

With a semistructured interview, it isn't a major problem if your respondent jumps ahead and gets to things that you were planning on covering, but later. Still, that can be a bit disorienting for you. You want to avoid flipping around a stack of papers madly when you're supposed to be listening. You can minimize this lurching about by having a good temporal pattern for the interview. That is, you should be going slowly enough so that you can always figure out where you left off. If you're feeling like you're on a roller coaster, you probably wrote your questions too "densely" and are moving through your topics too quickly.

Another reason you may need to improvise comes from misunderstandings. As I've noted above, question writers work hard to have language that is as clear as possible to as wide a range of people as possible. But it doesn't always work. Sometimes what you say draws a blank. You need to figure out different words. And you need to be able to distinguish between when your words just didn't make sense to the interviewee and when you've made an assumption that turns out to be wrong. In the first case, there is nothing wrong with adapting; in the second, if you go further, you simply start putting responses in your subject's mouth.

Here's a real example of the first. A student I knew was employed on a public health project interviewing street prostitutes. One of the questions she was to ask pertained to the last time that the respondent had "had vaginal intercourse." Some of the women, many of whom were recent immigrants, had no idea what this meant. In order to preserve comparability and keep the survey to the highest scientific standards, the interviewers were cautioned never to respond to requests for clarification but to insist that the respondent answer on the basis of "what this means to you." So, since the thing sounded sort of medical, some of the prostitutes answered that they had never had vaginal intercourse.

The idea that this was more scientific than saying "Oh, I mean scr——g" is pretty ludicrous. They weren't answering the same question as someone who knew what the term meant. You need to be able to rephrase things so that everyone can understand. But not to offend, shock, or disgust anyone either.

And for an example of the second—putting words in people's mouths by "clarifying"—look above to the section "Prompts" and see the example about whether democracy is working. The problem wasn't that the respondent didn't know what the word "democracy" means (the way the respondent might not know what the word "intercourse" meant). It was that you didn't know what you were talking about, at least, not with the specificity you need to ask someone else about it.

Ending It

Ending the interview can actually be very difficult for many of us. "Well, that's about it. I guess I'm all out of questions!" A sudden hard stop when you reach the end of the interview isn't the best way to bring it to a close. If you're sure you really haven't skipped over anything you need to get back to, this is a good time to tie things together in a way that helps you and the respondent. If you've talked about things that are upsetting, your IRB will insist that you remind them about follow-up counseling (not with you). But if you haven't broached any distressing topics, this an opportunity to leave the person feeling pretty good about things—which can be important in a setting where one respondent can talk to another potential respondent (e.g., you are interviewing members of a church) and you don't want him saying "what a creep!" about you. Rather than going gaga ("Wow! This was really great! Thank you!"), this is a time to reaffirm your professionalism and the importance of their contribution, and for them to learn about what you're doing.

Some methodologists suggest asking, at the end of an interview, "What should I have asked you about here but didn't?" There are some situations in which it's important not to look even the slightest bit lame, but I think this sort of question is appropriate in more settings than you might think—certainly in all pretests, but even in many standard interviews. I think it's also usually a good idea to ask, "If I have any small follow-ups, is it OK if I contact you?" And that's because, sometimes it's only after you've gone over lots of transcripts that you realize what you should have been asking all along. A short follow-up can do a lot here.

Going More Formal: Survey Analysis

Why Survey

I've been arguing that you need to think through the questions you ask a lot more like survey writers do. That doesn't mean that we don't see that there are going to be inherent problems with an interview that is completely rigid, no matter how well the questions are asked. Most obvious, we're going to have a hard time getting at more complicated and interesting parts of people's experiences and beliefs. There's a good chance we'll only be able to get these ideas if we carry out procrustean violence on them, forcing them into our boxes.

But a single person can only carry out so many in-depth interviews. Past a certain point, you need a team of researchers. And they tend to have a hard time pooling their data if they aren't strictly comparable. For this reason, researchers often end up "coding" the responses (see chapter 8). Well, there isn't always such a big difference between surveys in which the coding happens beforehand (and we give people four or five choices, plus "other"), and those in which it happens afterward (and we let people say whatever they want... and then reduce them to four or five piles, plus "other"). In fact, there are many advantages to the first: respondents might be better at coding their own thoughts than we are. The main advantage to us coding the answers afterward is that sometimes we don't know what the four or five top patterns will be. But with good pretests, we will.

The truth is that surveys give up the autonomous control of the individual interviewer because the interviewer is no longer the "head" but is relegated to a position of manual laborer, and surveys are in a way the Taylorist vision of research. And sometimes this does lead to pathologies. But what I think we've learned is that through a lot of good pretesting, we can get questions that succeed in measuring something very close to what we set out to measure. What we get may be useless in itself as a "point estimate." Saying something like "62.43 percent of Americans support the Affordable Care Act" is ridiculous, because how we ask the question will change this number. But these results can be fine for comparisons across groups and across time.

> **I'm always tickled to hear the scorn in the voices of graduate students who treat survey researchers as fools and charlatans for forcing people's complex ideas into five-point scales—when that activity's what they are aspiring to do as a profession (A, B, C, D or F).**

Further, what survey items measure may not be complex, but people aren't quite as complex as we thought anyway. So take a chill pill on the outrage you feel about forcing people's complex ideas into a five-point scale (see box). You can prove logically that the ten-point pain scale now used by doctors is impossible. But it works pretty well for all that. And the great thing is that Taylorist control project, unpleasant though some of the implications are for the peon, is good training in the self-control that you need. And that's what the great advantage of surveys are—the opportunity for a clearer theorization of the task—not their "representativeness."

As Allen Barton (1968) said, we wouldn't think well of an anatomist who took a random sample of cells from an organism and studied them all together—why assume the same for social research? If you ever served your time in the vegetarian hippie co-op house, you probably have now an instinctive aversion to brown lentil... soup? Stew? Mush? Call it what you want, it was always the same, the lowest common vegan denominator. Brown lentils, carrots, onions, bay leaf, salt, pepper, miscellaneous. It was basically a fair random sample of what was in the kitchen. Representativeness is that hippie stew.

Representativeness is that hippie stew.

So what we often think is best about surveys (representativeness) is not their strength; rather, it's what we often think is worst about them. And this is that so much is up for grabs. It's this that lets us use surveys to learn more about the response process, and produce findings that you should know about even if you are going to do in-depth interviews.

Response Process

A long time ago, researchers started to notice that how they phrased questions mattered to how people answered. For example, more people agree with policy *X* if you ask, "Do you agree with the president's policy *X*?" than if you ask, "Do you support policy *X*?" At first, researchers saw this in terms of contamination, and so they'd try to come up with good phrasings that didn't push responses around. But they often found that the phrasing mattered so much, that it seemed implausible that people had *any* real opinions. All there were, were artifacts. So if you ask, "Do you support the president's policy in Kreplachistan," 70 percent of Americans will say they do. Even though there's no such place. How can we study these "opinions"?

In trying to nail down these artifacts, researchers started putting together really good theories of response. And remember, that's what I've been saying we need to do—have good theories of the processes that produce our data. And as they pursued these, drawing on cognitive science and conversation analysis, survey researchers got more sophisticated, and stopped assuming that "real" opinions were something that people had all the time, even when they weren't being asked about them.

It turns out that it isn't just "contextual" things that affect meaning: it's prosaic matters, like giving someone a long list of alternatives, which means that they're more likely to forget some of them, especially the middle ones (and hence choose the first or last option). The sum total of these researches led to a Gestalt shift—sociologists realized that it wasn't that all these biases and distortions were things that kept us from understanding the logic of opinion—they *were* the logic of opinion.

So when Americans were asked in the 1980s whether they supported the rebels in Nicaragua, we got all sorts of crazy responses. And the reason is, most people had the sense that Nicaragua was a small country, probably in Latin America, and most of the time, rebels in such countries are anti–United States. Not everyone was sure about this, and some (correctly) believed that, in this case, the United States was *supporting* the rebels. But the same person could claim to be against the rebels and say that she supported the United States' policy here. She wasn't guessing randomly; she was trying to figure out what her opinion *would* be if she knew more. So when we say, "Do you agree with President Reagan's support for the rebels in Nicaragua?" someone like this would know exactly what her opinion would be.

Lessons from Survey Analysis

And it's for this reason that I think in-depth interviewers can learn tremendous amounts from survey researchers. It's easy to smirk at the bland way that survey questions are written. "Many people these days think that cannibalism is always wrong. Other people think that it depends. Given all the sides of this complex issue, would you say that cannibalism is always wrong, sometimes wrong, or never wrong?" But most student interview schedules I see have serious disaster areas, and they could have been avoided by reading up on the literature of question writing for survey analysts.

This is becoming ever more relevant, as students who never thought that they'd do anything like make a survey themselves are finding this a real option, due to new technical changes that allows for fielding small surveys relatively inexpensively. And so I want to end this chapter by talking about how these technological developments alter the field of possibility for the task of talking to people.

Brave New World

New Forms of Data

Recent technological changes make it more likely that you can do something like a survey. They also are allowing for changes in how surveys are done, and they even allow for you to use new techniques during in-depth interviewing, if you have the guts.

It's important that we separate different strands of these intertwined changes, as they have very different implications for research. Some of this really has to do with documents, and we'll discuss this in chapter 8. For the questions of interviewing and survey analysis, what is more important has to do with computer administration, which can allow great flexibility in who answers surveys and where. It also automates data collection, as opposed to requiring a separate data entry phase. And finally, it allows for new, clever, and invasive forms of data collection. With sufficient care we can...

1. tell where someone is looking on a screen;
2. see how long it takes someone to respond;
3. see, if she's talking, how excited her voice sounds;
4. see where geographically the respondent is;
5. and, very possibly, measure skin galvanic response, though fingertips don't sweat much.

We generally associate such computer-implemented tasks with Internet or phone surveys. But these are things that can be incorporated into an in-depth interview. And it's often actually fun.

Now some of the fun is only for the researcher—such as when we make programs that don't look like research and, in fact, spread themselves throughout the web. Or when we have things appearing on Facebook that look like ads but are really stimuli ("click here if you feel X!"). But there are also ways to make it fun for interviewees. There are well-known experiments that are games—for example, shooter bias games, like those used by Joshua Corell et al. (2002), to see if people are more likely to mistake an unarmed black character for an armed one than they are an unarmed white character. You wouldn't pause an interview to include that particular game, but other tasks can have similarly game-like qualities. There are few limits to the creativity you can use to incorporate enjoyable and revealing tasks into an interview situation.

You can embed experiments in your work by, for example, using vignettes in which certain aspects can be varied. You might think it's crazy to do this if you only have forty respondents. But it can't hurt, and something interesting might emerge. You can do more creative things. You can show respondents photographs and have them describe them or sort them. You can ask respondents to take pictures of things for you and upload them to your site. You can ask them to draw the route they take home and use different colors for different feelings. You can ask them to arrange cutouts of their family members to best represent the structure of their family. And if this is done on a tablet computer, all the data can be automatically coded and stored for you.

That's the unadulterated good news. Now here's the mixed news: this technology offers temptations to students to try to get a lot of information on the cheap, and it doesn't always work.

New Survey Options

Because of this new technology, students are actually collecting their own data with hundreds or thousands of respondents. Yes, the data are limited (sometimes only a few questions or simple experiments), but using such technology can be a nice way to move a research project forward. For one, there are time-sharing, Internet-based surveys that allow you to add some questions that will be part of a large set of questions randomly sent to different people.

There are also some less plausible ways people do this: at the time of writing, there is a web service called Mechanical Turk through Amazon, which I'll discuss more in chapter 7, since the biggest appeal here is for experiments. This service allows you to pay people a small amount to do almost anything, including take a survey. And these appear attractive to researchers who need a particular sample, like combat veterans. But using the Turk to find your rare population is a gamble you shouldn't take. The reason is simply that if respondents are doing the survey because they want the $5.00 in bitcoin you offer, when you ask as a screening question, such as "Are you by any chance a combat veteran?" there's a good chance that that twelve-year-old girl who needs a new Nintendo controller will say yes. So rely on these for experiments, maybe, but not to reach the hard to find.

Another option I'd warn you away from is the automated survey where a computer not only randomly chooses people to call but also asks them the questions—you end up giving your respondents that sort of experience that we associate with the kind of frustrating phone tree that makes us prefer to have no telephone at all rather than deal with Verizon. These surveys have response rates in the single digits. That's bad. There *is* evidence (Weinberg et al. 2014) that some forms of automated surveys like Mechanical Turk are no worse than somewhat more staid designs (where a fixed panel of participants is recruited), but when you can't answer basic questions about who your respondents are, even if you have good experimental designs, no one is going to believe your results.

So there are still good reasons to be afraid of certain sorts of easy-to-get Internet research. But some forms are better than others. And some are cleverer at making sure they're not being gamed. Some recruit people by e-mail, have a link sent, and keep track of who is whom by giving each person a unique identifier to click on; Matt Salganik's keeps track of the Internet Protocol address used to access the survey.[9]

---

9. Of course, like with all intelligence wars, every solution is temporary. Take for granted that if someone has an interest in cracking a code, they're working on it right now. It's spy versus spy: if the information is good, someone else is using it. And that means that the pattern you find may be about to be neutralized.

Don't be afraid of technology; or actually, do be afraid. But don't avoid using it in interviews; it can make them better. The biggest concern is simply losing control and visibility over what is happening.

TAKEAWAYS

- Your questions are tasks. If you don't theorize properly what task you have set, you can't interpret the results.
- If you can't pretest it, don't do it.
- Take for granted that the Clever Hans effect will occur if you don't take steps to prevent it—exert yourself!
- If you are sloppy, all your evidence will come from the like-likes.

If you were going to read more...
You've probably noticed that I really like Weiss's book *Learning from Strangers*. And the best book on question writing that I know of is still Stanley Payne's 1951 *The Art of Asking Questions*. It also has a cool cover.

* 5 *

Hanging Out

You will need to teach yourself how to see. And, if you don't bring too many hang-ups, just spending time with others can be a remarkably effective way of learning about them. But don't ignore the variation among those you study.

What Is Ethnography?

Origins Of

Now we're going to talk about hanging out with people as a strategy of data gathering. Why am I calling this "hanging out?" Not to belittle it, but because I'd like us to get a little clearer about what we mean when we use our terms, and I'm not crazy about the tendency to use the terms "fieldwork," "participant observation," and "ethnography" interchangeably. What are these? Let's start with ethnography. When ethnography really meant ethnography, it was a way in which powerful, usually colonial, cultures objectified those that they encountered, largely for their own uses (though ethnographers as individuals were often fierce defenders of the cultures they studied). They turned a bunch of people into a map, sort of like a "users' guide" for invaders.

But as anthropologists morally purified themselves by vilifying their forefathers and foremothers, one branch decided that they were actually the ones who, far from objectifying the others, were helping oppose the trend of objectification in the social sciences. To a large degree, this was because cultural anthropologists made the convincing argument that to really be able to explain what was going on in some culture, you needed to be able to *understand* it, that is, to make sense of the motivations of other people. In practice this meant, first of all, an emphasis on seeing things as an insider would. This has been assumed to require learning about the group and being accepted as an honorary member by the group.

Second, it is assumed that when you see things from within the group, you are entering a whole mindset (we call it "culture") that makes things reasonable that don't seem reasonable to others. This made a great deal of sense for the earlier anthropologists, often confronting behavior that was radically different from what went on in their home country. But because of this legacy, our discussions of it in sociology are often confused, as we let ourselves get drawn into family feuds of long-dead ancestors. Here I'll try to make sure that you start in a position to think through what you are doing without battling ghosts. There's one part of this legacy, however, that I'll keep for brevity of explication, and this is the assumption that you are studying some "group." This isn't always the case—you may be studying a less-organized social environment—and you'll need to adapt these ideas accordingly.

Ethnography, Participant Observation, and Fieldwork

So the word "ethnography," originally meaning to describe a people, is now often used interchangeably with terms previously denoting very different endeavors. "Fieldwork" means that you go out of your own territory into the field to study people. "Participant observation" means that you study by doing. Many people call themselves "participant observers" but they don't really participate at all. Instead, they watch and take notes on what happens and ask participants questions, both individually in interviews and sometimes together in informal field settings.

Others really participate. When Michael Burawoy studies workers, he works right beside them. He hangs out with them afterward. He doesn't just watch and talk. Of course, the scope of the researcher's participation is always limited in some ways. First of all, it is almost always limited in duration. Unless the group is an unusual one with a short life span, the researcher's participation will be shorter than that of other members. Second, usually there are a number of occasions when most group members, but not the researcher, will participate. The researcher is back in the research environment, at the university, say, and so is unavailable for real participation.

But there are also times when you only will be observing. I'm going to discuss observation first, and then turn to participation.

Structured Observation

Learning to See

Students often plunge into some sort of fieldwork—setting out to participate *and* interview *and* observe—before they really even know how to observe. That's like starting out juggling and unicycling and yodeling before you know how to juggle. A lot of dropped balls.

Observing is hard. Most of us don't do it well, or at least we don't do it well without training or after a lot of trial and error. And almost no one can actually observe well while also wandering around and talking. You may leave your site with the illusion that you have seen things, but a tremendous portion of these will have been "filled in" and very possibly not have happened at all. If they *did* happen, still, chances are, you didn't *see* them happen. So we're going to do a crash course in close observation, which is when you actually use your eyes to gather these data by seeing—yourself—what is going on.

> **"You can see a lot just by observing."**
> **Yogi Berra**

I was able to reduce what was originally a whole separate chapter into this section because of a marvelous book that came out right before this one, namely, by Christena Nippert-Eng (2015). It teaches exactly what I'd want to say here. My approach starts from the same inspirations she does, which is to say, animal ethology, and it helps to open with a brief discussion of what this is.

Animal Ethology What

While the "ethno" in "ethnography" comes from the Greek word for "people," the "etho" in "ethology" comes from the Greek word that means "character," and the word "ethology" was invented in nineteenth-century France to describe the study of the characteristic behavior of animals. For example, one might look at chickens and notice that they scratch the ground, feed, and chase and peck each other.

This is a different way of looking at people than classical ethnography. While ethnography might involve systematic observation, it always assumes that people are conscious actors, and that to understand their action we have to understand its *meaning*.

In ethology, it's the opposite—there was an emphasis on recording action and explaining its *function*, without assuming that the animals knew what they were doing. Much of ethology involved filling out what became called an "ethogram"—a checklist of when the animals did which of the dozen or so things in their behavioral repertoire.

Such an ethological approach has rarely been applied in sociology (though see, e.g., McGrew 1972). This is quite a shame, because there is a lot we don't know about people because we never look very closely at them and record exactly what they do. The few mavericks like Erving Goffman who did might become famous, but they were rarely imitated. Goffman actually said that he stopped reading sociology and only read animal ethology. (Did I mention that Nippert-Eng is a grandstudent of Goffman? It's her mentor and Goffman's student, Eviatar Zerubavel, who told me that story about Goffman and ethology.) We'll see why in a second.

In the 1970s there was a rise of interest in nonverbal communication which directed attention to various subtleties of behavior, but most of that was pop psychology, and whatever wasn't, was assumed to be and was drawn down the sinkhole with it. Since then, relatively little work has been done in the area of nonverbal communication, and so even though we've had a hundred years of systematic sociology, probably more is known about interactions between chimpanzees than interactions between humans. We know a bit about our touch initiation patterns, but maybe more about theirs.[1] We may assume that our interactions are too culturally variable to be studied in the way that chimps are studied, but this is only an assumption. That is, we know that there is indeed plenty of variation, but that doesn't mean that an ethological approach is impossible. You'd have to try to see.

> **Neo to Morpheus: Why do my eyes hurt?**
> **Morpheus [*sadly*] to Neo: Because**
> **you've never used them.**

Why don't we know more? One serious reason is that it's considered rude to stare at people: to train your eagle eye on someone who is picking his nose and wiping it on the desk, or pulling on his lip, or scratching her butt. So we automatically look away from others regularly. It takes some effort to learn to actually just stare at people and look for minor actions. And when we do, we often want to stop. Because, truth be told, when you start to learn how to read people as if they were animals, it can be kind of creepy. The actions that we normally don't "notice" (although in everyday life we react effortlessly to them) now jump to the front of our attention, and it can feel like the volume of nonverbal communication has been turned up to a deafening degree. Most other people seem clumsy and exaggerated in their gestures, and their nonverbal actions embarrassingly

---

1. There's also been some work on eye blinking and interactive dominance orders (see Mazur 2005).

amateurish in comparison to those of, say, a gorilla. Further, if you are observing adult humans closely, it is far from impossible that one will come
up to you and punch you in the nose. I'm going to go on to talk a little bit
about how to observe closely, but do remember: it *is* rude.

How to Observe Closely

In some methods classes, you will have an exercise to carry out some
observations. Say, sit outside for an hour, watch some people do stuff,
then write it up. This is usually good only for showing you what you *don't*
see—which only starts appearing at the fourth time you watch. If you are
lucky, when you're done, and going over your notes, you'll realize what you
should have been looking for. The most important thing for you to learn
is how to minimize the number of visits that it takes before you can do
real observations; once you have this down, you can work on making your
observations and records as good as they can be. And that means, don't
count on just appearing one day with a pad of yellow paper and a pen.

1. *Case the Joint.* It rarely makes sense just to plunk yourself down. The first
   time you go to your site, you should wander around and try to figure out
   what you *would* want to see. What is happening? When does it happen?
   Are there signs that it's about to happen? And so on. And then you can
   try to figure out, what's the best place to be to actually see this stuff
   happening? And what do I need to do to get ownership of that space?
   Sometimes you'll need to appear at the café at 8:00 A.M. to get the best
   table to conduct your observations at 11:00.
2. *Make a Template.* Nippert-Eng is great on note taking, and I refer you to
   her for particularities. I'll focus on one thing that many students figure
   out for themselves, at least to some extent, and this is the advantage
   of having some sort of prefabricated form, which Nippert-Eng calls a
   "template," to use in taking notes. Sometimes this is a floor plan, with
   a notation system so that you can turn movements into arrows; sometimes it's a matrix, with persons or times as rows, and possible outcomes, events, or actions as columns.

   Think through your notational system before you begin, because it
   is hard to change in the middle. The best ones are going to involve the
   fewest changes of "state" as you go from vision to hand movement.[2] So
   if you are trying to describe people moving around, the simplest way
   is to have a line represent a distinct person, with perhaps a different
   pencil color for each. Person moves left, line moves left. Person moves

2. In the terms of Peircian semiotics, you want your scheme to be iconic, not symbolic.

back, line moves back. The worst is an arbitrary code that requires that you look things up. "Tony ran right while Tabitha walked further back. OK, Tony is P18, and 'running' is motion 3, while walking is motion 2, and right is in degrees, I guess 90, so P18M3-90. Now walked is M2, but who was it that walked, anyway? Now I forgot...."

Even if you're not doing something so structured, it can make sense to construct your note taking "pad" in a useful way. The simplest is just to have a line down the middle with observations on one side, reflections or interpretations on the other. But you might also have special places for times, participants, or other things that you might expect to repeatedly note. If you are using an electronic device—for example, a tablet and a stylus—your templates can be very well developed, going right into a database. A few kids really used to doing everything on their phone may actually think that they can take notes this way. Don't. It will take your eyes too long to adjust from staring at the bitty screen to looking at the people you're observing or talking to. It will take you a lot longer than you think to switch back and forth. If you are interacting with others as well as taking notes, they may get irritated or bored (unless they're also checking their phones). Many of you will even have this trouble with a tablet because we automatically become a bit more passive when we turn our eyes to an illuminated screen. Anything that sucks you in is to be avoided like the plague. Otherwise, a tablet, especially with a specially made input program, can be ideal.

3. *Structure, Structure, Structure.* Your first few visits to your site, you may need to be doing relatively unstructured observation—you're still seeing what can be seen. But after that, at least sometimes, you're going to need to force yourself to observe in certain ways. Why? Because you'll tend to direct your gaze one way and not another. Most important, people observing groups (especially meetings!) tend to look only at the speaker. But you can't understand the group that way. People observing classes tend to look at the teacher; people observing performances tend to look at the performer; and so on. You need to give yourself rules like: "Today I only look at students" (perhaps, "today I only look at boys in the last two rows"). Or: "Each time there is a new speaking turn, I will alternate between looking at the new speaker or looking at everyone but the speaker."

Further—and this sounds weird and mean, but seasoned observers will recognize this—chances are, you avoid looking at some people. Maybe because you sense they don't like you, maybe because they stare back, maybe because you are afraid of your intentions being misunderstood (like you have a crush on him or her), maybe because this person stands out (the only white person in the room, the only one in a wheelchair, or someone with no ears, say), and you don't want to be seen as gawking. And finally, you actually might be less likely to let your eyes fall on people whose overall appearance you just don't like.

Sometimes your instincts are right—at least, right for you. You can't really look at the person who is staring at you to see if you are going to stare back without a fight breaking out, say. Of course, you should always try to observe as evenly as you can, but you need to remember the bias that comes from you not looking in certain directions.

4. *Record, Record, Record.* If you can, you want to record whatever it is you're observing, so that you can compare your initial notes to what you would produce if you got to watch the same thing over and over again. Never underestimate the importance of really, really, really, really watching that thing. Sure it's boring. But as John Cage (1961, 93) said, "If something is boring after two minutes, try it for four. If still boring, then eight. Then sixteen. Then thirty-two. Eventually one discovers that it is not boring at all."

Jack Katz (1999) was interested in where emotions become visible in human interaction; they're interesting in that they are somatic and mental simultaneously. He looked at videotapes of people crying. Over and over again. One regularity that popped out was that people were likely to break into crying when they were under a high emotional load, were speaking, and started a word that began with an *H* vocalization—most importantly, "heart." I'll refer you to his work for the explanation! The key is watching closely, over and over and over, which requires recording.

5. *Reduce, Reduce, Reduce.* Close observation produces a lot of data. When you have started with a focused data collection project—what Nippert-Eng calls a "mission-oriented" approach—you don't have quite so much, but it isn't uncommon for researchers to really feel like they are drowning in data. You need to reduce it—either zero in on a few aspects of what's going or have your templates be something that you can actually compile in a way such that you are already reducing the data to forms that you can compare to bring patterns to the surface.

In sum, you need to be able to see like an artist in order to write like a scientist. That's what Evelyn Fox Keller (1983) wrote about the great corn geneticist Barbara McClintock. It's what you need to learn.

Getting Your Mind out of Your Eyes

One of the wonderful things about being a human observing other human beings is that we are able to see meaningful behaviors as a whole. Instead of having to describe each movement of a finger, wrist, elbow, and shoulder, as well as each object that comes into contact with the body parts, for a page or so of notes, we can write "she lit a cigarette." We know what this act is as a whole, and we know this whole in a way we don't know about the parts.

I'm definitely not saying that you should try to ignore the meaningfulness of actions. You can't, and if you tried, you'd end up wasting a lot of time. However, such understandings of meaning fall on a continuum. Sometimes we are sure about how to interpretively "chunk" a set of observations (e.g., lighting a cigarette). Here we often can't find any other way than a meaning-laden one to describe the action. Some other things we see we're somewhat sure about—for example, we see "one person running after another down the street." But we understand that we might be wrong. (Maybe they were both running from someone else, say.) And so if your notes only contain your interpretation rather than what you truly saw, they're incorrect. It would be nice if I could tell you never to make such assumptions and always to question your interpretation—and that in your notes, you shouldn't include such interpretations. But I'm going to be honest—most of the time you just won't be able to do this. It's too cumbersome to keep track of all the events without imposing structures of interpretation.

Observation is not mind reading.

Still, other times you will witness happenings where you might want to add an unnecessary interpretation. And that interpretation often requires you relying on things you didn't in reality see. For example, you might *believe* that someone was now talking with "renewed confidence." But why would think you know the person's emotional state? Maybe you can keep track of what you literally did observe—a more even tone, fewer false starts in speech, steady eye contact—without the interpretation.

Focused Contrasts

And now here's the best part of close observation. When you do find yourself making an interpretation, and you realize that it's relevant for your arguments, you can—sometimes—check it using comparative observations. That is, during your data collection, you will do the sort of analytic work that other sociologists do after the data is in. So, for example, let's imagine that you are watching people "learn the ropes" at some new institution that they are navigating (say, people going to the employment bureau in your city). You see people who, two weeks ago, looked nervous now looking calm and confident. You think that because they now know how to get things done, they are feeling more confident and agentic.

But of course, you don't see their feelings. What's another possible explanation? Perhaps it is simply that they are habituated to the physical contours of the space. How can you check? Well, are there some people who aren't actually succeeding in the institution? When they are called up to the desk, they have the forms filled out wrong and so on. Do *they* look the same as the people who have learned the ropes? If so, change your interpretation. Thus, focused observational contrasts can allow you to develop some checks on the interpretations that you are likely to be developing.

Stage magicians always work by having your attention in the wrong place to catch them. Reality will do that to you as well. It will have you looking at one thing, the part that happens to interest you, and, if you don't fight against it, you'll make a mistake. Look at the other thing—the thing that is necessary to *test* your interpretation.

You won't be able to do all of your analytic work while you are observing. So what you want to do is keep your notes as interpretation free as they can be, and then to check your interpretations, when you must make them, by doing focused contrasts. Then you'll have data you can rely on when it is time to analyze them away from the field site. And you can also use the results of your observations to help improve the quality of your data gathering when it comes to hanging out.

Learning Through Doing

Hanging Out

This is the core of what is properly called ethnography. But this term contains a wide range of different endeavors that can be arranged on that continuum introduced in chapter 1 between "front-loaded" and "back-loaded" research designs. For a long time, the classic anthropological ethnography was very back-loaded; though there was a research design guiding the research, it was dry (e.g., to investigate gardening techniques), and the classic book has to do with very different matters (e.g., how the investigator became an initiated witch). That is the origin of one polar position in sociology, which I'll call "heroic" ethnography—the idea is that the researcher goes alone into a potentially hostile environment and, through trials of strength and courage, proves himself to the denizens and emerges their defender. I don't mean to make fun of this: it actually happens—a lot.

There's more of a move now toward front-loading in ethnography, with perhaps an extreme being the Harvard model where the researcher is like a Navy SEAL paratrooper—GO IN GET THE DATA MOVE MOVE MOVE WE'RE OUTTA HERE! Stealing the term from Nippert-Eng, I'm going to call this mission-oriented ethnography. It's often shorter, involves fewer "sleep-overs," and has a clearer research design. There are many good things about this movement, if only because it inherently tends to combat some of the illusions that are apt to spring up in heroic ethnography.

Finally, there's something a bit in-between, namely, the organizational ethnography. Here the researcher observes people as they go about their work in an organization, such as a firm, a school, or a political group. The nine-to-five aspect can lessen some of the "baggage" issues we'll look at in this chapter and the next and also give the field-worker time to rest and write up notes. But the temporal limitation means that there is less of an opportunity for the researcher to see many sides of people. In a few cases, this doesn't become a problem because the researcher really is only interested in what happens in the organization. Yet it's hard not to draw on your ideas of people as a whole... and you haven't seen that whole. Often students who do such an ethnography come in with the crisp front-loaded research design of a classic organizational ethnography ("compare two organizations...") and are worried because, to make their arguments persuasive, they feel tempted to rely on all those informal data that aren't part of the research design.

Thank God for little favors; this is one of the times when yielding to that temptation will increase the scientific merit of your work. Most of the time, as we'll see, it doesn't work that way.

One last thing—it's become increasingly common for people to proudly announce that they have done an "auto-ethnography" or a "constitutional ethnography" or a "digital ethnography" (lurking on the Internet). What they seem to mean is the following. (1) They think ethnography is cool. (2) They think they're cool. (3) Therefore, what they did was an ethnography. Ethnography is a serious, difficult, and rigorous job. People who call things ethnographies that aren't are more likely to have done something shoddy, easy, and lame. Otherwise, why wouldn't they call it what it really is?

Hanging Out and Experience

One of the most impressive characteristics of good ethnographies is that the field-worker can get the answers without having to ask the questions. First, it is true that certain kinds of questions sometimes make people clam up and that it's better to let people answer them by their assumptions or actions than through explicit questions. Even more impressive, sometimes you can get answers handed to you before you understand what the question was. This clearly isn't going to fit most of our ideas about research design, but it doesn't completely skirt around them either.

Let's think about this issue of being handed the finding on a platter. For a while this was often called "serendipitous observation." A classic example is William Whyte ([1943] 1981, 320) having a breakthrough about social structure while he was bowling—which he was only doing as a means to what he had thought was the focus of his observations.

But the most interesting thing is that Whyte's breakthrough didn't come because he just observed bowling. He also bowled. And when he was bowling, Whyte actually felt in himself the confidence of the others coming from his relative closeness to the group's leader, and hence—buoyed up—bowled a great game ([1943] 1981, 319). Without that, he probably wouldn't have developed his interpretation. Similarly, the sociologist Matthew Lawson (1999) participated in charismatic Christian groups and felt himself being carried away by the Holy Spirit. While he interpreted this as the "collective conscience," a sociological concept from Durkheim, his respondents would (I think) agree that the feeling was the same thing they were talking about.

> **Never forget the difference between *experience* and *interpretations of* experience.**

Interestingly, students often imagine that they can't share this sort of experience with their subjects, because of their lack of the "cultural background"—they have no real understanding of what the activities in which they are engaging "really mean." Only when they learn more do they (or so they believe) really "get it." We need to make a distinction between experiences and practices (on the one hand) and meanings and interpretations (on the other). I don't think it's at all implausible that, regarding the former, the ethnographer is basically similar to others in, say, somatic feelings (e.g., being buoyed up with confidence). And when it comes to practice, one can check whether others do the same thing. When Michael Burawoy (1982) worked in a factory to figure out why workers work as hard as they do, he found himself getting caught up in what he called the Game, and found himself working harder than he had to. And he could check to see whether others felt this way too. They did.

That doesn't imply that the "meaning" of the feelings or practices is the same. And in fact, although this goes beyond the bounds of the current work, I'd suggest that we are often wrong in assuming that there is a consensus on what something means among the subjects. People often don't talk about meanings with one another. They can have very different interpretations of something that you would imagine should be the subject of wide consensus. Chantelle Marlor (2011) studied how First Nations clam diggers and Western-trained biologists viewed the same issues having to do with clams. She found that the diggers all shared *experiences* but had very different *theories* about clams. That's because there was no institutional structure that would lead them to share or argue their points out with one another. This might be an extreme case, but it might not.

Participant observation, then, does give important data when the participant undergoes experience; further, there are good reasons to think that the ethnographer's experience is going to have a great deal in common with that of others. Sure, reject the hypothesis that it's exactly the same as "theirs," but there's no reason to think that any two of "them" (the subjects) have the same experience anyway. What's important is that the researcher's experience can sit in the same general universe as that of others. When Erika Summers Effler (2010) participated in an anti–death penalty group whose members powered themselves with feelings of righteous anger, she could feel the righteous anger within her. Anger, like other emotions, can be termed a "spectrum disorder"—there are many shades of what we call a single emotion—but it's not the broadest spectrum in the world. Not nearly as broad as our theories and interpretations of it.

That doesn't mean that you don't need to deal with interpretations—your own and those of your subjects. Many will tell you that you need to immerse yourself in your subjects' "way of seeing." But it's not that simple. You need to avoid two things: one is having an idea that is really different from that of the group, and the other is having an idea that is really the same as that of the group.

Analytic Independence

Of course, I'm joking a bit, since this seems to leave no options. But my point is that just as you need to realize that your formulation of what's going on can be different from that of others, so, too, you may easily lose analytic independence and rely on your subjects to tell you how to interpret what's going on.

The strongest form of such loss of independence is often taken to be what anthropologists used to call "going native." Sociologists don't like to use this phrase any more, but the problem remains. This can mean actual defection from the research team. If you're a researcher—especially a relatively young student—the group you are studying may be more fun that the group you're currently in. My friend Ben Zablocki lost a few research assistants to the religious cults he was studying. The ex-students seemed to be pretty happy there, and one commented that she considered the guru's teachings to be clearer and more useful than Zablocki's.

Still, there's really no scientific problem stemming from researchers dropping out. Go off and join the group and have fun! The problem is when you think you're still a sociologist but have lost the ability to think things through in a way different from the "group members." Sometimes, of course, that can be due to sheer laziness, but more often, and more insidiously, it comes from the fact that as bonds form between the researcher and the group, it becomes harder for the researchers to dissent from the group members' "self-conceptions."[3] Why? Because not accepting someone's way of explaining what they're doing is really equivalent to criticizing them, or implying that you think they are lying. This is considered extremely impolite. Some groups have been known to skillfully use ethnographers to communicate their self-vision by befriending them and taking hurtful offense at descriptions that they don't like. (Unfortunately, some of these groups also sue your ass into the ground if you so much as look at them sideways, let alone write something bad about them in print, so no references for these claims! Sorry!)

Ethnographers have talked about how they found it disconcerting when they felt the people they're studying and hanging out with withdraw their approval. This is true even for those researchers who are trying to observe at arm's length (e.g., Blau 1955, 197). The pressure is going to be much higher if you've decided, for whatever reason, that you want to feel accepted by this group.

And this can lead not only to a pervasive slant but also to huge misinterpretations, in which the researcher, in an effort to demonstrate how completely she or he is on the "group's" side, confuses official doctrine or justifications with what members actually think. That is, "the group members' self-conception" isn't usually as real as it seems. One of the results of the "myth of culture" in sociology is a tendency to homogenize the psychology of others, because we confuse a *public discourse* with *internal processing*. And so our portrayal of the group is overly consistent, overly optimistic, and so on. The problem with losing analytic independence isn't that the researcher is parroting the *members'* ideas. That wouldn't be so bad. Because the actual members (remember, now, we are talking about

---

3. Are you noticing the irritating quotation marks? I know I don't usually do this. You'll see there's a reason for this.

a collection of separate individuals) are usually able to see the downsides, the complexities, the inadequacies, and so on, that are inherent in this—like any other—group. The researcher who thinks he's giving the members' ideas may be parroting only the view of the minister of propaganda (whatever he or she is called [e.g., Davidson 1983]).

> **Defending "the group" is usually taking sides in a way you may not understand.**

So yes, peek behind what people say. But this doesn't entail a critical, destructive, or cynical relation to your object of study. You peek not to catch someone naked, but because you want to "walk all around" your object of study—see it from all angles. And only if you do this will you be able to see your subjects as the multidimensional creatures that they (like other human beings) are. A refusal to do this isn't polite or egalitarian or sensitive. It might be sloppy or lazy, it might be gullible, but it's certainly going to be trivializing and produce incorrect conclusions.

Take Note!

There are a number of well-known books that give systems for taking your field notes; I think that Emerson, Fretz, and Shaw's *Writing Ethnographic Fieldnotes* is the most often used. It gives a system associated with an analytic plan that I think is great, but it doesn't always work for those with a more deductive approach. Here I only have a few specific things to emphasize that are generally valid for nearly all sorts of notes. First, if you are doing observations as part of your ethnography, take your observation notes separately from other notes. Second, have a clear system for distinguishing between jottings made nearly at the time, notes made during a break in the field, and your synthetic notes, which you might make at the end of the day. If you want to correct or question something that you jotted down, never erase the earlier. Sometimes, a pattern emerges in the "corrections" you make.

Third, understand the difference between necessary brevity and prejudice. In your jottings, you may need to choose a simple way to remind yourself of who did what. This internal system is likely to be stereotyping (e.g., "a blk wmn came in…") and often cruel and offensive ("ugly boy enterd & sd smthng stupid & evry1 laughed"). You do what you have to in the moment to get as much real data down as you can. But you need to always fight against the tendency to have your notes turn into lies—which is what happens when we allow our memories to reconstitute the usual suspects. If you have to put a "jacket" on someone for purposes of identification (e.g., "the army guy"), supplement this, as soon as you can, with precise description of the actor. In the absence of this, all our research on memory suggests that you will use your general term to fill in details that you did not actually witness. For this same reason, go back over and critically examine any unsupported linkages you put in your notes: you didn't actually see that one thing happened "because" of another, and so that shouldn't be in your notes (see Emerson et al. 1995, 32, 80, 94, 112).

Fourth, if you are doing a real participant observation, and you want to focus on your own experiences—for example, learning how to be a cliff diver—choose in advance whether today you are taking notes on your own experience or on what others are doing. When you really pay attention to your own experience, the chances are you won't be in a good position to pay attention to others. And so the things you *do* note about them are likely to be wrong; conversely, when you're really paying attention to others, the things you "remember" about your own experience are likely to be reconstructions without a lot of validity.

Fifth, in going over your notes and adding reflections and musings, if you have questions for yourself ("cld it b th boys actually r frndly w/ the girls 1-on-1, jst nvr in gps?") come up with a plan for how you are going to answer it. And then link your later answers to this question so you don't replicate your work.

Sixth, you may indeed want some system for finding data among your amassed notes. Sometimes this is called "coding" your notes. For reasons that I'll expand on in chapter 8, I'm going to urge you not to *code* your notes, but to *tag* them. "Coding" implies that you say, with definiteness, *what* each bit is. A meeting you observed becomes "conflict over procedure." "Tagging" is when you are connecting issues, themes, persons, whatever, to parts of your notes, but there is no exclusivity. The same paragraph can be tagged "conflict over procedure," "spontaneous fun," "Miranda," and "beer." All coding platforms now will allow this sort of nonhierarchical tagging—the question is whether you remember that something can be kept in multiple categories.

Finally, make sure you keep track of your uncertainty. Here's one system in which

K said "we'll go out & fix his wagon"

means that you are totally sure K said precisely "we'll go out and fix his wagon"; that is, you recorded it or wrote it down at the time. But

> *K: 'we'll go out & fix his wagon'*

means that you are pretty sure he said just this; the phrase stuck in your mind, there was no confusion... but you can't claim you recorded it or were acting like a stenographer. It *did* get written later. And

> *K: ? 'we'll go out & fix his wagon'*

means K said words to this effect, but you're not sure these were the exact words, and

> *K: ?? 'we'll go out & fix his wagon'*

means you *think* K said this, but you're not sure. It seems weird that he would say something like this, or you had a hard time hearing, and you didn't get a chance to confirm that others heard this.

Why emphasize this sort of punctiliousness? Because you'll do a lot of analytic work outside the field, looking at your notes. You're looking for patterns. We tend to have a "downward permeability" in our interpretation of unique bits of evidence: that means when we're not sure about one particular piece of evidence, we tend to interpret it in line with the pattern we see emerging. And that means, with lots of ambiguous evidence, you make patterns, just like seeing a ghost ship in the fog. You need to be able to remember what is foggy and what is not.

Getting It Wrong

Hanging Out and Hanging Up

But sometimes the fog that leads to our misinterpretations isn't in our data—it's in our heads. We have a hard time seeing things clearly, for what they are, in close detail, because, for some reason, things are *too* significant to us. Bear in mind, a thing isn't its significance. That's true even if you take a rigorously phenomenological approach to things (and therefore you don't confuse an experienced object, like a jack-o'-lantern, with the physical object that chemistry might tell us about). When you have too many hang-ups, and things are too meaningful to you, they get replaced with their meanings (to *you*). The fact that you'll then use fancy theory to do the cognitive work to convince yourself that these are the same as the meaning to the group won't help. You'll only compound one problem with another.

> In your study, you're going to need to let
> things be what they are. Because that's what
> they're going to keep doing in the world.

Early ethnographies, precisely because they were trying to show how things made sense to people who seemed really weird to the intended audience, tended to fall back on the idea of culture, which is pretty reasonable. I don't deny that this is problem in many ways—for one thing, as a number of people, including Ken Dauber, have noted, "culture" then becomes a word we slap on a box in which we dump all our failures of intersubjectivity. "I understand. In *your* culture, that's considered good looking." (Silently: "Oh my God that is gross"). Still, all in all, it worked well to alert people that they needed to keep their dismissal engines in idle for a while and see if they could figure out what was up.

But the problem for the anthropologists using this was that their subjects got swallowed up in their own culture. It led to the assumption that (other) people's thoughts thought *them*, instead of vice versa. A wonderful story along these lines is given by Colin Turnbull in his *The Forest People*. Turnbull has gone to a forest in the Congo to study the BaMbuti people, generally known as pygmies. He is very excited to hear the *molimo*, the secret and sacred musical instrument used in special midnight ceremonies of the initiated men, kept hidden deep in the forest. The *molimo* is some sort of gigantic flute that makes beautiful clear tones that call softly across the forest.

> I suppose I had expected something elaborately carved, decorated with patterns full of ritual significance and symbolism, something sacred [etc.]... But now I saw that... it was a length of metal piping, neatly threaded at each end... I asked... how it was that for the *molimo*, which was so sacred to them, they should use water piping stolen from roadside construction gangs, instead of using traditional materials.
>
> ... They answered calmly... "What does it matter what the *molimo* is made of? This one makes a great sound, and besides, it does not rot like wood. It is much trouble to make a wooden one, and then it rots away and you have to make another." (1961, 70)

Anthropologists basically learned this lesson, but sociologists are not always on the lookout for the assumption that there is a true, harmonious canopy of meaning under which all true members live. They may tend to assume that two conflicting reports or definitions require "resolution"— that one person has to be wrong and the other correct.

Interpretations and Experience

And it goes a bit further than that. Beginning ethnographers are often remarkably casual in going from a datum (an experience, something that an informant has said) to an interpretation of the world that supposedly generated it. The recycling of official dogma as if it referred to everyday experience is only the most extreme form of this. More subtly, if someone opens up to you for the first time and says, "*This* is how we [First Nations in this tribe] *really* feel about white people moving here!" it seems awfully cold to refrain from simply accepting this as a deep truth (and a gift, and a mark of trust). But if you really are going to hypothesize (note—not "learn") that members (all? most? usually?) feel this or that way, and use this in your overall interpretation, wouldn't you want to figure out what would be a different implication of that theory that you can test?

Do you think I'm being persnickety? If that's how you feel, that means— I know this sounds a bit harsh—that you're not really ready to participate in an endeavor that ends in "-ology." We're supposed to put in the work that's required to get things right... and not just what's "interesting," or "creative." If it doesn't matter whether each particular thing you say is true, it isn't worth saying in the first place.

Subjects and Informants

Understanding the internal variation that every group has in terms of how experience is interpreted is vital for your everyday interactions with people, and, most importantly, the division of those you are studying into "subjects" and "informants." In chapter 3, I mentioned that researchers often use brokers to get access to ethnographic sites. But even afterward, many use some but not all of the people they study as "informants." A *subject* is someone who produces *data*... but not interpretations. An *informant* is different—she or he is given an epistemic privilege to tell you "how it is" and to give *interpretations*. Most ethnographers start out by finding some key informants early to help them get oriented. There's nothing wrong with that.

In fact, in the earliest days of anthropology, there was little else most did besides find an informant—sometimes a native who spoke the anthropologists' language and who was a broker for many things (and who was playing his own game!), or sometimes a missionary who spoke the natives' language. But rather quickly, anthropologists began to supplement this with their own interactions with noninformant subjects. Still, many made a simple two-class distinction between subjects and informants, with many of the former, and few of the latter (often just one).

Some sociologists still do things this way, but more and more will agree that you should get over the informant/subject distinction pretty quickly. In a way, you want to make *all* of your subjects informants. Not that they can guide your interpretation, but you want all of their interpretations. Because there isn't one "right" one that you are supposed to get. Your job is to systematize the variation across these. But it's just as true that you shouldn't have *any* informants—if by that it means that you are collecting their interpretations where you should be getting data. If you do this, and not because you're treating the interpretations as data, you're basically trying to get some of your subjects to do your job.

Put another way, there is an aspect still of describing—graphing—a set of people in ethnography. Imagine that your job is something like making a map of a park. You can't see it from above, only by walking around inside, but you can't walk everywhere, only on the paths. Those paths are individuals—the more paths you walk down, and the farther you go, the better an understanding you will have of the whole.

So sure, you'll have subjects who are special to you. They may become friends. You might talk to them more. And you might tend to agree with them. But if you are discounting how one subject sees something, because it's "wrong," that's sort of like throwing away data that disagree with you.

Hang-Ups and Freak Outs

I talked above about the importance of not having hang-ups. If, indeed, you yourself (body and soul) are your instrument of research (as Wacquant [2005] would say), you want it not to have a glitch, in the same way as you don't want your tape recorder to have a restricted frequency range. Yet students beginning ethnographies often have all these weird hang-ups about it, thinking that it will do stuff it really can't, both wonderful (change the status of the subaltern) and horrible (disrupt their natural lives—which, come to think of it, would be the result of changing their status, wouldn't it?). And this can bring that fog that interferes with you being able to understand what you're really doing.

Do Observers Change Things?

One weird hang-up is the idea that it will be terrible if the ethnographer "affects the participants" and that doing this would make the research nonobjective. It seems that this has turned into a moral principle of non-interference (which they called the "prime directive" on *Star Trek*).[4] As far as I can understand, two utterly different yet historically connected feelings are behind this. The first is a purely scientific one—you don't want to interfere in the lives of the people you are studying because you might change them, and then you won't get a proper understanding of *them* (as opposed to you). For early anthropologists, this was a major concern: the only reason they'd hauled their asses to some faraway place was their conviction that if they saw people who were really different from Europeans, and who hadn't yet had their society destroyed by Europeans, they'd learn something about human beings in general. But (as they knew), they were in fact studying societies that were in the process of changing, and what might seem to a novice as a minor interference—say, providing good informants with metal axes as an inducement for participation—could radically destabilize the society.

But since many anthropologists saw an inherent value in the social and cultural organizations they were learning about, they saw the kind of interference that Westerners tended to bring as morally wrong as well. And not just such interferences as forced relocation, conversion, conscript labor and kidnapping, which sometimes came with colonization, nor even the provision of goods that were mostly bads (knives, guns, liquor, venereal disease, and—in the eyes of some—Christianity), but even the attractive options (cotton clothing, e.g.) that tended to draw folks away from their previous ways of life seemed, to many anthropologists, bad.

Whether that's defensible, I don't know. But when sociologists make the same assumption, it rarely facilitates clear thinking. In particular, it leads students to assume that (if/since) they were good people, they won't affect their subjects. But since they also tend to be of the general do-gooder variety of social researcher, they want to "help" (a feeling encouraged by moving down the class ladder, which tends to put researchers in contact with people who, if they don't objectively need "help," at least are often having a tough time). And the third "but" is that they are also trying to be "egalitarian," which they often interpreted as meaning "not different" from their subjects, which rules out the one possible resolution, namely, behind-the-scenes paternalistic manipulation.

Now, I think that there are some actual resolutions that were worked out, such as Whyte's "participant action research" and that of Desmond

4. Did you ever notice that, despite all this talk of the "prime directive," Captain Kirk *never once* holds back from putting other cultures back on the proper path of capitalist development? Spurred by the moral outrage of seeing a whole planet full of good-for-nothing hippies, he'll turn the *Enterprise* into an overpowered crop duster and spray atomic paraquat all over the damn place! What's up with that?

(2016), though there were plenty others that were convoluted and weird and (as we'll see in the next chapter) quickly degenerated into narcissism. In the next chapter, we'll think about some real limitations to participation that are necessary for ethical reasons, but this idea of "changing" usually turned out to stem from a dramatic and implausible estimation of the effect of observers.

And this gets back to the first issue about the presence of observers changing the site that anthropologists struggled with—not that such change was ethically bad but that it was bad for learning. I think that complete noninterference made some sense for what early anthropologists were trying to do (even if it was impossible), but it rarely makes a lot of sense for sociologists. I'm not denying that you can, if you want, totally wreck the group you are studying—and the lives of each and every member. Of course you can—destruction is pretty easy. You can probably ruin the department you're at right now if you really have a mind to. But most probably, you don't ruin it just by showing up for classes every day.

Anyway, the question is whether your mere presence will change the group. This is something that students seem to take for granted. I'm going to call this the "Heisenberg uncertainty principle," after Belinda Heisenberg, who was in one of my classes a long time ago and thought that whenever she was watching people, they did something different. In the California college she came from, this was considered epistemically advanced. In reality, however, it's called *paranoid schizophrenia*, and she got a 5-year funded fellowship to the booby hatch.

And the truth is that, with a very few exceptions (such as criminal conspiracies), your presence usually just isn't a big deal, at least, not for long. Of course, the ethnographer might change it a little for a long time or a lot for a short time, but most folks tend to get used to an ethnographer just like they would anyone else. People habituate to observers very quickly. And almost no one can preserve a deception plan in the face of their normal routines. Usually if something's important for some group, it's going to come up, over and over again, whether or not the ethnographer is there (as we recall, Duneier [2000] calls this the "Becker principle").[5]

Or put it this way: your presence might, every now and then, change things dramatically, but usually not in a different way than any other person's might. And when it does, chances are good that it leaves a lot of smoke behind: someone uses a racial slur, then looks at you and blushes.

5. Alice Goffman (2014, 235, 237) points out that there are times when *not* "intervening" would be far more noticeable and altering of the way things were going, than would intervening—for example, when a young man would begin a cycle of threats, presumably expecting that others would interfere, thereby allowing him to save face without initiating a dangerous sequence of events.

Or someone picks the steak from the floor and is about to put in back on a plate when another worker says "don't *we always* wipe it off and re-sear it?" in a deliberate and pointed fashion. The guilty party is confused, looks around, sees you, and immediately agrees that they always do this. And so on.

So the question isn't really whether you change the universe but whether what you are studying is robust enough that you should walk away with a clear argument about what happens. If it's so sensitive to *your* presence, it's also probably sensitive to others' presence and, therefore, maybe not something you should make a lot of assumptions about.

In sum, unless you come to your field site seeming (correctly or not) to possess a lot of resources that folks there are in competition for,[6] if you conduct yourself with reasonable prudence, reserve and dignity, you usually don't need to be worrying a lot about how your presence "changes" things. People get used to you. And this turns out to be crucial for the second major hang-up that students tend to come with, specifically, the worry about being "accepted."

We Accept You—One of Us!

Because a second set of problems ethnographers often make for themselves comes from the idea that they need to be accepted as insiders to know the "true story." The classic examples here come from anthropologists who, before they can, say, go into the men's house, need a formal consecration as a "true" member. Until then, they are just in a trial period. Often this transition was marked though a ritual that would heighten the sense of a sharp division between the two worlds. And that's true—there *is* a sharp distinction—for ritual purposes. The problem was that then sociologists looked for similar watershed events in their relationships with their subjects that they could interpret as rituals of acceptance.

But actually, membership is not all or nothing. First, I mean that literally: in many sorts of groups, there are various forms of semi-memberships, including being a novice and being an honorary member. Just like universities will present honorary doctorates to people they think are cool, so groups can bestow honorary membership on people without forgetting that they aren't real members. An honorary member is treated like a member for many purposes and allowed access to some things that members have, but doesn't have all the rights and responsibilities of a true member.

6. As many field-workers learn the hard way, if you appear to be a walking chum bucket, then yes, you'll change things, and you'll make life miserable for yourself. It might feel stingy, but you won't get much done until you figure out how to dial this back.

The anthropologist Derek Freeman (1988, 1998), for example, went to Samoa, where he wanted to collect data that would disprove what another famous ethnographer, Margaret Mead, had written about Samoan youth. There he was made an honorary chief, and his new chief buddies told him how Mead was full of baloney. He proudly displays a picture of himself with another chief smiling for the camera to prove that because he was now a big-ass guy chief, we could trust that he really knew his stuff. (He didn't.) I think if he followed the principles outlined here, he'd have not made the same claims, which assumed that there was really only one inside story, and it went to the insideriest insider of all.[7]

But even when there aren't multiple levels of formal membership, it's still not an either/or. Thinking that it is tends to go along with reifying "the group" as something with clear boundaries, unambiguous membership, and generic commonalities. This, of course, increases the conviction that it is vital to be an "insider." "We accept you, we accept you, one of us! One of us!"—the famous pinhead chant from the movie *Freaks*—was imagined to consecrate the ethnographer into an inner circle in which all pretense was dropped.[8]

This just isn't so. Groups have internal differentiation, all the time. If you assume that now you are a homogenized insider, you'll tend to take your own ideas, or those of your informants, and project them to all others, because you'll assume there is only one group view, which you now have access to.

The best learning experience on this score is reported by Mitchell Duneier in *Sidewalk*. He had long since been accepted among the street vendors he studied. He considered them friends and felt that they saw him as one. One day, he walked away, leaving his tape recorder going (to which the men had long become habituated). Later, he played it, and found to his surprise that when he was out of earshot, there was an interesting conversation in which the men theorized about what he was really up to, with one saying he's there to steal the secrets of street vending, as the Jews are always wanting more, which is why they brought the Holocaust on themselves (2000, 337). He realized that there isn't an "all or nothing" accep-

---

7. Actually, Mead ([1928] 1967) herself played fast and loose with honorary membership. She allowed herself to be made an honorary *tapou*, which is a special kind of ceremonial virgin. She never let on that she really had a fiancé back home and wasn't much of a virgin. That's the kind of thing about her that drove Freeman crazy. But she loved dancing and by all accounts made a wonderful *tapou*—it allowed her to see things that she wouldn't have been able to otherwise, and she actually never forgot the difference between being a real *tapou* and an honorary one, as far as we can tell.

8. Gabba gabba hey!

tance whereby you become "one of us"—because even "us" badmouth each other, sometimes. That's just the way it is (also see Desmond 2016, 322).

Getting In

Now that we aren't fetishizing the process of "getting in" to the group, let's take a look at it in practical terms. This is going to sound very presumptuous, but it's a bit of advice that will help you for a few of these issues (though, sadly, not all): don't listen to ethnographers. Listen to me. Why? Because some parts of ethnography are very personal, in the sense that they make use of each person's particular profile of personality, skills, history, and knowledge; they also depend heavily on the target community; and they also involve a lot of luck. And a fair number of ethnographers only do one real cold entry in their whole careers. Yet some (not all, and, it seems to me, fewer as time passes) insist that what worked for *them* is the only way to do it. If you are talking to someone who met his gangs via a broker and long negotiations, and you explain, say, that you simply started hanging out with some of the Gangster Disciples, and it worked out naturally, he'll stare as he tries to decide whether you are lying or just insane. But in talking to someone who had made a different entry, if you say you are using an Operation CeaseFire activist as a broker, she'll be convinced you can't be doing a *real* ethnography. And so on. I'm not saying that you should ignore what they have to say. But you do need to bear in mind (1) selectivity and (2) subjectivity. (A thousand people can have tried this person's pet technique, and 999 times it led to disaster, but guess why those folks aren't talking to you about it? Because they work at Starbucks.)

I think if you're looking for some things that are common to great ethnographers and successful ethnographies, you are going to find only a few. Let's take a classic example, the story of William Whyte ([1943] 1981, 288–89), who knew he wanted to study a slum. But how to get access? His first try was by helping conduct an official survey on housing conditions. That didn't work. His second try was just to walk up to people in a bar and ask if he could join them. They threatened to throw him down the stairs. His third try was through the settlement house, and this only succeeded because one worker introduced him to Doc, the leader of an informal gang.

But was it really only luck that got Whyte to Doc? In a way, yes, but after all, this was Whyte's third try. Most people would have given up before that. More than any other thing, this sort of tenacity is what you need to be a serious ethnographer. A capacity to resist discouragement, to respond to rejection with a new attempt, to always dust yourself off.

What is it that gives workers this tenacity? Some field-workers don't really feel as if they fit in with anyone in particular, so they're equally happy with everyone. Some are really desperate and have no choice but to go forward. They get kicked out of school, fired, whatever, if they don't go on. Some are fundamentally oblivious—strangely enough, the socially insensitive person can be a good field-worker. And some are totally confident about themselves as persons and so don't mind looking like fools in front of others.

There's an inspirational speaker for businesses who carts out his huge collection of four-leaf clovers. He's got to be the luckiest guy in the world, you think. But his point is that anyone can find four-leaf clovers. You just have to patiently scour a field of clover. It takes hours. But if you're systematic, you can get 'em. Sometimes fieldwork is like that.

Establishing Trust

Another myth that ethnographers tend to reinforce is the need for "trust." As I noted in chapter 3, criminals, say, will want to make sure you're not a cop, and workers might need to really be sure that you aren't a stoolie for the management. But the idea that you get the position of trust is just like the idea that as an honorary member, you're now an insider. It just isn't that way.

Rather than it being an all or nothing thing, it's usually the cumulative experience of seeing you behave a certain way that makes people forget about your weird status for stretches of time. A great example here is Jankowski's work on gangs. The gang members did, in fact, initially test him to make sure he wasn't a tattletale, and they also had the initiation ritual they use for real gang members, which is to beat the crap out of them (Jankowski 1991, 11). But most important, he says, they'd get into tough situations together. They'd see him behave more or less like they would, so they naturally started to become habituated to him. They didn't *promote* him to the status of "trusted insider." But they could stop wondering about what he's doing to do.

What's less important than getting them to trust you is simply not getting them to think you're a prick. And actually, a fair number of sociologists communicate just that. Why? Because a lot of us are judgmental people, and you have to be a really good actor to smother all signs of judging others. Now I'm not talking about being a good person or a moral person. This seems to be relatively independent of judgmentalism. You can be good and judgmental, or bad and judgmental. But a judgmental person moves really quickly to put other persons, or at least their actions, into a "good" or a "bad" box. If you're a judgmental person, you're going to have an uphill battle being an ethnographer. If you don't really stifle yourself, you're going to see a lot less than you should. And you won't be able to observe that people aren't being totally forthcoming when they assure you that they like you and are really happy to share with you and all that.

Being Yourself

The desire to be a part of those studied, and the (false) belief that this is necessary if the researcher is going to get the true story, often lead students to try to "fit in" by changing their behavior and appearance. This is not good. Of course, that doesn't mean you wear a tuxedo to an iron foundry or use language (whether formal or informal) that your subjects don't. But it means that if you want to be accepted, it has to be *you* that is being accepted.

And you need to understand that what's prompting any change in your behavior isn't a scientific necessity; it's not much different from the first day of kindergarten. Will I have a friend? (See Cohen 1967.) And just like the other kids at kindergarten don't like a phony, neither will your subjects. Anyway, you have to be yourself as opposed to copying them—because probably none of them are copying them. (Or, if they are, they're appearing foolish for doing so.) Mitchell Duneier, I think, gives us the clearest understanding of this. When he goes to hang out with largely homeless street vendors, he dresses like he normally does. Does he fit in with them? No! He doesn't fit in, but it's Mitch who isn't fitting in, as opposed to it being his fanciful idea of what-a-guy-who-fits-in-is-like who isn't fitting in (2000, 336).

Trying to be someone else to fit in isn't just bad acting—it's a way of fundamentally trivializing the dignity of other people. Because you're basically saying, they're not people—they're just a role that anyone can put on. You may really change as a result of your fieldwork—and you might even become more like your subjects in real ways than you ever imagined. But this isn't about aping others.

I've been emphasizing that all these hang-ups interfere with your scientific task. That's because if you—a human individual—are yourself the data-gathering instrument, having illusions about what you are doing means you cannot calibrate your instrument. You can't successfully "think through" what you are doing. But this also brings us to ethical issues that are so fundamental that I'm going to start a separate chapter.

TAKEAWAYS

- Observing is its own task, and you probably can't do anything else at the same time.

- If you have illusions about yourself, and you interact with and study others, you will need to construct illusions about them in order to preserve those about yourself.
- When you reify a group, you are almost always siding with some against others.
- You are what you are: whatever that is, for better or worse.

If you were going to read more...

Regarding observation, clearly, read Christena Nippert-Eng's *Observing Closely*. You've probably noticed that I *really* like Duneier's book and his methodological writings. And Matthew Desmond's *Evicted* sets a new bar; it's a must-read, and his methodological appendix is excellent. I also strongly recommend his piece, "Relational Ethnography." The only nice thing about the distrust that ethnographers have of one another (coming from the personalism of the work) is that they have had serious critiques of one another that most sociologists avoid. You can learn from these.

* 6 *

Ethics in Research

*Ethics is the study or practice—sometimes both—of defensible interpersonal
interactions. It shouldn't be shocking to learn that bad ethics leads to bad
sociological research practice. If you are willing to cut out all the bullshit, it turns
out that it isn't that hard to determine how to be ethical.*

Why Discuss Ethics?

Bad Ethics Makes Bad Science

I'm a pretty hard-hearted guy in most ways. Oh, I'm nice enough, all right,
and I'll throw you a rope if you're going down, but if you don't make it, I'll
have a steak dinner and sleep fine. So when I spend a lot of time talking
about ethics in research, it's not because I've been waiting for my chance
to be the Sunday school teacher and give you all lessons in saying please
so that you can go join the choir in do-gooder heaven. It's because I've become increasingly convinced that bad ethics leads to bad research.

The reason is, in a nutshell, that few of us are OK with being bad people.
We want to be good. Which is fine. But that means if we *are* bad, we have
a problem, and the way we are tempted to resolve the problem is to come
up with reasonings, tendentious derivations, implausible observations,
and so on, to prove that we aren't really doing what we really did and are
about to do again. That means we are lying to ourselves. And lying is a
bad place to start a science. Especially when (as I've been saying), you really need to be correctly theorizing your own actions in the production
of data.

So if you actually have no problem being a bad person, go right ahead.
Push that old lady out of your way and charge on! You'll not only probably be a good liar, and hence an effective one, but you'll happily admit to
your sins (at least to yourself) and won't distort things. But if you aren't
like that, you need to read this chapter.

Science versus Morality, and Other Tough Decisions

Gotcha. Because the first thing I'm going to say is, watch out for times when you feel you have a "tough decision" to make. Probably you don't. And if you find yourself putting "science" on the balance, that is a really bad sign. Here's a typical example, from Bosk's dissertation work. Bosk was wondering what he would do if he saw a patient harmed by bad doctoring and no one was saying anything. (Remember from chapter 3 that Bosk did this research to see if doctors were really able to police their own.) Should he fink out on the bad doc? As a young student, Bosk convinced himself that, really, he *shouldn't* say anything. Why? Because he would be able to do more good by shedding light on the situation in medical research and by not jeopardizing the access of future researchers.[1]

> **Those who weigh science against ethics usually have neither.**

Hmmmm.... let's put them on the scales. Which side goes up, and which down? Do you really think that anyone can figure out how likely their work is to transform the world so that it will be better for enough unspecified people in the unspecified future? Because you need to be able to do that if you're going to weigh these hypothetical benefits against the more specific, limited, here-and-now people that Doctor Nutsy might be killing. Will your work really make the vague social change that you anticipate as an indirect effect of the increase in "knowledge"? I don't know if it will make any change, but I am pretty sure we can't *weigh* it. And if we can't really do this weighing, pretending to is a bad sign. It suggests that you are starting to lie to yourself about what you are really doing.

Feeling Bad

So if we aren't able to use a moral calculus to guide our ethical behaviors, what *are* our moral principles? Here, as often, I think it helps to follow the

1. Bosk ([1979] 2003, 200) wonderfully wrote: "In fact, it is hard to imagine a field-worker, insistent on imposing his definitions of justice on a scene, completing his work." I get the point, but now imagine hearing it from a defendant: "In fact, it is hard to imagine a burglar, insistent on imposing his definitions of justice on a scene, completing his work." And anyway, presumably if in his written work Bosk eventually told the truth about what he saw, then the doctors wouldn't let future workers come humiliate them, and so to ensure future science, he'd have to lie... to make *what* future work possible? More lies?

thoughts of someone you feel you could take as a role model. Let's go back to William Whyte. When he reflected on his work much later, he found times where he believed that he had done the wrong thing. One such time was when he joined a group of men doing "repeat voting"—voter fraud. This involved swearing falsely before a vote warden. At the time, he might have thought it was an invaluable research opportunity. But afterward, he realized that he didn't have to do it—other people said no. He just got caught up—like someone else could have—in a particular group's momentum. He could have continued to rationalize this as "worth it in the balance" because it made possible his deep access leading to findings that would help transform the world and make it so that such a thing like repeat voting never happens again. But he didn't.

Even more, it's interesting to see which of his acts weighed upon his conscience the most: it is when he interfered in a group decision as to whether to invite a certain politician to speak at a club ([1943] 1981, 170). Come again? *That's* what eats at you? Whyte had a hard time explaining why he considered this such a serious blunder; he says that he may have changed the way events unfolded (336). Yet Whyte once organized a march on the part of the residents to demand political change, and he never regretted *that*. If he was so worried about changing things, why didn't the march provoke a guilty conscience, given that the interference was so much more extensive? The difference is that in the former case, he had made his suggestion to bring in a competing politician so that he could build a bridge to another faction he wanted to study. In other words, he was only using their decision as a means to *his* end, as opposed to an end in itself (like the march).

In a sense, Whyte stumbled upon Kant's categorical imperative—the only way to act in a consistently ethical manner is to treat each person as an end in him or herself and not as a means to an end. The problem is that you *are* trying to use people as a means to a different end—don't deny it. Can we work this through? Let's start with the most unpleasant case—using your good friend, even when you try not to.

Relations with Key Informants

It definitely happens that some field-workers have a central informant who takes the worker under his or her wing, not just introducing and protecting the field-worker but offering interpretations and explanations, sometimes almost even cowriting portions. Doc for Whyte, Hakim for Duneier, and so on. The sad thing is that if you have such a buddy, you're going to have to be prepared this relation to go sour, even if you try to head it off by being "better" than all the other field-workers ("*I'm* not going to use him; if I get anything, I'm going to make sure I give enough back!").

But the preservation of good feeling in this relationship rarely seems to be helped by going as far as possible in recognizing the authorial contributions of the sponsor. Whyte and Duneier both brought their informants to speak or conduct college classes. Many researchers try to "give back," sharing royalties and authorial credit, yet rarely does it prevent a break.

Why? I think there are two reasons. One is that these sorts of sponsors sponsor others because they like being sponsors. When you try to "give back" you are suddenly turning into *their* sponsor. You started as a little ugly duckling, but suddenly, you are now some big swan. Further, and I think this was especially true for Whyte and Doc, bringing the informant into academia as an equal highlights something really sad. You, as ethnographer, can go in and out of the field, nearly at will. But the informant, who might have been a local intellectual in his own realm, transported into the "big pond," realizes that he can't come and go at will. That this is indeed something that he *could* have done—by virtue of his own smarts, he's equal to anyone there—but it is forever closed. It's a *Jude the Obscure* moment, and it really stinks—as does unfairness in general, almost all of which was there before you started your work and will be there when you are done.

So it may well be that the more you try to do for your sponsor, the worse your relation will be. That doesn't mean you shouldn't do it. A sponsor relationship is, when it works best, a self-negating thing. A sponsor *gives*—refusing to "use" this isn't being noble, it's being ungrateful. "Using" someone in the bad way isn't about getting something from them or having more than one purpose in hanging out with them.

Really using someone is being *duplicitous*. Letting them think you're doing one thing when you're doing another. Telling them it's a good idea if they call Marcy and see if she wants to hang out, when actually, you're only trying to get in better with Marcy's clique. If you don't do things like that, you're in pretty good shape.

Decide Beforehand

But there are other problems. In particular, if you are going to be a real participant, it can be hard to know where to draw the line if you're trying to go along with the group, but suddenly it looks like they're starting down a path that will lead to them doing something you think is wrong. For this reason, it makes sense to think about this in advance and make decisions about when one will stop participating, when one will call the cops, and so on. Martín Sánchez Jankowski (1991) made it clear when he did participant observation in gangs that they wouldn't expect him to go along with anything illegal, and he didn't kill anyone or rob or sell drugs.

In contrast, Sudhir Venkatesh (2008, 119), admits that he just winged it with his normal moral compass and that this compass wasn't always very reliable. (For example, he once kicked a guy who was down in the stomach.) He had the guts to admit it and give a warning to others to think it through first. Walk it through in your mind, so that when it happens, you know what to do. As Aristotle says, ethics is basically a matter of habit.

What's the Rule of Thumb?

Still, we can't always work out everything in advance. And researchers can easily get carried away with the thrill of their research and start to feel like they're James Bond, or perhaps Che Guevara. Is there a good rule of thumb for making decisions on the fly about ethical versus unethical behavior as a researcher? I think there is, and it's so simple and works so well that I can't believe it took me twenty years to figure it out.

Remember to think of yourself as just a regular person, with a rather low-paying academic job (or none at all), among thousands of others, also trying to write books, articles, and papers, all by studying people. What you're doing isn't necessarily so important that you have to hurt people's bodies or feelings in a way that you wouldn't if they were your neighbors. You are not 007, and you are not licensed to kill. (Kai Erikson [1995] made this point nicely.)

And so if something isn't right for you in your everyday life, there's no way it becomes right in the course of a study. In general, abstract values are the worst things in guiding our behavior, concern for people is a lot better, and fundamental principles of action are best. Those work because they can be internalized and guide us when things are tricky. It's hard enough to be decent. It won't get any easier if you start making "ifs, ands, and buts" to ease your professional life or boost your standing in your own eyes.

> **If it wasn't right before, nothing makes it right now.**

That doesn't mean you turn into Jesus. If you're hanging out with a gang, and they're beating the crap out of someone, chances are good you won't throw yourself in their way and say "over my dead body." Maybe that's the right thing to do, but you wouldn't do it as an ethnographer for the same reason you wouldn't do it as a regular person, namely, that you're scared. Not the worst thing in the world to be scared by a bunch of tough people. But very bad if you then start to convince yourself that this was your duty as a good scientist and will be made up for by the wonderful effects your glorious science will have. That's the "weighing" story we've seen people start to tell themselves as they psych themselves up for being bad.

Do you think that you have *more* of an ethical obligation than others? Fine with me if you want to take that on. But make sure you aren't inventing some new special morality that is supposedly binding on you to justify breaking some other, more everyday, rules.

Interestingly, a lot of our ethical problems only arise when we're writing it up. It isn't that they weren't there before. But they weren't visible. I want to turn to the issues of writing up original research based on participant observation, deal with some of the simplest problems, and then use this to return to these ethical issues … at which point, it will all fall into place.

Writing It Up

Promising Confidentiality

The simplest ethical problem for sociologists writing up their findings pertains to the disclosure as opposed to nondisclosure of information. It's not uncommon for students to plan on promising people "confidentiality" without really thinking this through. Confidentiality and anonymity are different—you can have one without the other. Anonymity means you don't give names, and you keep your subjects from being recognizable, up to a point. Confidentiality is that you keep stuff secret. Saying you'll keep confidentiality and meaning that you'll provide anonymity is a horrendous mistake. You can almost never promise blanket confidentiality—you're planning on writing a paper, a dissertation, an article, or a book, right? That doesn't sound very confidential to me. If you'll mean you'll keep confidential *who* said it, that's different.

You might say that you will keep *some* things completely confidential. But you do not have any particular legal right to keep things confidential from The Law. Some professionals, like lawyers and psychologists, have what is called "evidentiary privilege." This won't really work for us—this is a model in which the professional has clients, and the professional's interaction with the client must be protected if the professional is to truly serve the client. But when it comes to sociology, our subjects are not our clients—and really, we have no clients. We're *not* to be trusted to put the interests of the subjects first. That's not our job. Well, it's a moot point. You don't have evidentiary privilege.

That means that if your notes (or memory) are subpoenaed by a court, and you don't turn them over, you are in contempt of court, which means you get to sit in jail until you do what the judge says. There are, to be sure, certain restricted forms of evidentiary privilege you can get for certain types of studies. If you want to study drug addicts, for instance, and you can explain to NIDA (the National Institute of Drug Abuse) why it's important, they can give you a certificate that a judge will respect—but it will be limited. It won't cover all crimes you might witness, only drug crimes, say.

For a long time, sociologists were writing checks that they couldn't cash—promising that they could protect information that they couldn't. Nowadays, things are a bit better because of institutional review boards (IRBs). Most sociologists complain about them, and indeed, they often are set up in ways that aren't relevant for us, but I have to say that I think they've improved sociologists' previously sloppy ways of working.

Because what most sociologists do when they are dealing with interviewees or other subjects is to start by promising confidentiality without really thinking about it and then to take down observations that have explicit or implicit identifiers in them. And to talk about these observations informally, and even write up their first draft and pass it around to their writing group and their committee with no attention to confidentiality. Only at the very end do they make a revision with the lamest possible substitutions to "preserve anonymity." Very often they preserve notes that contain the identifiers.

And even where there is an attempt to give anonymity, graduates students almost invariably begin by keeping initials the same. Or doing something else that works as a mnemonic. A pseudonym that is too close isn't a pseudonym, it's just a fun game for readers, who try to figure out what your logic was in making the connections. Or students do a "search and replace" at the very end of their writing process. . . . so that when a reader notices that the bibliography has a work called *The Protestant Ethic and the Spirit of Capitalism* by Rocky Weber, she figures it out: oh, I guess "Rocky's" real name was Max.[2]

And you have to expect that in a fair number of cases, the participants will be able to do just this. In *Kitchens*, Gary Alan Fine (2008, 171) recounts a conversation with restaurant-worker Evan, who asks, "Are you reporting all this to the owners?" Fine "emphatically" says no, and the workers respond positively. But Fine did report the things in the *book*, and my guess

---

2. As I write this, I am reading a nice article in *Social Problems* that studies a "large California city." But in the footnotes, the name of the city is given! Why? Because when you do a search for a string in Microsoft Word, you have to do it for both the main body and the footnotes separately.

is that the restaurant owners bought that book (since he only studied four establishments, it shouldn't be hard to pick out which is theirs). Maybe he should have been less emphatic.

Further, sometimes sociologists try to disguise their site or informants by changing the details. Often this doesn't work at all. Recall that Bosk studied a large teaching hospital that he called Pacific Hospital. Isn't that weird? He's a graduate student at the University of Chicago, where there's an elite teaching hospital right down the street, and he goes all the way to somewhere on the West Coast to do this study? Did it fool you? It didn't fool anybody else. You can call it Pacific, call it Asian, call it Martian, but folks assume you're studying what's down the street. They instantly figured out what hospital it was, and if you knew the surgery department, it probably shouldn't take long to figure out the attending physicians.

So should you preserve anonymity by changing some details around? ("I'll turn anesthesiologist Bruce Zhang into a pediatrician I'll call Marsha Gupta"). Unfortunately, no. That's faking the data. If specifics aren't real, they shouldn't be there.

Even more, are you really sure that you *should* make people anonymous? We often assume we should but for no clear reason. Many people actually want you to cite them by name—sometimes for good reason (e.g., an expert in a field might want to have control over what other people think she said). And as Mitchell Duneier (2000, 348) argued, giving names can force us to hold ourselves to higher standards. As he realized, "When I have asked myself whom I am protecting by refusing to disclose the names, the answer has always been me."[3]

Key thing here: we need to be able to correctly distinguish when we are thinking about ourselves from when we are thinking about others. I'm going to go over a reasonably famous case to work this through and bring some general principles to light.

Disclosure and Discretion

I'd like to introduce this topic with a true example of an ethical train wreck, generously shared by the ethnographer herself, Carolyn Ellis. She did an ethnography of some basically poor white folks in a fishing community that she called "Fisher Folk." She was first introduced to them by her mentor, a professor ("Professor Jack"), as his "friend from college." She

3. Also, think twice before allowing your respondents to choose their own pseudonyms, or you may find yourself in the position of Philip Goodman (2014, 372), who had no choice in his excellent ethnography of a very serious issue—race tensions in different types of prisons and prison fire camps—to cite the words of his subject "Poopy."

told them that she was writing a paper on fishing, but she never really said, "I'm studying *you*." Yet she did study them, for over a decade, while she became especially close to one family with whom she regularly stayed.

And then she wrote her book, which described them with what can tactfully be called an outsider's eye. These are some excerpts. "Most Fishneck women wore pants and often knee-length rubber boots and layers of unmatched clothing.... By age eighteen, many of them weighed two hundred pounds or more..." "Scarcity of plumbing meant baths were infrequent. That combined with everyday work with fish produced a characteristic fishy body odor, identified by outsiders as the 'Fishneck smell'" (Ellis 1986, 14). Out of context, this might seem mean, but her portrayal is by no means an insensitive or trivializing one. However, it was part of a comparison to a somewhat richer community, and Ellis certainly focused, as would most comparativists, on the contrasts, thereby accentuating the slovenliness of this community.

Further, Ellis (1986, 144) didn't work very hard to disguise the identity of the places she renamed, as she cited historical work, including the mention of the chief settler by name, that allows identification if one is willing to walk over to the library. And because she had invented names for the characters that all began with the same letter as their real names, it was perfectly easy for any community member to figure out who was whom (Ellis 1995). She took it for granted that her subjects wouldn't read it, as in fact, many were illiterate. Yet her confidence seems a bit strange in retrospect, as she included (1986, 171) a discussion of how, when two newspapers printed features on the community a few years earlier, "Fishneckers found parts of these to be derogatory" and "were the focus of local gossip and agitation" as well as a letter to the editor.[4]

In any case, her subjects did learn about her work. They were furious, telling her, "You said we're dirty and don't know how to dress." And that they had sex at ten years old. Now some people had, in fact, told her these stories about *some* people in their town, but after it was published, they felt as if it reflected on *all* of them. But more to the point, they felt betrayed and spied on. Ellis felt bad about her indiscretion, but I don't think she ever questioned whether her research-via-spying actually led her to incorrect conclusions. I think it did.

Imagine that you (if an American) were being interviewed by a sympathetic Parisian interested in American culture. In part to show how much

---

4. In this letter, a resident, using excellent logic though poor grammar, pointed out the hypocrisy of sensationalizing her community. "About the Saturday night feuds don't we all have them? There is stealing, killings, robberies, men running after other men's wives going on elsewhere other than in just [Fishneck]" (Ellis 1986, 182).

you appreciate art, as you two are bonding by running down the uncultured, you talk about how some Americans don't care at all about art, how they can't tell a Manet from a Monet, and never go to a museum except to use the bathroom. Then you find that the person you were talking to doesn't write, as you would have guessed, "many Americans actually care a great deal about art like this fine fellow I talked to." Instead you read, "most Americans can't tell a Manet from a Monet, and never go to a museum except to use the bathroom. That's how dumb they are." You'd feel pretty betrayed, probably. So, too, Ellis's reports weren't always contextualized thusly. She reports that children "told many stories in graphic detail about 'slipping off into the woods' for causal sexual liaisons. Note a description of a sister by a ten-year-old boy: 'She is off in the woods with prick [*sic*] right now. Screws all the time, she does.'" Ellis did not properly theorize the type of discussion she was having and assumed that the further "insider" she was, the truer the reports were. It isn't just that people didn't realize they were giving reports to Ellis when they made these statements; the context was such that they weren't necessarily the full story. The ethical problem indicates the presence of a scientific one. Now let's follow Ellis as she confronts the question of what do to about this.

Denial

To set the context, let's back up a bit. For a while, in anthropology, the favorite solution to these sorts of puzzles was to try to deny them. The problem was believed not to turn on ethics so much as power differences, and so the way some researchers dealt with it was to decide that they would see things through the eyes of their subjects. And as you can guess from chapter 5, I'm pretty skeptical that this is anything other than an exercise in homogenizing at best, stereotyping and projecting at worst.

But when Ellis tried to figure out what had gone wrong, this is where she started from—and that she should have seen *herself* through the "Fishneck eye." The basic problem, it seems to me, was indeed that she really didn't look at things through the eyes of her friends. But not in the sense of "they have a different worldview"—rather, in the sense that she just wasn't sensitive to their feelings in an everyday sort of way, and hadn't behaved according to normal rules of decency. As she makes clear, she quieted initial reservations by focusing on herself—her desired self-image as a good ethnographer, which led her to act without discretion. When things went badly, she didn't think about her *behavior*. Instead, she thought about her *self*, and in ways that increased the abstractness whereby she thought about the human beings she had been messing around with. They were still a means to her own end, and she didn't think this through.

The reason to pursue this case isn't to make Ellis appear worse than everyone else; it's because she was honest enough that we have this document. You might think this is an extreme case, but I continually find novice researchers who are surprised that their subjects cut them off and hate them after reading the work in which the researcher has strung together bits of data in a one-sided way to implicitly morally elevate herself over her subjects. Of course, the researcher never sees it this way—because she hasn't thought through her data collection and doesn't face the reality of what she is doing.

> **Run, don't walk, from anything labeled autoethnography.**

You can't be a good student of other people if you are only interested in yourself. I've listened to many people who thought they were ethnographers, and who have sophisticated notions regarding how one always sees through a "lens" of one sort or another, when actually what they were holding was a mirror, not a lens of *any* sort. It's hard enough to learn about people through hanging out. Narcissism just kills the deal. It isn't sophisticated or smart; it's juvenile and should not command the attention of serious sociologists.

So you probably don't think that Ellis's choices were right. (Neither did she, which is why she gave us this information so that we could learn from it.) But the problems she fell into are simply an unusually visible case of a more common problem in our approach to ethnography, one that can lead to questionable results.

Baggage

I think a plausible hypothesis is that part of the problem here in figuring out a response to an ethical quagmire comes from spending too much time dealing with one's own hang-ups and not enough listening to others. I increasingly feel that you just can't do good ethnography if you have too much personal baggage. (Hence the section titled "Hanging Out and Hanging Up" in the previous chapter.) Now plenty of sociologists, perhaps especially ethnographers,[5] come with *some* baggage—they think they are boring, or their lives are sheltered, or they want to bring back something good to the place they came from, or what have you. Here's how I'd say it:

5. Sorry! I call 'em like I see 'em.

you're allowed one piece of baggage and one carry-on. But if you're drag-ging around a steamer trunk of surface-to-air missiles that you want to shoot at others, that's not good.

Anthropology as a discipline nearly died in the 1980s because you had a collection of five thousand anticolonialists, coming from a strongly anti-colonial heritage that was completely bound up with colonialism, no lon-ger knowing what was good except to be more anticolonial than everyone else. It wasn't a field—it was just a demolition derby. If your big moti-vation in doing your research is to prove (again) that other people were morally wrong because of romanticizing or this-ing or that-ing you won't get very far.

And yet, we all are going to have a little baggage. If you're traveling so light that you don't even have a carry-on, you might have your own troubles (i.e., you are a sociopath). Sometimes there's something in that little bag that we should pay attention to, even if we can't defend it con-vincingly with arguments.

Queasy Feelings

Sometimes we really have a hard time justifying our feelings about what's good and what's bad. A great example here is seen in the reaction to Laud Humphreys's ([1970] 1975) important observational work that became *Tea-room Trade*—observations of men who had anonymous sex with men in a public bathroom. Now assuredly Humphreys did some things that were really beyond the pale, such as having a friend at the department of motor vehicle run plates on people who went to the "tearoom" so that he could then interview them as if they had been randomly picked for a poll.

But even putting that to the side, other sociologists still had major problems with his surreptitious observations. At the tearoom where he ob-served, there were three main roles among participants (with potentially more than one performer): someone performing oral sex, someone receiv-ing oral sex, and a "watch queen" who observed and in return alerted the actors if there was police presence. Humphreys served as a watch queen, and was taken by the participants to be one. The others didn't know he was doing research on them.

Other sociologists were outraged.

"You observed people having a private interaction!"
"No, it was in a public place."
"But they assumed privacy!"
"No, they knew I was watching. They like being watched."
"But they assumed that you were watching because you were gay!"

And that isn't even true—lots of folks at a tearoom like the ones Humphreys studied are bisexual, or in the process of changing from one sexual orientation to another, or just curious, and the participants surely knew that. But Humphreys wasn't in any of those categories, and so many sociologists were outraged at his snooping, even if they couldn't quite explain who had been harmed.

Well, Humphreys *was* gay. When he came out of the closet, it changed how a lot of people interpreted his research. Now that seems really funny. The idea that doing a certain thing is bad, *unless you actually enjoy it*, is a tough ethics for a profession to start with. Yet I actually think that the sentiment behind it isn't crazy. When others didn't know that Humphreys was gay, they probably assumed that he was looking at this behavior with disgust or negative judgment, which meant that the participants were somehow being lessened in his estimation. And for this reason, many sociologists felt that he was doing something bad to his subjects, whether the subjects knew that or not. I'm not sure that notion's correct, but I *am* sure that it isn't *crazy.*

The arguments about his research tended to turn on that mythical weight of the pros and cons, the goodness that would come from the ends versus the badness coming from the means. No one could make much sense of that. But I think that, in reality, they were stuck on something simpler—whether or not it was a gross to watch people do something you think is gross. When Humphreys came out of the closet, the trade-off between harm done and benefits reached didn't change at all, yet our evaluation of his behavior did—I think because it was really about the sense that it would be uncool to spy on people in a way that lessens them in your own eyes. I think we should take seriously those queasy feelings we have and not always try to argue them down.

The funny thing is, whether or not they had heard rumors that Humphreys—an ex-priest—was gay, many readers somehow knew that he didn't despise the men. Even in the coded language of the early 1970s, you can feel the sympathy and his fundamentally human relation to the subjects. I don't know what to make of this.... But perhaps, again, it's a feeling to be taken seriously.

Public Data

And this brings us to a new sort of issue where standards haven't completely gelled, and there's the chance for us to set things right. One of the many unpleasant parts of the new world order is our susceptibility to constant surveillance. The problem is that there is a range of responses to this. Some us shrug, and say, well, let everyone know my purchasing preferences—send those targeted ads my way. Others try to blind cameras with laser pointers. Because of this, we don't all have the same instincts when it comes to the use of new forms of public data, such as those that you can find on the web. You may have a *legal* right to use certain forms of data, but that doesn't mean that it's right. If there is a site that people have set up to allow them to communicate about something of shared interest, and you want to study them, you may need to think about how you can do this in a way that doesn't make their lives worse.[6]

I think an admirable example is the recent work of Bakker and Paris (2013). They studied the postings on a website where religious people who had lost children (as in, they died) talked about their relation to God. This is a public website. You can find it if you try... but you probably won't. Bakker and Paris decided that when they quoted text, they would quote exactly, except for any place where names were used. Here they would put in pseudonyms. The reasoning I think is as follows: first, we are interested in their words—not the gossip. Second, although the information is legally public, given the sensitive nature of the topic, we don't want to pull personal feelings into the light if we don't have to. And I'd also add the following: people have shared information with others for a reason; although they didn't go to any steps to ensure their privacy, we don't really want to help contribute to a world in which, unless you're paranoid all the time, someone gets to put your personal story on the front page.

Luckily, IRBs will often stop you from doing things that you have a legal right to do. For example, a student interested in a hard-to-reach (but not particularly vulnerable) population realized that she could use freedom of information requests to get the names of those she was looking for from the government. She thought it might be sketchy, even though it was completely legal, and asked the IRB. They (properly) said that this was wrong—because they don't want the university to be seen as harassing people. Discretion is the better part of ethics, and talking to IRBs before you start will help you err on that side. Because once you are in the field, discretion becomes harder and harder.

Realism and Discretion

When we can look at ourselves realistically, we can go further and be reflexive without being narcissistic. This involves, to use Bourdieu's (Bour-

---

6. The question of whether "terms of use" that are posted (even if you haven't consented) are binding on you as a researcher is currently being argued out at many universities. Note that if there is a difference between what is legal and what your university says is acceptable, you probably need to go with the more conservative opinion.

dieu and Wacquant 1992) language, not pretending that you aren't objectifying your subjects but objectifying yourself as well—seeing yourself and your relation to the subjects as they really are.

One of the dirty little secrets of ethnography, which Whyte pulled out into the open, is that ethnographers are often people who are attracted to those having a dirtier, more dangerous life than they themselves, which they romanticize. Romanticizing isn't necessarily so bad, and can be compatible with objective reporting, but it can put the interests of the researcher—who generally isn't going to suffer any consequences—against those of the subjects. There's a cute part in Short and Strodtbeck's book on gangs where they describe their efforts to find drug-using gangs through an ex-convict middleman. (This was the 1950s when drug users were a bit harder to find than now.) Their ex-con friend found one group, but then they got busted and straightened up. "Shortly after this the [informant] reported excitedly that he had located a group of pot smokers in the same general area of the city. We were elated and so was he. His parting shot as he left the research offices after his usual weekly interview was, 'Don't worry, Doc, I'll keep them on the stuff until you can study them!" (1965, 11).

That's a funny story, but it's not as funny when the enthusiastic and supportive interest from a sociologist might help sway the balance of someone sitting on the fence, who might get a job at Kmart or instead stay involved with behavior that the researcher sees as "resistance" and the judge sees as a third strike and mandatory twenty-five years in jail.

In sum, having contempt for your informants sucks, but so can thinking of them as some sort of hero in a movie you're writing in your head. But worst of all would be letting those thoughts start your gums flapping. Keep it to yourself.

The Need for Symmetry

So why not just be honest: portray them as they are, warts and all, and let their feelings be *their* problem? If being honest and hurtful is the package deal, it's hard to fault someone like Ellis for the effects of her writing. But I've come to be convinced that it just isn't so hard for a sociologist, even an ethnographer, to be both honest and not hurtful. For one thing, as I said, it often turns out that discretion is the better part of ethics. You do not need to report everything you see to be a good scientist. Many of the things that ethnographers report, which end up hurting their subjects' feelings when divulged, are completely irrelevant to the claims being made. So why is the author repeating these stories in print? Sometimes for sensationalist illustrations; sometimes to prove that the ethnographer got "real" inside access; sometimes to lift the ethnographer over the subjects by showing that they are morally blameworthy in some way.

Salacious stories are one thing—you can leave them out. But in some cases, you're going to have a fundamentally negative view of a person or a group. You can't sugarcoat the truth, true. And you might imagine that this implies that you can't be honest without making some folks look bad and hurting their feelings. What I am about to say is going to sound really idealistic, and many of you won't believe it, but I am increasingly convinced that there is something scientifically compromised about work that hurts your informants' feelings. That doesn't mean it has to make them look good, nor that they should have a veto on your conclusions, or even what you write.

But I do mean that if you have the feeling that if they read what you wrote, they'd break off relations—it would amount to a huge change in how they see you—there's actually something wrong. What's wrong isn't necessarily what you are saying; it's that if they suddenly have the idea that your relation with them was not what they thought it was, you've already done something wrong in your research process, and if you've done that, your data aren't actually going to be as good as they should be.

You might be scandalized that I'm suggesting that you need to treat the jerk-offs you are studying as seriously and respectfully as you do the cool ones. Am I saying that the Klansmen are basically good people, just a bit misunderstood? No, it's the opposite: most of the so-called good guys aren't actually so good. That is, they might be on the right *side* (yours), but most of what determines what side we're on is where we're born and stuff like that. It isn't closely correlated with our moral status.

The distribution of moral status among human beings is narrowly distributed; most of us are together in the fair-to-middling range, sides be damned. The problem, then, isn't that you aren't lauding the jerk-offs. That's fine—they get what's coming to them. The problem is that, at the same time, you give a pass to the ones you like—including yourself. As Charles Kurzman (1991) shows in a wonderful article, this leads us to actually invoke different classes of explanatory factors for what Kingsley Amis called "the two great classes of mankind," those one likes, and those one doesn't like.

And even more, when you think that you can dismiss someone, you stop listening carefully. You've reduced them to a caricature, so you just seize on the few things that support your thumbnail simplification and ignore the rest. And so you are going to be doing bad science. Not because you are being selective, but because you are being selective without knowing you are. I've noticed that when a student gets to findings about a group she or he really dislikes, the findings get less interesting. The treatment is shallower, there is more confirmation of what the researcher always expected, and there are fewer surprises (a point also made by Desmond 2014, 561; Hyman 1954).

If, when your subjects read what you wrote, they are shocked and feel betrayed, this isn't due to an inherent problem in *social research*. It's rather due to an inherent problem in *social interaction*. Your problem was that you hadn't figured out how to be able to look someone in the eye and tell her to her face something that you were planning on writing. Don't confuse normal, and understandable, embarrassment with some sort of research imperative.

For this reason, it's often a help to assume that you are going to show all your informants anything that you write. This isn't always applicable—often you are dealing with technical issues that are of no interest to them, or they just don't care. And in no way should you think that they have any rights over your interpretation. But I suspect that you'll actually hold yourself to somewhat higher standards if you tell everyone you're happy to let them see your penultimate draft. You're less likely to rely on shaky interpretations, less likely to twist the evidence, and less likely to make contestable imputations. When push comes to shove, you have to accept your notes, and your interpretation. But push doesn't always need to come to shove. If your subject reads (about himself), "... he said slowly, as if considering the issue for the first time" and protests, "What do you mean, 'first time!' I think about this lots! I was just trying to figure out how explicit to be!" there's a good chance that you'll realize that you didn't have enough data for your interpretation. Think about showing your work—if there's interest—not as a presentation to a tribunal of censors, but as a final round of interviews.

If you are implicitly criticizing what your subjects do (perhaps they simply had poor information), they may accept what you say but be upset that you withheld this fact as opposed to giving them this useful correction before. Here you need to emphasize that when you are in the field, you gather lots of data, and while you might have a suspicion that something isn't working for your subjects, it's only when you can really go over it altogether that you can be sure enough to commit to an interpretation. They'll probably accept that and forgive you for letting them go on doing something stupid.

In sum, it's become common for researchers to invoke trade-offs. There's the trade-off between the harm done to research subjects and the good done by the knowledge produced. There's a trade-off between reporting things honestly and respecting the feelings of others. I no longer believe that either of these is true. We are striving for that spot in which we treat those we deal with eye to eye, using them for data without disguise, apology, or manipulation. When we deal with them, we tell the true story, but not the "whole" story—instead, the relevant story. And finally, we act as professionals and do not dabble in things beyond our training. That's the last point I want to make.

Interview Style

I've been focusing on the sorts of ethical problems that arise when you are around your subjects in an informal social setting, such that they (reasonably) imagine that you are treating them as friends. But there are also some problems that arise in interviewing, even though the relation is quite different. Indeed, it often stems from the opposite sort of illusion about what we are doing. Many students start off thinking, "I'm never going to treat my research subjects just as data. They'll always be people first to me, and I'll be responsive to their emotional needs, not just taking measurements from them."

This can lead to interviews that are both bad science and bad practice. Helen Rose Ebaugh made a distinction between a therapeutic interview and informational one. In the former, the interviewer makes suggestions; she is nonjudgmental but not wholly reserved. "Many of the interviewer's activities at this point serve to gratify the patient's emotional need to feel protected or loved" (1988, 215). In an informational interview, the researcher should not give such positive feedback.

Many students, especially those dealing with subjects who they see as having undergone upsetting experiences, are tempted to dabble with a therapeutic style of interview. I'm here to say that's wrong, wrong, wrong. First, we might be surprised, but it turns out that people often love an informational interview precisely because of its neutrality. It's rare that we have the chance to think out loud and to take back ideas we've thrown out that, once we hear them, no longer sound right. Indeed, as Ebaugh found, people used this freedom to talk to a neutral party quasi-therapeutically. It isn't just that they liked the fact that someone is interested in them—and realizing they aren't alone and odd in the world, simply by the nature of the questions. It's that the very neutrality allows respondents a chance to rehash things and create a nice narrative that makes sense of their feelings, often arrested by pressures of day-to-day life—and by the fact that most of our friends tend to jump in and affirm whatever stupid thing we have just done, even when we're possibly trying to rethink it. The informational interview has quasi-therapeutic effects without the interviewer being supportive in anything other than the most generic way.

One implication is that you shouldn't assume that a straightforward informational interview doesn't help people. But it also means that subjects may be far more sensitive to your input than you might think—and possibly more likely to fall into a therapeutic mode than you understand. Trying to be a "little bit" helpful and supportive of specific things your respondent says can have strong implications for how the respondent decides to walk through that forest of memories and thoughts. This is not simply questionable methodologically: it can be mildly dangerous for the mental well-being of your interviewees (and hence constitute a form of malpractice), and in a few unlikely but real cases, may be dangerous to you.

Taking the latter first, real psychotherapists are trained (hopefully successfully) to anticipate the establishment of a strong emotional bond from someone undergoing a talking cure to the listener. They are supposed to handle this (if it ever happens) so that it does not become a source of psychic agony for the patient, when she or he realizes that the listener does not actually love the patient. In a few cases, patients become obsessed with the therapist and will stalk him or her, and that can happen to you if you play therapist. More likely, you could find that you have a new "friend" who is not really your friend, and who may make you feel extremely guilty for eventually cutting off the relationship, if you must. If you are interested in persons who are at all mentally ill or undergoing a major transition in their lives—such as if you were interviewing people who had just joined or left a heavy commitment religious group—you can imagine as a worst-case scenario that a casual approach to emotional bonding might have more serious effects, like the use of suicide attempts to keep you near.

These are unlikely, but a real therapist would learn about them, and if we want to play therapist, we need to consider them. More prosaically, it simply may be that we don't really give very good therapy at all and are inadvertently using our reputation as "knowing what we're doing" to act incompetently. When a person you are interviewing "gets clear" on something due to the interview process, they will probably feel elated and will thank you. (Sudhir Venkatesh [2013] has a hilarious story about this in his most recent book.) If they act on this new vision, and later regret it, they will—quite properly—blame you, even if all you did was reinforce their self-esteem.

IRB

One last thing about ethics: IRBs. Everyone complains about them, and says they aren't really useful for most sociological research. But try to go around one at your peril. (Undergraduates don't normally need to worry about these unless they are planning on publishing their research, but graduate students always should, regardless of whether they are planning on publishing.) Even if your research is unfunded, even if it is not your dissertation research, if you do social research while you are affiliated with your university and you do not have IRB approval, you can have your PhD turned down. Give yourself time to have your project actually reviewed before you plan on starting. Go to them with questions, early, and have them tell you how to write your stuff up. And you know what? Your work—and your soul—just might get a little bit better as a result.

TAKEAWAYS

- Don't pretend to weigh things that can't be weighed. Lying to yourself is a bad way to start your day as a scientist.
- Of course you are using people to make your research. That doesn't mean you're abusing them.
- The moral status of your acts does not change because you are a sociology student or some other type of scholar.
- Discretion is the better part of ethics. Blurting is not the same thing as discovery.

If you were going to read more...
Don't. Some things you don't get from reading. Look around. Who are the people you like and respect as human beings? Who do you think God will let into heaven? What do they have in common? Go thou and do likewise.

* 7 *

Comparing

Sometimes rather than be systematic and use the logic of sampling, we use strategic comparisons to winnow out possible explanations. This gives us tremendous opportunities for doing terrible work and, also, opportunities for doing excellent work.

Here I'm going to be talking jointly about two things that are often considered antithetical—social psychological experiments, first and foremost, and comparative historical research (in its Skocpolian variety). I'm doing so because both start with the same sort of table of comparisons and try to make causal claims. And I'll argue that taking this parallel seriously helps us improve both.

Experiments in Sociology

The Classic Experiment, the Demonstration, and the Miniworld

To sociologists, the classic experiment is based on a socio-biomedical vision and involves the following:

1. random allocation of units to treatment and control categories;
2. the infliction of the treatment on some;
3. a delay to see what happens; and then
4. a comparison of the treated to the control.

Not all interesting experiments have all these features; in some, the key thing is in *demonstrating* a phenomenon, the existence of which might otherwise be denied. One very famous example of this is Stanley Milgram's (1974) experiments on *Obedience to Authority*.[1] Milgram was interested—

---

1. My take on this comes from Ann Swidler. Thanks, Ann!

like most social psychologists after World War II—as to why regular people could join or help the Nazis slaughter civilians who posed no threat to them. So he designed an experiment to look at these processes.

The true subject (the person being studied) is brought into a lab and told that he has the (somewhat unnecessary) job of administering electric shocks of increasing severity to a "learner" as part of a conditioning experiment. Each time the learner (actually an actor) gets a question wrong, the voltage on the machine is increased until the learner starts screaming and begging to be released, while an experimenter repeatedly instructs the subject to continue giving the shocks. It's all a fake, but it speaks volumes about American psychology that this struck everyone as plausible—it's just the kind of thing psychologists *would* have done, a nice stimulus-response experiment with Bzz! Bzz! shocking equipment. Most people really hate giving the shocks—they protest, they are anxious, they argue with the experimenter—but a large chunk go all the way to the maximum of 450 volts, obeying the instructions of the experimenter no matter what (Milgram 1974, 22).

Although Milgram did, in fact, conduct variations that produced insightful data on situational effects, the most impressive aspect of the experiment was demonstrating that most of us have the wrong theory of the human actor. We assume that, in Milgram's words, "unless coerced by physical force or threat, the individual is preeminently the source of his own behavior. A person acts in a particular way because he has decided to do so.... The behavior itself flows from the inner core of the person" (1974, 31). But he showed that people will violate their own moral standards, and do things that they don't enjoy, when they are under no physical compulsion to do so (1974, 41, 6).

It's a proof of possibility—we don't necessarily understand the reasons for this phenomenon, but we appreciate its existence. If the production of this phenomenon is itself theoretically significant, as it is in this case, that's great. And if it isn't, an experiment may mislead us. And this might be often true of the sorts of experiments that we can consider miniworlds.

Here the experiment involves a rhetorically effective mock-up so that a more important social process can be studied (e.g., we want to see whether people will contribute to a collective goal or fink out on everyone else). Such experiments may not involve any treatment at all, although usually, there is some sort of random allocation, perhaps of subjects to positions within the miniworld or to various different conditions or rules.

Miniworlds are the most common sort of experiments that graduate students are likely to do, and they're the most hazardous scientifically. To really understand why, we're going to start with the attractions of the experiment, and only after we see the offered rose will we know where to expect the thorns.

Universal, Cheap, and Subject to Manipulation

I hear people say that we use experiments when "we really want to get at causality." But you can always want to get at causality, just like you can always want to be rich or play shortstop for the Red Sox. That doesn't normally affect what you do. Experiments are used when we can intervene, when we're strapped for cash, and (usually) when we think what we're interested in is universal. Let's quickly walk through these, starting with the last.

Universality is great, because often with an experiment, we're using a convenience sample, like using the undergraduates at one's institution. Universality implies that you don't have to worry about whether your particular undergraduates are different from the rest of the population. And since we usually assume that social-psychological processes are relatively invariant across Western culture, that's where experiments abound. Note that this is an *assumption*—it may not be true. Leon Festinger (1957) proposed in the late 1950s what was to become, for around fifteen years, the most important theory in social psychology, namely, the theory of cognitive dissonance. The idea here is that people don't like to have two ideas that contradict each other, and they will act to bring these ideas into harmony, either by changing the world or by changing their ideas.

Interestingly, these experiments were at first done only on male college students. When they were replicated with female college students, not all worked the same way. So it isn't necessarily true that it doesn't matter who we study in experiments. But we wouldn't do an experiment on just anyone if we didn't believe that we were studying something pretty universal. Our current assumption—and one that I have no objection to—is that, in general, the closer we get to something that could be recognized on a biological level, the more universal it is.

Now there are times when we don't make this assumption: for example, when we do field experiments. Rather than rely on a convenience sample of undergraduates, we go to where we think our real subjects are. For example, Delia Baldassari and Guy Grossman (2013) were interested in factors promoting social contributions to collective goods—a question often explored using undergraduate (or even high school) students. But they wanted results that would have more external validity, so they went to Africa and studied members of agricultural cooperatives. Traveling to a specific population can avoid a lot of the problems I am going to talk about, but such work can be very expensive and out of the budget for most students' projects. I'm going to be focusing on the cheaper approaches, but don't give up: there are students who get the funding to do their research in a big way. It's worth a try.

But I've emphasized that one of the reasons we turn to experiments is that we're actually a little short of cash. If we're interested in how managers judge female as opposed to male applicants, we can try to put together a research team, wriggle into a bunch of firms, try to sit in on their meetings, and get enough data that we can control for various other hypotheses that might arise. Or, for a hundredth of the cost, we can have undergraduates judge other undergraduates. And, we think, rather than have to wait for our phenomenon to happen, we can (as Francis Bacon emphasized) *make* it happen.

Not all social phenomena, even those that you might think of as involving causality, can be investigated via manipulation. But some can, at least if they are scaled down so that our causal treatment is a fraction of the real world strength. There's nothing wrong with this in theory, but here is where the problems arise: sometimes what we theorize as a mere change of *degree* is actually a change in *kind*. And we can be so wedded to a chain of deduction that we don't stop and really think about what we are doing—and that is manipulating other people.

Making Stuff Up

Artifacts

I don't mean to make this sound morally bad. We're just going to think it through, rather slowly. The first thing is that this basic impulse of the experimental approach is one that, as Bruno Latour (1987), in particular, has emphasized, is fundamental to modern science. What we try to do is to go out into the big, crazy, messy world, and grab some of it, and run back with it to our laboratories, where we can take control over it. We bring it to our home turf, where we are the bosses. We scale it down, strip away its "allies"—turn a disease that leads to pus, vomit, screaming, and death, into a colored splot on a sealed glass petri dish.

There isn't anything wrong with the impulse to do this with aspects of social life. However, I think that, in the past, we've made some serious errors in our understanding of what happens when we do this. And I think the biggest problems have come from our idea that we should be "testing theories" in experiments.

If you think you're testing, or even "building," a theory, then your big worry is that your results are "artifacts," not aspects of the real world, but something you made happen. That's wrong. Sociologists have been confusing *contamination* with *artifact*. Experiments are artifacts. Everything in them is artifactual.

There's nothing intrinsically wrong with that, because this gets to what's distinctive about the kind of experiments that are done in physics, where researchers attempt to produce a phenomenon under controlled conditions—because success in that situation would be theoretically significant (see, e.g., Schaffer, Pinch, and Gooding 1989). If you're studying cold fusion, you *want* to make it happen. If you do, that's a point in your favor—no one complains that it was an artifact; they just want to make sure it was the right one.[2]

In good experiments, you are aware of the artifact, and you're basically trying to demonstrate that it is there—that you *can* make someone do X. That's why Milgram's demonstration is a good experiment. Because it was working *with* the artifact. In bad experiments, we're trying to pretend that it isn't an artifact, that it wasn't us who got the subjects to do X. Another way of saying it is that, unless we are really wondering whether we can make an artifact of type X, then, really, the fact that you *did* make one *can't* have any theoretical importance! Simple, but true.

Because experiments involve manipulating others, they tend to be much better at investigating phenomena that bring out the passivity in people than they are dealing with the more active sides. Let's say you want to use a rigorous experimental situation to see whether "power" or "achievement" affects whether people do some X, and so you randomly allocate subjects to power or achievement. But if you can manipulate one person into thinking he has high power, and another into thinking she lacks it, really, the one who has the high power is *you*, so the best thing is to check out whether you're doing X! Like the interview, the experiment is a social situation, and you can't really take the experimenter out of it and still understand what's going on.

This isn't a logical problem. It's a real, practical, and social psychological one. And it's also one that can, to some degree, be solved, so long as you are willing to look carefully at what you are actually doing. When scientists need to heat something up to start a certain kind of chemical reaction, they pay very close attention to how much heat they put in.[3] We, too, need to study how we shape social situations. And sociologists have often been dreadful at this.

2. Even so, we often have a real puzzle when it comes to interpreting the "fun-size" effects that we see in Miniworld experiments. The fact that we can make a small effect sometimes seems to us to suggest that in the real world, scaling things up should lead to a bigger effect. But some sorts of effects cumulate, and some dissipate quickly; to some, we even get inured. It's not always easy to know what kind we have.

3. And, actually, it looks like this was the problem with the cold fusion experiments of Pons and Fleischmann—they didn't correctly calculate this.

Labelmakers

Let's take a step back, and follow the career of an imaginary sociologist. Let's say it's a he, and he goes into sociology because he is struck by the great and, so far as he can see, unjustifiable inequality in life chances of the people all around him. He learns different theories of "inequality," and he'd like to know which is right. But it seems impossible to really test these, especially given that he has only eighteen months to do his dissertation. But then again, that very confident professor in the department has a very impressive, general theory about inequality. Perhaps *that* can be tested.

This theory says that people induce differences in competence when they see differences in rewards, and then this shapes how social interaction proceeds. Those who have been unrewarded won't seize opportunities to demonstrate competence, and those who have seized these opportunities will feel justified withholding rewards from the others. And so the cycle is reproduced.[4]

We can't study that directly, so we make up thirty pairs of undergraduates. We tell them they have a task to do together, involving estimation of crowds. They'll be paid corresponding to a fee schedule the lab has. Then we tell them that recent psychological research has found there are two types of people in the world, in terms of their spatial perception: gamma types and zeta types.

Then we have them take some fake test that we score, and let one person see that he or she is a gamma type and is to be paid at the bottom of the scale, while the other turns out to be a zeta type and gets paid a lot. Well, people assume that they're paid less because they're gamma types. And they figure gamma types aren't good at estimating crowds anyway, so they should let the partner make the decision.

Aha! Now we can substitute any favored category (white, male, educated) for zeta and any disfavored (black, female, uneducated) for gamma and have a theoretical answer to the problem of inequality! Even if this doesn't tell us about the initial generation of some inequality, at least this tells us about its reproduction. What can be wrong with this?

> **Let things be what they are. Because they sure aren't something else.**

---

4. Yes, this is a real theoretical approach, although the actual one often combined a lot of implausible precision with these very reasonable claims. For years, this really was a degenerate research paradigm, but recently, the leaders have shifted to doing what I'm going to advocate here. I'm not just saying this because I like them. It's a real happy ending.

Two things. The first has to do with the problem of labeling (and we're going to return to this in even greater detail in the last chapter). We easily confuse the actual phenomenon that we've created with some *terms* that we are interested in. This mistake is very easy for us because of our ideas about theories and because of our tolerance for abstractions that don't have clear referents. "Inequality" is a single word, true, but it's got to be just about the most general term in the world. There's no reason to think that there is anything so fundamental to the set of things we could use the term to indicate that we can really study "inequality" as a natural kind. So what happens when we try to scale it down?

We end up studying one thing, but *calling* it something else. And if our results have a lot to do with what we *call* our findings, they're almost certain to be useless. Can I prove this philosophically, beyond the capacity of a sophistical rebuttal? Maybe not. But it doesn't make it any less important for that. You might be studying something that has to do with the interaction of groups of American strangers in a safe environment. There's nothing wrong with that. Very interesting. You might learn about attribution processes, eyeblink hierarchies, all sorts of things. But you won't learn them if you insist on calling them something else.

And if you don't understand what you are studying, you don't understand what you are doing. And this gets to the second problem.

Did, Does, and Can

Our imaginary researcher somehow slipped from (1) "what's up with this?"—a prescientific question, to be sure—to (2) "how *did* this arise?" to (3) "how *does* inequality arise?" to (4) "*can X* lead to inequality?" One of the problems with theory testing is that it tends to blur the difference between these questions and, again, leads researchers to lose interest in what they are actually doing. But if you are testing a "theory," as long as your "predictions" are confirmed, you're delighted.

Confirming predictions in an artifactual situation isn't always necessarily flawed, but for a long time in sociology it was more or less shooting fish in a barrel. And researchers were honestly ignorant of this, because—given their attention to abstract theories as opposed to scientific knowledge of local interpersonal processes—most remained, to the best of my capacity to judge, ignorant of the work on demand characteristics (which I'll get to soon; this has to do with how situations guide conduct).

But even without that, logic should have indicated one of the problems with the experiments, since they went from "did" to "can." Suppose that twice in one month, we come to the university and see that a number of the windows are smashed out. Clearly, we have a problem on our hands!

The police are already at work, but, with a supercilious wave of the hand, we dismiss them. This is human action, our specialty. We'll give a scientific answer.

There are debates; different theories abound. One of them is that it is caused by eight-year-olds with baseballs and bats, proposed by a researcher who just happens to have an eight-year-old who recently broke the garage door window playing baseball. This researcher gets ten eight-year-olds, puts each in an empty room with nothing but a baseball bat and a baseball, and locks them in for the night. In the morning, indeed, six of the rooms have broken windows (and two eight-year-olds are missing!). The theory is supported!

The problem is that if you put someone in a room with nothing else to do but, most probably, smash that window, they're going to smash the window. The fact that baseballs *can* break windows was never in doubt. The question was whether they *did* break this window. There are three parts of this lesson. The first is that if you find yourself wanting to test the hypothesis "Can *x* cause *y*?" almost always, you should stop right there. The answer is yes. If you're even thinking this, you can reject the null hypothesis that *x* never, ever, even *can* cause *y* (and that's why I said this in chapter 2). Once you've asked it, it's just a game to see if you can come up with a setting in which it will. That would be fine for an applied question, like "Can we increase tolerance by getting kids to run relay races?" But if that isn't your focus, walk away.

The second lesson is more particular to the case of experiments. Very often, we give the people nothing else to do *but* work with things. All they know about each other is that they're gamma and zeta; that's especially true when we have them interact with computer terminals. They get it. They're supposed to use that to do something, and usually you've given them only one thing to do. Yes, you have proven that people can break windows with baseballs, or set up hierarchies based on task contributions. Riiiight. They can do lots of things.

> **Just because they *can*,
> doesn't mean they *did*.**

Remember this from chapter 4? What people are is potentialities for action. If you're closing off all of these potentialities except for one, it's not surprising that that's the one you'll see. It's not going to confirm a theory that it did or does happen. So rather than "deduce and test," we want to make our artifact, and then think about what's going on. If we can think of a few possible explanations, and we often can, then we want to eliminate some of these others. How are we going to do this? Through successions of other experiments with variations. And I'm going to argue that this way of working—making a series of strategic comparisons focused on eliminating plausible counters—is something we can learn from in non-experimental comparative work.

If experiments aren't great at testing theory, they're even worse at face-off attempts. In conventional numerical sociology, that's often what we do in a typical paper. We have different theories competing to explain the same phenomenon, and it's a match to see who can explain the most variation. I think that this way of working is more defensible than it seems—in part because there are pretty clear standards for how this sort of battle is conducted. Experimentalists often try to do the same thing: we'll try *your* cause in one-third the subjects, *my* cause in another third, and keep a residual third for control. Guess what? I win again! Always, I am the winner.

Why? Because if there really are treatments, they don't just differ in kind, but in intensity. If you are free to choose the intensity of the *other* guy's treatment, chances are, consciously or not, you'll make it on the weaker side. Drug companies often test their drug against another company's. But they have to use the recommended dosage determined by previous research to set the intensity of the competitor's treatment. *The fact that we have no way of even thinking about what this means for us is itself conclusive proof that we cannot engage in such face-off research.*[5] And that's the third lesson.

School Subjects

Bad Subjects

I haven't held back here on the problems that were, for many years, legion in sociological experiments. It was truly that bad. The problems I've identified in experimental work, however, turn out to be generic to social inquiry that involves interaction with subjects. Usually in class, students love when I go over all the problems with experiments. But then someone says, "Gee.... doesn't this imply the same problems are seen in, say, ethnography?" You bet it does. And they're harder to identify, there—and harder to fix. We'll look here, where the looking is easier. These lessons, then, are for all of us.

For a long time, other sociologists dismissed these experiments as "undergraduatology," because almost all experimentalists were running ex-

---

5. If we do want to compare treatments, we're best off doing so by comparing the mediators that they seem to employ.

periments on undergraduate students at their own institutions (if not in their own classes). And that indeed is a problem, but not, I think, for the reasons that were often raised (e.g., being unrepresentative). Instead, the problems have to do with the specific social relations and social situations that produce the data, which we need to think through.

It's been a dirty secret that subjects in experiments often don't necessarily really care about what they're doing. They usually know that they are the subject of research and know it is an abstract situation. That in itself isn't so bad. But many also don't believe the researchers are really studying what they claim to. They are often asked about this afterward, and most swear that they never suspected that the wool was being pulled over their eyes.

But they're generally at universities that specialize in experimental social science, where researchers have been doing similar work for years, and often, the students are taking classes where they *read* this stuff. If they're so stupid they can't figure this out, they're not good subjects. And, in fact, graduate students in my classes who were in such experiments as undergraduates often say that they all knew the experiment wasn't really what the experimenter said it was, but when debriefed, the students would lie: "Oh my gosh! No, I never guessed you weren't really interested in what I would bring to the moon!" Why did they lie? It's hard to give disappointing news to someone's face. If you did, you'd ruin that person's day. Why bother?

Often the research is fun, or at least fun compared to sitting in lectures by sociologists. Still, think about this: you teach a class on, say, social psychology to students. And you give them tests. And you teach them your ideas. And if they don't understand your ideas they get bad grades. And you give them an experiment. And you lie to them about what it is about. Well, there is a very good chance that they will do whatever it is they think you want them to do. You've increased the susceptibility of your subjects not just to the construction of an artifact but to the active construction of precisely the artifact that you want (which they may have a good sense of)... unless they hate you enough to try to bring it crashing down.

And sometimes they do. One prominent sociologist, Anthony Oberschall, in a review a few years ago (2000, 1188), revealed that when he was a student at Harvard, he was a subject in some of the classic studies of group behavior carried out there, because he needed the beer money. "They [the experiments] were so simple minded... that to overcome boredom my peers and I sought to create paradoxical and absurd results. I have no regrets about it; it was retaliation against insulting young people's intelligence."

And this hostility has been noted by the other side. In one article, the great Stanford researcher Morris Zelditch (Zelditch and Floyd 1998, 363) noted in passing that the "other" category to questionnaires that subjects filled out includes irrelevant responses to the questions. Some of the examples he gives of irrelevant responses are "'hi'; or curses" (presumably, things like "f——k you this sucks"). Why the hostility? Because a great deal of experimental research comes from subjects who are basically being coerced to participate.

Now you might think that rebellious students sabotaging the results will just lead to meaningless results. But here's the trickier issue—the researcher gets wind that this sometimes happens. He has a theory (which is, by the way, totally wrong). He does his experiments. The results indicate that his theory is wrong. But he thinks, "You know, I think this is the result of sabotage. That class had an attitude problem. Let me do it again" (and, at the same time, the researcher unconsciously changes his way of presenting the experiment). This time he gets the right results. So we have a strong bias toward positive findings.

New Subject Pools

Got it, you say. Don't use undergraduates. Well, good! Perhaps you were thinking of using a different subject pool anyway. Because now there are firms that will deliver respondents to you, as it were. For example, Amazon.com runs a wonderful little thing they call Mechanical Turk, as mentioned in chapter 4. You can give people any task that can be done via the Internet and offer money, and some will accept. This could be counting the number of pins in a photograph of a pin pile or answering survey questions.[6]

The problem is that such experiments are best at getting at core psychological processes, those closer down to the meat of the brain. But with "M Turk," you really have no control over the setting, and you can't be sure what's going on (though you can eliminate people who take too long to answer on the assumption that they are also watching *SpongeBob* [here see Peterson 2015]). So the setting cuts against one of the strengths of experiments. And remember from chapter 4 that we don't want to use them to find rare populations—or any particular population at all.

---

6. The reason it's called Mechanical Turk is that in the eighteenth century in Europe, some folks unveiled an amazing chess computer, a full-sized robot of a Turkish man who could mechanically move the pieces and play a great chess game. If you are wondering how this slipped your notice, that there were chess-playing robot computers in the eighteenth century, it's because it was a delightful hoax. A midget was stuffed into the box, and he manipulated the arms. So the idea here is that there are actually people doing something somewhere, but you can't see it.

Good Subjects

OK, you think, point taken. You need to avoid both coerced subjects and bought ones. Always use volunteers. Nope. There are really big problems with relying on volunteers; these problems, by the way, are by no means restricted to the case of experiments, and working this through can turn out to be very useful for interviewers. Basically, we're back to the problem of selectivity. It turns out that volunteers are very different from other people, both in general and in particular. In general, they score lower in authoritarianism, which tends to be correlated with hostility to academics (Rosenthal and Rosnow 1969, 87–91). They'll generally measure higher on intelligence tests, and almost certainly will be better educated and of higher occupational status than others. In medical research, they have more psychopathology. And of course, folks who volunteer for a particular experiment are likely to be interested in the topic, in agreement with the general approach of the researcher, and, indeed, possibly trying to suck up to this researcher.

The point isn't that they're not "representative." The point is that they're almost certainly different from other people in ways that are especially likely to be related to the theory being tested. And even worse, they're more likely to be extremely susceptible to the biggest problem with all experimental research, to wit, the problem of "demand characteristics."

Demand Characteristics

This is a term coming from social psychological field theory and hence largely forgotten with the eclipsing of this by the trivial social psychology of the 1980s. It refers to when, basically, something about certain situations tells you what you are supposed to do. You don't always know *how* you know it, or even *that* you know it, but you know it. It's what Milgram was playing around with when he got people to obey authority.

The most straightforward form of the effect of demand characteristics in experiments comes from the cues that experimenters give off that indicate how they want people to behave. That is, it leads to confirmation bias. This has been proven—by clever experiments—to affect experimental results. In one wonderful case, half of the experimenters are given subjects (really accomplices) who confirm the experimenters' hypotheses, and half are given subjects (really accomplices) who disconfirm the experimenters' hypotheses. Then all the experimenters are given a second batch of subjects—this time, real subjects—and what do you know? The unlucky ones got stronger results from the randomly allocated subjects. In fact, their subjects recorded different personality tests (Rosenthal 1969,

191, 222). And these sorts of effects persist when someone else does the checking.

Such experimental artifacts can be very strong. In some cases, researchers experimenting with rats, told that one rat was the smart one and the other stupid, eventually found the rats diverging in their performance so that the one labeled smart got better and better and the "stupid" one became stupid. The same pattern has been found with short-term experiments on human beings. And, it has even been found to hold in an elementary classroom, when the teacher is told to expect "blooming" from some children but not others. Those kids' IQs went up more than the others (Rosenthal and Jacobson 1968).[7]

In another study, half of a set of graduate students learning how to read Rorschach tests "happened to hear" that better researchers were likely to elicit from their subjects more answers involving humans than animals, while the other half heard the opposite. All were sternly warned to make sure that they did not coach their subjects. All the interactions were tape-recorded. Listening to the tape, the researchers don't seem to be giving the subjects any guidance as to the "right" answer. Yet there was a statistically significant difference in the ratio of animal to human answers across the treatments.

This shouldn't be an excuse for us to dismiss experiments as artifactual. Because the same sorts of things happen in other forms of research. You think there aren't demand characteristics in in-depth interviewing, which is a joint production of two persons having a conversation? In ethnography, which can be totally undisciplined and idiosyncratic? In surveys, in which we ask people dozens of questions that mean nothing to the respondents, and they may be looking for situational cues to tell them how to answer? In all cases, we need a lot more sociology to understand the production of the data that we use to make our sociology. And experiments themselves are one of the best ways of understanding what is messed up with the production of data.[8]

To do this, we focus on the phenomena that we create artifactually, and propose multiple explanations. We then try to eliminate some, by conducting a *series* of experiments. You might need one to first "establish the phenomenon"—demonstrate that the artifact can be reliably produced. But, if you really want to convince someone who knows his or her stuff, you're probably going to need to do three or four more, where you now

7. This research is controversial, and some replications have failed, but replications cannot now be of "full strength."

8. And the results can help us attenuate the effects: earliest responses are usually most affected, and removing the physical presence of the experimenter also attenuates the effects (Rosenthal 1969, 249–50; also see Hyman 1954, 179).

successively eliminate other possibilities, zeroing in on what's going on (look at the work of Robb Willer as an exemplar). That's not the way we're generally taught to think in sociology, where we favor a single set up and a decisive test. But that's basically ridiculous. The experimental version of successive comparisons is better, more scientific, and can be used in other types of research.

Toward Comparative Historical

Motivation

And this brings us to comparison in historical sociology. There's been a school in sociology that insists that comparison on nonrandomly allocated cases can be used to good effect to uncover causality (or something a bit more obscure that is functionally equivalent). Indeed, it was an enthusiasm for causality that led to their focus on comparison. The problem they started with is that, when it comes to history, many extremely interesting things only happen once. Yet they might still have a question about these things that is (more or less) causal: the kind of question that normally sociologists answer via comparisons. But here, they have just one case, and so they have nothing to compare to.

So, for example, suppose someone says, "The cause of the French Revolution was that the French government was too deep in debt, couldn't afford to pay its army, and couldn't raise taxes, and that leads to revolution." There isn't really any comparison we can do within France that will help answer this question. We aren't saying that people more concerned about the state's debt led the revolting, and it won't really even help to look at the rate of increase of debt over time. So what do we do?

The Use of Counterfactuals

Max Weber ([1905] 1949b, 164–66.) had a suggestion here, which he called the notion of "objective possibility."[9] We first come up with "imaginative constructs" to help us get a handle on the manifold nature of reality. Then we come up with alternative scenarios involving the removal of some element in our picture of the world (173). And we hopefully have some empirical rules that are attached to the presence or absence of such an event.

9. He took this from Johannes von Kries, a biomedical theorist. It is related to von Kries's notion of "adequate causation"—causation that is both actual in some instance and general.

For example, in 1995, the fifty-year anniversary of the end of the Second World War led historians to consider the question of whether the dropping of the atomic bombs on Japan caused the United States to win the war. Now in one way, we'd have to say yes, because in short order after the bombs, Japan surrendered (nearly) unconditionally. That works as part of a narrative and assumes that causality is *sufficiency* (after the atomic bomb, no chance of not surrendering). But Weber's (180) approach, like that of sociologists in general, prefers *necessity*. Thus the Weberian method is to ask, "Were we to imagine the basic scenario in the absence of the atomic bombs, could we, according to any empirical rule (which doesn't include "freaky accidents happen") project that Japan would have been able to escape (nearly) unconditional surrender?" That is, were enough objective factors present to make reasonably plausible an alternative outcome? Historians agreed that the answer was no. The bombs were not necessary (even if sufficient) and hence, in this understanding, were not the "causes" of the United States' triumph over Japan.

This seems like a marvelously successful application of the method. But that's because it's a pretty easy case—it's hard to find reasons to think that Japan could have led to a negotiated outcome that preserved its regime. When we all agree, we can identify such causes. But that's not when we need science—when we are already sure of things. When it comes to the more interesting cases—like what was the cause of the French Revolution?—at least some of us disagree. Then it seems we're stuck.

But what if we could find an actual alternative case, which *did* indeed have the other objective factors that, we hypothesize, in the absence of the crucial factor X, would have led to a different outcome? Then we could see whether our hypothetical reconstruction really is consistent with another outcome.

This is the most direct, and, I think, justifiable derivation of a comparative historical endeavor. We are finding plausible illustrations of our hypothetical reconstructions to demonstrate that they are not inherently contradictory. It is important to understand that this is closely related to the increased interest among quantitative researchers in ascertaining the degree of support in their data for answers to causal questions—basically, it's again about finding close comparables. There we reduce things to a single number (in many cases), namely, propensity to be treated. Here, we look for a single close matching case.

Now, we may not be able to find such a case; and to do so, we may have to look far and wide. But this gives additional plausibility to our argument. It is this that brings us to comparative historical research as it was boomed by Theda Skocpol (1979, 1984).

Table 7.1. Hypothetical Data Supporting Method of Difference

Variable or Factor?	Case 1	Case 2
x (bankruptcy)	Yes	No
y (revolution)	Yes	No
v (monarchy)	Yes	Yes
w (current war)	No	No
t (peasant unrest)	Yes	Yes

Note: This implies x uniquely necessary for y.

Comparisons and Causality

Here, rather than focus on one event, and use comparisons to illustrate other possibilities, the researcher claims that this event can be treated as a particular case of a more general category of events. She seeks to explain not "*the* French Revolution" but *a* revolution in an agrarian bureaucracy. What Skocpol did was draw on earlier comparative traditions in historical explanation but try to crisp them up, to what is now widely accepted as an improbable degree. But that's good—it's only when we're crisp that we can get clear on our problems.

She turned to J. S. Mill's work on explanation and seized, in particular, on what he called the method of difference. We are trying to explain some outcome y and we have a candidate cause x. We will accept that x is the cause of y if one case has x and y, the other has neither, and the two are the same on everything else (see table 7.1). (Less commonly used is what Mills called the method of agreement, namely, that two cases have only x and y in common, with everything else being different, so we think it must be that x is the cause of y.)

This sort of comparison relies on us being able to establish that our two cases are different on everything else but x and y. Unfortunately, no set of cases can have the right patterns of variation on all possible alternative explanations. So some variation will remain that is logically implied as a possible cause. That is, it turns out that there was some factor z (e.g., political centralization) that, say, case 1 had but case 2 did not (see bottom row in table 7.2).

For this reason, Mill himself, though extremely interested in and sympathetic to a search for social laws, concluded that these methods were not suitable for the social sciences. Even in the natural sciences it was nearly impossible to find two cases that satisfied the methods of difference unless it was due to experimental manipulation, but the possibility of finding such cases for comparative historical investigation was "manifestly

Table 7.2. Hypothetical Data Frustrating and Adapting Method of Difference

Variable or Factor?	Case 1	Case 2	Case 3
x (bankruptcy)	Yes	No	Yes
y (revolution)	Yes	No	Yes
v (monarchy)	Yes	Yes	Yes
w (current war)	No	No	Yes
t (peasant unrest)	Yes	Yes	No
z (polit. centralization)	Yes	No	No

Note: Cases 1 and 2 support both that x is necessary for y and the alternative that z is necessary for y. Adding case 3 suggests that z is not necessary for y.

absurd." "Two nations which agreed in everything except their commercial policy would agree also in that" (Mill 1872, 257, 575).[10]

So we know our cases will never fit the requirements of the method exactly. Now logically, this means that the entire effort is wasted. But not all logically possible variables are equally compelling. Those that remain that have to be dealt with by other means. Most importantly, we can bring another case into the comparison. So we find a case 3 that lacked z but still had y (the third column in the table 7.2).

This is where you, the comparative historical researcher, come in. You're not working on the abstract logic of inquiry, you're trying to make some argument, and you're trying to assemble some cases to do it. Can you still use this approach to support your claims? There's a fork in the road. One way leads us back to Max Weber and to seeing your case as illustrating an objective possibility. I think that's pretty smart.

The other way is... not so smart. That way is to squinch up your eyes and try to use the comparison itself to prove your argument. There are two problems with this. The first is that this relies on the dubious assumption that what we happen to have lumped together as a set of "identical" outcomes really are identical, and, even more, that they all share the same cause. But we know that, in reality, Mr. Green can die of one thing, and Mr. Black of a totally different cause. Since I've said that elsewhere (2015, 71),

10. Indeed, Mill had a rather sensible understanding of the nature of social organization and its study, most notably, that "it follows... that unless two societies could be alike in all the circumstances which surround and influence them (which would imply their being alike in their previous history,)... no cause will produce exactly the same effect in both. Every cause, as its effect spreads through society, comes in contact with difference sets of agencies, and thus has its effect on some of the social phenomena differently modified; and these differences, by their reaction, produce a difference even in those of the effects which would otherwise have been the same" (Mill 1872, 586).

I won't go into that here and, instead, grant that assumption. The second problem is, even if that *were* true, how can you "kill off" all the potential z's that could interfere with your planned comparison?

Survive the Terrible Twos

Neutralization via Comparison

First of all, we recognize that not all logically possible variables are equally compelling, and second, the researcher can try to deal with those pesky z's by other means. And in fact, most of the serious methodological work of a comparative historical researcher falls outside the method of difference, and is a set of strategic attacks on z's to make them go away (cf. Nichols 1986, 174–75).

Of course, we generally choose our cases in advance to try to minimize the number of z's, remember? Which means that when it comes to comparative historical research, no one samples randomly. Rather, one samples strategically—to make a certain point. (The exception is when we have *all* the cases of some type, which I'll get to later.) And so depending on what you want to find, you select your cases differently. That is, if France had a revolution, and a strong king, and a centralized polity, and sale of offices, if you pick a country to compare it to that has no revolution or strong king, but a centralized polity and sale of offices, then you can seemingly prove that it is a strong king that leads to a revolution. But of course, if you pick a different case, one with no revolution or centralized polity, but with both a strong king and sale of offices (but no revolution), then you prove that it is the centralized polity that leads to a revolution. This is a fundamental problem regarding a pathological research design—if you are allowed to select your cases to prove your point, your work means nothing.

I want you to take seriously this critique: the mere conjunction of cases, like one of those in tables 7.1 and 7.2 above, has the same scientific status as the Ouija board. Yet a principle that we considered when thinking about experiments turns out to be very plausible here. And this is that what we want to do is to use successive comparisons to zero in on what's going on.

A wonderful exemplar is found in Richard Biernacki's (1997) *Fabrication of Labor*. Most of the book compares England and Germany—not in the form of just "making a table" but compiling and organizing many different kinds of primary documents, demonstrating two different patterns of associations in the two countries, representing two different ways of conceiving of the relation of labor to its products. In England, labor is understood through the lens of its physical results; in Germany, it's understood in terms of the *time* it takes. Then, when it's time to make sense of it all, Biernacki's got the typical problem—a contrast of two cases has a near infinite number of possible causes, and he can't really rule any out. And in fact, his historical research suggests that there are really three critical differences between England and Germany that lead to the variation in their conceptions of labor. There's the timing of the emergence of labor markets as well as commodities markets; there's the survival of guild organizations; and there's the role of cultural models from a feudal past.

How to demonstrate that? Well, in Britain, there was a market in goods long before there was a labor market, and labor was, therefore, assimilated to the case of goods. That's how they saw it. But let's look at France—there, the guilds were no longer powerful, and their notion of labor lacked the German focus on authority. And now let's compare France and Germany together to Italy, which lacked feudal agriculture when wage labor was being organized; here the notion was, somewhat like the British, that labor was embodied in an object, but to them, the value came in the labor one is willing to expend for it. Each comparison focuses on separating themes that are collapsed in the original comparison, and allows us to bring new forms of data to bear on the question. It's not exactly the way an experimentalist works, but it's pretty close.

And there are other ways of pursuing the finding through different comparisons. Most commonly, if the theorized explanation involves lower-level actors (e.g., individuals), then you can try to go down a level of analysis within your cases to prune away contrary explanations you think are wrong. Yes, case 1 was high on z and y, while case 2 was low on z and y, but look *within* case 1. The subsections of case 1 that were highest on z weren't highest on y.[11] I think that this sort of thing can work very well— because you are going to let your evolving argument push you to make the sorts of comparisons that are most relevant for weeding out possibilities. It might seem less scientific, because you're changing what you're doing on the fly, but as we've seen, that's what experimentalists do.

What's less scientific, though it often seems more scientific, is to take all the cases and do a sophisticated comparison of them all. Let me go on to scare you off of that.

11. James Mahoney (1999) has pointed out that comparative historical researchers tend not only to use the Millsian method of presence/absence but also to bring in both narrative and ordinal comparisons (e.g., both England and France had tension between the nobles and the king, but England had more tension). I'm going to try to steer you away from that way of pursuing your finding, on the basis of the Tigger principle (see below, n12).

To Larger Case Comparisons

My colleague Terry Clark talks about the "danger region" of having more than nine but less than a hundred cases—too many to really grasp as individuals, too few to use statistical theory. I think that's right, and I suggest we call these the "terrible twos" (two-digit numbers). In order to make comparisons using data sets of this size, sociologists make assumptions that are stronger than those used when the comparison is really a rhetorical scaffold. Let's consider some of these assumptions.

Beware of the terrible twos!

The first has to do with interchangeability. We've come to accept that it is fine to pool human beings, giving each an equal weight, despite how different they might be. We don't care that some are more important than others. But when it comes to historical analyses we often want "wholes" as our units, and we've decided that it's more of a problem to pool these—to treat Togo and China as just two instances of "country." Togo, as Allan Silver once mentioned, doesn't even make its own stamps or control its own currency. That seems like a pretty damning critique, though I bet we could say the same about people if we were being tactless. ("Really? Tim doesn't even comb his own *hair* or make his own *lunch*. Are you really going to count him as having an opinion the same as me?")

A second supposition is that most of our statistics assume that our cases are independent in some way. However, if we are making comparisons across the eighteen founding Organisation for Economic Cooperation and Development states (excluding the United States and Canada, that is), almost all are part of a transnational European Union. But then again, that's true of people, too. We're all in the same boat.

There's nothing, then, incredibly wrong about using these assumptions for entities like countries. But even being not-incredibly-wrong can be bad enough. When you're in the terrible twos, you don't have a lot of science to waste. Every dumb move can cost you badly. If you forget about person ID #1659 in a survey, probably nothing happens. You forget about Germany in an analysis of Europe, and that's a different matter.

The biggest problem, however, has that been that in applying variable type analyses to small sets of countries (even if you call it case based), we have moved from a rectangular matrix (many more cases than variables) to a squarish one (around the same number), which forces us to change our theory of causality. We can afford to be probabilistic with the "large

N" world of many observations, but, as Stanley Lieberson (1991) in particular has argued, we can't do that with the small N one, or we'd be forced
to admit that we don't really have much grounds to conclude *anything*. So
we end up moving our sense of causality toward determinism. (Further,
we get pushed to assuming that our measures are perfect, which is even
sillier.) But we shouldn't be able to simply declare that the event we're
studying was deterministically caused by its antecedents, just because, if
that *were* true, it would make our job easier.

> **Just because it happened, doesn't
> mean it *had* to happen.**

A key part of the assumptions used to justify such comparisons is of
course that the same general historical plots should play out the same way
in different places. Greater tax pressures should lead the Han dynasty and
the Roman Empire to change in similar ways. And here we are in a difficult
position. Almost everyone believes that there should be *some* similarities
and regularities, otherwise studying history would be basically impossible.
But no one thinks that the regularities are simple, obvious, and foolproof.
We are stuck in a nether ground, and it is tempting to assume that there
is just the amount of regularity required to make our analysis work.

And it gets a bit worse. Even if we assume that our results are driven by
deterministic causality, so that a terrible-twos comparison can unveil it,
we also have to decide whether we accept only a simple world or a complicated one. In a simple world, our comparison has to give us a simple causal
recipe: for example, revolutions are just caused by debt. If that seems implausible to you—or, more likely, you're just unable to find any results
like this—then by all means, allow for complexity. Let there be multiple
pathways that can produce the same type of event in different cases. But
then there's nothing to stop you from identifying every combination of
independent variables that is associated with a positive outcome a "cause."
That is, we actually assume something along the lines, whatever is, had
to be. For this reason, we are guaranteed a finding for every data analysis.
Hmmmm... be suspicious of anything that seems too good. It is.

What Kinds of Causes Should You Look For?

Further, the causes we can find are only the causes we have. That's of
course always true, but it becomes more critical in the terrible twos, because we're more likely to find *something* that explains our outcome. And

chances are, we've only looked at the potential causes that are big and obvious, the sorts of elephant causes that are fun to go after. Constructing a column labeled something like "strong civil society" makes you sound smart and scientific. Making a column labeled something like "leader has tertiary syphilis" or "paper shipments delayed due to fungus" with only a single numeral "one" in it, doesn't seem very sociological. Of course, you could bundle these together (perhaps the great factor predicting state breakdown, "bad luck"), but, after all, you're hunting elephants, not fleas.

Big effects don't necessarily have big causes.

That's in large part because fleas are hard to see. Your comparison can't possibly say that the actual cause was a corn blight in one particular region you don't even know about. And you won't even look for such flea problems, because we generally assume that big effects have to have big causes. Yet in our own world, we know that this isn't always true.

The 2000 U.S. election is a great example—some of the causes of the current configuration of global politics really, undeniably, owe their existence to the decisions of a relatively small group of political actors in Florida. If this turned out to push the United States down one road—for example, sustained, ruinous conflict with Muslim extremists and, who knows, perhaps a nuclear war—and twenty-fourth-century sociologists were trying to understand why the Middle East War involved the United States, as opposed to Russia, chances are they'd be looking at the elephants, not the Florida fleas. Yet no Florida win, no Bush; no Bush, no second Iraq War, no successful September 11 attack, no war in Afghanistan, and so on.

But of course, if your comparisons are such that you are guaranteed a "finding," you're always going to reinforce your assumption that big effects always have big causes. You and your friends will just argue about *which* ones. But there's a very good chance that you'll all be wrong together. As Goldthorpe (2007, 1:58) says, maybe things like revolutions and other exciting transitions just aren't going to be the kind of phenomena on which sociological theory can shed light. It never came with a guarantee that it was good for everything.

What Is A?

So far, we've been focusing on the comparison part—and not what we are comparing. But very often, that's where all the problems enter. This point was first made by the philosopher William Whewell, in his critique of Mill. Whewell argued that the problem was not in the rather elementary logic, but in all the work necessary to get the data ready for the application of the method (here also see the discussion of Brown [1984, 222–25, 245, 263–64]). (To put this in context, we need to understand the notation Mill used, according to which we seek to determine the effects of occurrences A, B, and C, or the causes of occurrences a, b, and c.) But Whewell ([1860] 1971, 263–64) pointed out that "they take for granted the very thing that is most difficult to discover, the reduction of the phenomena to formulae such as are here presented to us. When we have any set of complex facts offered to us... when, in any of these cases, we would discover the law of nature which governs them... where are we to look for our A, B, C, and a, b, c? Nature does not present to us cases in this form, and how are we to reduce them to this form?"

That is, if it was clear on inspection what constituted meaningful units of analysis, and what their properties were—for example, which nations had strong executives and which weak, which had feudal traditions and which did not, which were militaristic and which were not—everything would be easy. But all the important methodological work enters during the process whereby we summarize huge amounts of complexity into simple binary codes. After this, the methods of agreement and difference are simply a mopping up.

And this work of summarizing (which we'll explore in the next chapter as "coding") is likely to be tendentious—in line with our hoped-for conclusions. In the wise words of Howard Becker (1992, 212), we may indeed see two ways of working in sociology. Some researchers take big gobs of data, accepting that some cases are measured with error, which means that any relations are, at best, probabilistic. But you can't really do this when you have few cases; one "bad" one can wreck your theory, and you don't have enough data to estimate a probabilistic relation. Then, you may need to decide which cases to accept as valid and which to throw out. "Not exactly throw them out but, rather, decide by inspecting them carefully that they are not after all a case of the sort of thing we are explaining."[12] This sounds corrupt in the abstract, but in concrete cases it is reasonable. Was England in 1840 a democracy? Did India have a war of independence? In practice, there are good reasons to doubt the exceptions. But everything is an exception in some way.

> **Applying a rigorous comparative method to seat-of-the-pants dichotomizations is spackling over the holes.**

12. This reminds me of when Tigger tells Pooh and Piglet that Tiggers eat everything, especially thistles, until he tries one and redefines "everything" not to include thistles. Hence calling this the "Tigger principle."

And that means it is easy for researchers to make their codings be just those that help them say what they want to say. And the take away is this: putting an unambiguous process (like a mechanical comparison) on top of ambiguous coding decisions is not moving in the right direction. It's simply covering up the truth.[13]

Pathological Methods

You might think I'm being pretty hard on this one methodological approach, when "nothing is perfect" and "every method has its pluses and minuses." Of course that's true. No horse runs at infinity miles an hour. All have their pluses and minuses. But that doesn't mean you need to buy that bandy-legged one that is coughing in the corner. Anyway, I'm going to argue that the formal comparative approach is actually worse than most other methods. Because, the more seriously you take it, the more it channels you toward inferior work habits.

First, this sort of deterministic comparative approach will push us very quickly to emphasize more and more proximate causes. But this lowest common denominator, the one thing that all the cases with an outcome have in common, is rarely a *cause* of the outcome—it's rather its *foreshadowing*.

But there's a bigger problem. Taking the method of difference seriously pushes us to making the strong (perhaps indefensible) assumption that history works according to discrete necessary causes. And that these causes are big things. The problem is that if this is true, the method of difference eliminates more possible causes the more cases you bring in; the most complete research is going to be the one where you can't make any conclusions at all. And so you are going to be tempted to ignore evidence because the only way you can work with your assumptions is to not know all the counterevidence.

There are two ways of responding. One is pseudostatistical, and this is to maintain your ability to come up with a strong finding for any set of data. This also turns out to be pathological, but I'll get to that in a different work (tentatively titled, "QCA: It's just like statistics... only without

---

13. One more thing on codings and comparisons: it's important to realize that in this world, there isn't an intrinsic difference between a simple coding and an interaction. So Ragin (1987, 37) isn't quite right to say that the classic Millsian methods, as put forward by Skocpol, are unable to deal with multiple causation when either x or w leads to y. It does so all the time, and we don't recognize it because we've fetishized our labeling. For example, the dichotomy "state debt high" can be seen as an interaction between "state expenses high" and "state revenues low." "State breakdown" can be understood as an interaction with many OR functions, where we simply put a "1" down for any of the many ways in which a state can start to dissolve.

the statistics!"). The second is to back off on this idea of using the comparison to prove or uncover the truth and, instead, use it as a scaffolding to pursue your research.

Rhetoric and Scaffolding

To remind ourselves, we've seen that there is an important justification for normal sampling procedures, and comparative historical work usually violates it (the exception is when the universe of possible cases is so tiny that we study them all, like 1950s' "superpowers" where there's only the United States and the Soviet Union). Because of this, the comparative schema cannot be understood to be one that can actually test a theory. At best, it organizes the mass of data that is *also* presented. Look at Biernacki's (1997) *Fabrication of Labor*. The formal comparative part takes up a few pages. The rest of the book is a mammoth, and time intensive, exploration and organization of evidence. The comparative schema is really a rhetorical exercise, a framework that helps in terms of persuading the reader.

That's not bad. That is, if comparison is a framework that we use to illustrate objective possibility, and to sharpen our focus, it's all for the good. Dylan Riley (2010) uses this sort of approach in his comparative work on fascism. He looks at three different countries, not to see what "caused" fascism, but to see how the divergences across fascism point us to look at some configurations as important and not others. Rather than have to assume that fascism was the "same" outcome in each country, his comparison pushes him to explore how it differed.

Comparison to Experiments

When we were thinking about experiments, the cleverness in crafting a comparison seemed only good. Yet now, it suddenly appears bad. Why? To some extent, it's pretty straightforward. History is over, by definition. The data are in. Experiments don't start out that way; the treatment has yet to be carried out. That means when we set up our comparison for historical research, we've already peeked. It's a lot less impressive to call a coin flip after it's landed than when it's still in the air.

But there's something else about experiments that gives them an advantage. The active nature of the interaction means that we can attempt to slice things finer and finer. Is the effect of reading propaganda as opposed to *The Tale of Peter Rabbit* associated with the arguments being made? Or with the emotions aroused? We redo things again, now making two different treatments, one with the arguments but not the emotion, one with the emotion, but not the facts. Unfortunately, in comparative historical work, France stays France, and Germany Germany.

For this reason, we often find that the most impressive comparative analyses are those that assess subunits of a relatively homogenous unit. For example, Guy Swanson's amazing (1967) *Religion and Regime* showed differences in the religious affiliation of Swiss cantons that corresponded to their local political structure. (Yes, there are some problems with the historical chain that accounts for these differences, but it's still a fabulous work.) Michael Rogin's (1969) analysis of county-level variation in support for populism, McCarthyism, and progressivism in Wisconsin won a debate about the nature of populism by examining finer variations than did other researchers.

In too many other cases, we basically know the variation before we start. If you're studying those eighteen Organisation for Economic Cooperation and Development countries, we know the three clumps they almost all fall into (Scandinavian, Anglo, and the rest). We *call* these clumps different things depending on what particular difference we're trying to explain, but that's really a bit arbitrary. Variables, remember, are simply bundles of cases. And no important finding can come from what we call things.

And that's going to be one of our lessons in the next chapter, where we deal with documents.

TAKEAWAYS

- Experiments are artifacts. Don't forget that, and don't deny it.
- "Can" doesn't mean "did"; "did" doesn't mean "had to."
- Comparisons are where rigidity is deadly.
- Seek research designs that encourage you do to more, and better, work.

If you were going to read more...

If you wanted to read further on comparative historical work, I'd urge you to stay away from anything written by the self-identified comparative historical types. Fine fellows all, and great researchers, but not to be trusted here. I'd start with Ronald Breiger's work, especially "On the Duality of Cases and Variables" (2009).

* 8 *
Dealing with Documents

Most of what a document means isn't contained within it. Rather, it's about the processes that led this document to be created in the first place, with the particular form it has, and to survive in a place that you can find it. Thinking this through is usually necessary to know what's in the document, anyway.

Types of Documents

I'm going to begin by discussing how to use documents as data. This is a subject most often associated with historical sociology, but such documents are also used by organizational analysts and cultural analysts, and most demographic data come from historical documents. Still, I'll tend to use historical sociology as the assumed method in question, since the thing about a document is that it's already been made (in contrast to interviewing, ethnography, or observation, where you make the data when you want it).

Currently, there is an explosion in the breadth of different types of documentary data accessible to students. One reason is simply *digitization*—more information being put in digital forms. Some of these are old documents that exist on paper; some are documents that previously would have been in paper in some archive. (And there are also images and sounds, including oral histories.)

A second is the presence of what are called *big data*—new types of large data sets, from telecommunications technology, from invasive businesses, and from the government, many of which are documents (even if rather short ones, like tweets). A third is the existence of *by-product data*: data that is automatically produced by computer games (as in some great work by Ronald Burt [2012]), sales, searches on the Internet, or Wiki development, such as Wikipedia or open source software creation. Even the path people take for searching, including clicking on articles in a database—all can become a meta database for you to analyze. And many of these are more like documents than anything else.

And a fourth change is *open access* and *user-generated content*: there are more and more venues in which people are (finally!) proving the sourpuss economists wrong and doing hard work for free. And there are new sources of data springing up for the creative scholar, often produced by aficionados who want to share their knowledge of the ins and outs of their hobby. We have strange, sprawling, and multiauthored documents. Not all of the principles that we derive for more traditional documents are applicable to these types of data, but the most important ones, having to do with sampling and selection, are.

Sources

We traditionally sort documents into two types, though I'll propose that we see these as poles on a continuum. On the one hand, there are documents that we would call secondary sources: for instance, historical works written by others basically of our own time (e.g., a history of the French Revolution written in 1995). On the other hand, there are documents like diaries, account books, and church records, which were written way back when. We call these primary sources.

But there are things in between. Consider, for one, historical treatments of an event written pretty much at the time of the event (i.e., some history of the French Revolution written basically at the time of the French Revolution). We can treat these as original (primary) documents if we are doing a history of historiography, but if we are trying to use them for facts, we treat them as somewhat in between. A different sort of in-betweenness is sometimes seen in oral history. Here we find some old folks and ask them about what things used to be like. It's the inverse situation—now in our time we have the primary source, as opposed to the secondary source back in the "original" time.

> **Your generation's supply of old people is a nonrenewable scientific resource. Run out and grab some now because they're going fast!**

And I don't know where else to put this, but it has to be somewhere. If you are looking for information on things that happened fifty to eighty years ago, you have a potential source in the memories of old people. Don't overlook them. Oral histories are something that few sociologists consider as a method—they'd rather make up stories about what life was like than spend some time with the geezers. I think that's a huge mistake and that oral histories—whether new ones or ones that have already been archived—are treasure troves for historical sociologists. If you do oral histories, you should try to be in a position to have them fully transcribed and archived for the use of other social historians.

To learn how to do oral histories, you may need to be steered to a folklore department. Of course, you can try to figure it out on your own. But few sociologists know much about this, and since I sure don't, I'll continue here assuming that we're dealing with sources that you see, not hear.

Personal Documents

We also divide documents into another set of two categories, personal and public. We usually make this division less by the source of the documents than by their target—who ends up keeping them. A letter from the parole board to you becomes private; a letter from you to the parole board, although initially perhaps treated as confidential, if it is available at all, becomes public. And this is key because it affects our sampling: chances are we're either going through your boxes or those of the parole board. But in most cases, when we talk about personal documents, we are usually thinking of documents that were created outside of an organizational context.

These personal documents include things like letters, diaries, and inscriptions in the family Bible. This often strikes us as the "best" data. Why? Because we are very often interested in culture and motivations, things like how people thought about X and why they wanted to do Y. For example, Max Weber claimed that Puritans actually felt anxiety over the question of whether they were predestined for heaven. But he just asserted that. A steady stream of researchers (e.g., von Greyerz 1987) has sifted through the evidence, including diaries, to ascertain whether this was true.[1]

But then again, are we really so sure that something in a diary is always reliable? We often assume that diaries are true because they are intended for the writer's eyes only. But many of the people who left diaries were pretty sure that they'd be read by someone, sooner or later. And even if it is just for the writer, what does that tell you?

Goethe (1987, 241) remembers his visit to the Dresden art gallery: "I visited the gallery at all the permitted times, and continued rather assertively expressing my rapture over various exquisite works. Thereby I defeated my laudable intention of remaining unknown and unnoticed."

1. In general, I think it's fair to say, researchers do find all the religious ideas that Weber talked about. But at least for the English Puritans, there wasn't much evidence that they were staying up nights worrying about the state of their soul. Mostly they were pretty sure they were going to heaven, though plenty felt guilty about this and that ("Misled by the *devil* I did loathesoamely helpe myself to a somwhate larger *piece* of bread *pudding*. . . .").

Really?[2] What we read in diaries or journals is often less a record of what happened than an attempt of the author to do some sort of "self work." We probably all understand that if we open a diary and read "I do not care about Tammy Faye, I *do not care about Tammy Faye*, I DO NOT CARE ABOUT TAMMY FAYE!" we should not walk away assuming that the writer doesn't care about Tammy any more.

When it comes to letters, things get exponentially more complex. Very often we only have one-half of a correspondence. Without the other half, we may have a difficult time understanding where this letter fits in the story of an unfolding relationship. And in turn, this can make it very difficult to really figure out what the writer is trying to accomplish. And without this, we may understand the "meaning" of the words but not the meaning of the whole—because we don't yet understand what the writer was *meaning to do*.[3]

> **Personal documents are not CAT scans of the writers' brains.**

Even with the full correspondence between two persons, we often need to see some of their other correspondence to contextualize this one dialogue. For example, it is extremely common for academics carrying out international correspondence with other bigwigs to be extremely cordial and to understate their disagreement. Person A writes to B, "Your letter of 4 February was immensely clarifying. It is increasingly obvious that we are indeed on parallel paths, and only a few small points still divide us." And then A might turn around and write to some C, perhaps a countryman—and rival—of his correspondent B, with a very different tone: "I see indeed why B is referred to as a 'puddinghead' in your country; he just sent me another boatload of the most arrant nonsense to leak out of a pen." To contextualize a letter, then, we sometimes need more than we might initially think.

> **"People say things all the time. And you can never tell if they're telling the truth or not."**
> **Andy Warhol**

2. For an even better example, see Samuel Butler's ([1903] 1945, 17–18) wicked analysis of Felix Mendelssohn's reflections upon entering the Uffizi Gallery in Florence.
3. For this reason, some of the best letters for general social history are ones in which siblings simply try to entertain one another (Alice James to her brothers, or Susannah Darwin to her brother Erasmus).

Of course, sometimes we are looking through the correspondence for incidental facts. But when can we trust such documents? Just because everyone says something, doesn't mean it's true. There is no easy answer—a source that is valid for getting some information is not valid for getting other information. Indeed, when you think about it (and see Gottschalk 1950, 150), the most reliable information you might be able to find in a diary usually will have to do with matters of common knowledge that the writer didn't much care about. But that's the last thing you'd expect to find.[4]

Further, people make errors about the information that they should know best. On his deathbed, Alexander Hamilton tried to clear up the issue of the authorship of several of the Federalist Papers—which ones he as opposed to Madison had written. He got this wrong, and almost certainly not because he was trying to claim credit for something he hadn't done, but probably because his original number system was different from the final one. Many people get their age wrong, and a fair number in the world don't know their birthday, and really, the rest of us just believe what others told us about our birth dates (being too distracted to take notes at the time).

So, do you want to use a rich set of personal documents to re-create the everyday lives and ways of seeing and thinking of regular people? If so, this is likely to be the most exciting and rewarding project you will ever do. Because chances are good you will never do a second one. *If* you finish this one. *If* they ever find your body. You are diving headlong into a screaming confusion of silences, a madhouse of bathetic inconsistencies, and traveling over swaying bridges of aporia linked by coincidence. Best to use these for more specific and delimited purposes, at least for a while.

Public Documents

When we consider public documents, we're usually (though, as said above, not always) looking at things that come from an organization. First, there are publications produced by the private sector (media, advertisements, quarterly reports, press releases, manifestos, platforms, and so on). Second, there are government documents that are also published, some of which are statistics, some propaganda, and much in between, as well as reports, minutes, and, in many cases, records of their own proceedings. And third, individuals create public documents when they try to broadcast

4. Maybe this is the place to say that I'm having trouble tracking down the original of the quotation I attribute to Warhol. I do still insist that he said it, but I suppose you'll never know if I'm telling the truth or not. Still, feel free to cite me as demonstrating that he did.

their ideas, whether in letters to the editor, comments on government proposals, petitions, tracts, or Weblogs—otherwise known simply as blogs.

We often, with some justification, treat government documents as if they were entirely trustworthy. For sociology, this trust is most notable for the data that we might call demographic. Although these aren't delivered to us in the form of documents, usually there *are* underlying documents, and it turns out that in more cases than we might hope, we need to go back to these originals. For most of these statistics, the individual is usually the ultimate unit of analysis, but (without going back to original documents, if preserved) we may lack data on specific individuals. Thus, we may simply have the number of marriages in a county in any year. They are what might be seen as "objective" statistics. Not that other statistics are fake or biased, but in that they don't have anything to do with people's subjective states—opinions, beliefs, values.

Even if the data are the result of determined, objective, and well-funded organizational efforts, they can have errors in them—often quite high degrees of error—and for the same reasons that other documents do. And because we often use these data when we are interested in "mild" effects or rare events (and so we need a lot of cases), and because we often have millions of observations (and hence believe that our measures are very "precise"), bias that wouldn't make a big difference in a social survey can make a big difference here. And for this reason, more often than you might hope, one needs to either be able to trace these back to the original documents or find someone who has already done so. Often the nature of many of these sorts of errors is well known to experts, and they may even have worked out standard corrections. But you might not be as aware of the contingency that goes into its creation as you would if you had done the survey yourself. For example, as we'll discuss below, suicides may not be reported as such; those whose children have died early may not report the pregnancies; and people who claim to be unemployed may be working in the informal sector.

And sometimes, these sorts of data don't seem even remotely related to anything that we would think of as reality. But this can work for us, as we can make use of historical sources to uncover the cultural categories that historical actors must have been using. This is in effect to try to do an anthropological analysis (in the sense of Roy D'Andrade [1995]) of the past—how did these people see the world; what must have been their fundamental assumptions if they produced this document? For example, John Mohr (1994) studied the ways in which charity organizations classified recipients, not to find out how many people in 1907 were really "tramps" as opposed to "paupers" but to see how an emphasis on one way of categorizing people shifted to another.

The very unreliability of sources, then, can be used to study those who wrote them—it's sort of like a Rorschach test (or any other projective test)—the ambiguity in the world lets the fundamental structures of the author come through. This can also apply to personal documents, but I think people have been using it more for public documents, in cases in which we think the document is giving us a sense of "public ideas" that are shared even if they are wrong.

Finally, there are other indirect ways that documents can tell us something different from what they were intended to record. If firms keep track of the race of applicants, this might later be used to determine racial disparities in hiring. If churches have people sign a book when marrying, this can be used to estimate literacy rates.[5] The key task for us to think through, then, is to determine what sorts of claims we can link the documents we have to.

Linking Documents to Claims

And this linkage is where our problems start. Of course, this isn't different from what we find with other forms of data, but where we are collecting our own data, we're "going downstream." That is, we have to figure out how to get the data that will answer our question. But in this case, the data are already in. So the linking process goes upstream, and in a nutshell, the secret to using documents is just this—to realize that you have to go the other way.

These key linkages should be the subject of widespread consensus. I don't deny that it can be cool to be the first person to think of a new linkage (e.g., to be the first to realize that average bone length could be used to measure nutrition, and hence dispersion of bone lengths in archeological ruins could indicate inequality). But you want to stay away from any "creative" linkage that requires a long chain of logic connecting data (especially well known data) to your theoretical constructs (especially idiosyncratic and abstract ones). Look for new data and shared concepts instead.

How do we come up with plausible linkages? Sometimes we are using these documents to characterize places, times, or groups in some way, and we are trying to get at attributes that can't be directly measured. So we are likely to attempt to measure these attributes indirectly, by what we may, perhaps speaking a bit loosely, consider to be their causes or their effects.

---

5. This can also be true for personal documents, where the most interesting things may be left by *other* writers—annotations made by a reader, Post-its that say "this could land us all in the clink," or notes to children that say "make sure you burn all Grandma's letters to someone named 'Elvis' after I die."

For example, we might be interested in seeing whether increases in poverty make revolutions more likely, but we can't measure poverty itself. So we use grain yield—we assume that years when less grain was grown were years in which there was more poverty because we assume that harvest size *causes* wealth or poverty. For earlier periods, we might not even be able to get information on grain harvest, so we might use rainfall, as computed from trees (now we're going beyond documents, I guess). We figure that years where there was more rainfall (and hence tree rings are bigger) are years where there was a better grain harvest, because rain causes the harvest, which causes general good times.

The second creative way of proceeding is to use an *effect* of the thing we are interested in. In looking at which areas of eighteenth-century France were most revolutionary, John Markoff wanted to see whether degree of modernization or degree of market orientation—the extent to which a community bought and sold things on the market, as opposed to being self-reliant—affected the chance of an insurrection. How can you measure such orientation? You can't. So instead he used the length of roads in an area and the number of intersections (Markoff 1996, 380–81). That might seem very different, but he has some good justifications for the choice of measure and why it would matter. First, in a town where there are enough market sales to support merchants or craftsmen, they tend to live on little streets clustered around the main intersection—increasing the number of roads and intersections. Second, what goes over the roads in a big town may be grain shipments, and near big towns people no longer have subsistence agriculture, so if there are hard times, they may starve.... and watch the grain go by.

Sometimes, unfortunately, your attempts at linkages all fail. Sometimes, when you finally get permission to use an archive, and actually get there, sitting down in front of all those yearned-for boxes, your first two days tell you that these data are not going to do what you hoped. Sometimes you are even sure that the pages are stained with the tears of the last graduate student who used all his grant money to fly here, rent a room for a month, and realize that these records just don't hold what you'd think they would.

> **Keep your chains of reasoning as short as you possibly can; aim for parallel, not serial.**

Then what? There are two options. The bad one is to try to still make the data bear on your question. You need more herculean assumptions, longer chains of reasoning, and a lot more rhetoric and "theory," and you are basically putting yourself in the position of trying to sell a car with no engine. What's the good option? You throw out your previous question, and say, well, what questions *could* these data answer?

Many people who do not actually carry out sociological research—or only do research that is a foregone conclusion and, therefore, not very exciting—will tell you to plug up your ears and run away screaming from this advice. They'll pompously tell you that good research is theory driven (as opposed to bad research, which is empiricist, opportunist, fact-grubbing pointlessness, fit to be undertaken by only those too stupid to understand theory).

That is not true. A theory is a claim about how the world works. If you knew how the world worked, you wouldn't bother doing exhaustive research (if you were rational, that is). There is nothing wrong in being led by your findings to make a theoretical claim. If people didn't, there'd be no progress in knowledge. There is no shame in learning.

Theorizing Documents

All use of documents is a sampling procedure. And here I don't mean when you have more documents than you can actually read. I mean that even when you get "all" of them, you're looking at a selection of all possible documents. That's because originally, there was probably an almost infinite amount of possible information. Which documents are left for you to study can be related to the question you are interested in answering. Hence before you try to answer your question using your data, you need to question your data. Since the sampling procedure is largely not in your control, you need to think through all the stages in the selection process.

Why Are You Reading Them?

The most obvious source of bias here is similar to that in interviewing, but so fundamental we often miss it. And this is the question of why you have chosen to look at these particular sorts of documents as opposed to others. Have you perhaps skewed your answer before you even begin?

For example, here is the second page of a very important and influential work by a historian of the United States, Bernard Bailyn. He began editing a collection of documents written around the time of the War of Independence, found them fascinating, and ended up writing a major book on *The Ideological Origins of the American Revolution*. Here's what he says: "Study of the pamphlets confirmed my rather old-fashioned view that the American Revolution was above all else an ideological, constitutional, political struggle and not primarily a controversy between social groups undertaken to force changes in the organization of the society or the economy" (Bailyn 1967, vi).

You can see the problem, right? You can't really counter a Marxian explanation of the Protestant Reformation as related to economic transformations by studying theology. But lots of times, our main conclusion is that what we are interested in is important, because we spent so much time studying it.

So the first layer of bias (or selectivity) comes in what we are looking for. The second comes in what we find.

Who Made Them and Why

We then need to ask, who made these documents, and why were they made? Most obviously, were they made to be seen? We might imagine that documents made to be seen by others are less trustworthy than ones without this public relations slant, but this isn't always the case. And even if there is deliberate slanting, the clarity that tends to go along with a purposeful creation often makes it worth it.

The problem usually isn't that they're made for others to read but that often they were precisely made to influence the interpretive process of later readers. Official organizational minutes are a good example. For example, King-To Yeung (2007) studied the Qing dynasty response to the Taiping Rebellion, reading (among other things) all the official memorials that state officials created to report what was happening.

You might think this would be the perfect way of reproducing the actions at least of the state agents. But the bureaucrats knew that these memorials would be used to construct an official history that could then be used to determine who had screwed up. And so they worked hard to craft documents that were fundamentally ambiguous, that always alternated between "fortunately, this happened, unfortunately, that happened," so that by the end you are totally confused about who did what.

In general, when authors of documents are attempting to influence the reader's interpretation, we need to stop and theorize this before we go any further. And sociologists have, as I've said before, been very sloppy about this. I want to stop here and address this issue in greater depth, dealing with the particular case of newspapers and similar outlets.

Excursus on Newspapers

Sociologists often display a surprising naïveté when dealing with documents in which one person expresses an argument. Here as a running example I'll be talking about political "actors," by which I mean those who are taking a stand on public issues, whether as government officials, candidates, pundits, social movement organizers, or the like.

First, we often want to use these sorts of statements not as data about what an individual thinks, but what some group thinks. Even when a person is actually empowered to speak for others, and indeed, intends to speak for others, it may prove impossible to be clear as to who those others are. Is a congresswoman speaking for the American people as a whole? Her district? Her party? The people who voted for her? Even when we are clearer on who the "followers" of a spokesperson are, what she says is unlikely to match the thoughts of the people she supposedly is speaking for. In most cases, the beliefs of spokespeople are likely to be more consistent and more extreme than those of followers (though sometimes, where spokespeople need to present an extremist movement as less extreme, their pronouncements to outsiders may be less extreme than insiders' discourse).

Well then, you perhaps conclude, I suppose all we can do is use this spokesperson's words to understand her own opinions. No, that's usually wrong too. Spokespeople say something in response to a reporter's question, usually an argument that supports their side. We take this to be their motivation and forget that people making an argument often use the logic of those they are trying to convince, not their own logic. So liberals trying to sell a program to reluctant conservatives talk about eventual tax savings. We shouldn't code this as evidence that liberals care about tax savings.

We've seen something like this in our analysis of the bias in interviews, where we realized that desirability bias can't be counted on to elicit what the *subject* values, but elicits instead the subject's theory of the values of the *interviewer*, a theory that may be incorrect. So, too, political actors who are giving speaking points are rarely giving evidence of their own values; usually, they're giving their theory of the values of the "swayable." They're not talking to their enemies, but they're talking to those who aren't on their side, or not firmly, but might be brought along. Those theories are not necessarily accurate. Very often, political actors—like sociologists— underestimate the decency, sophistication, and guts of those who aren't on their side. And so they tend to evoke rather crass values, missing other values that are present.

Of course, political actors aren't always talking to the "others"— sometimes, they are deliberately preaching to the choir. That is, they are simply talking to their own supporters, repeating the ideas that they all accept. Why? Often it's because they fear that when preaching stops, the choir starts backsliding. Or they think that their adherents may need to be refreshed with emotional charge. Or they may think that they need to provide their supporters with talking points to use in arguments around the water cooler. Or they're just trying to make a buck for themselves by telling folks what (they think) these folks want to hear.

Can we tell from the text itself when we have one type of argument as opposed to another? Not always, and so we often rely on context (what we know about the actors). However, I think there's reason to think that when spokespeople are given more time or space, they're more likely to try to sway, and when they have little time and space, they're more likely to fall back on a "power up" for followers.

Finally, it is increasingly common for actors—and not simply elected officials—to work hard on saying precisely nothing. It's a national disgrace that we cut down trees and make wood pulp to print this sort of nonsense, and it's generally a waste of your time to study it, but you need to know in advance, that sometimes, the content of a statement is precisely zero.

> **Treating arguments as opinions is putting your brain in reverse.**

Given this sort of dispersal of the orientations of political actors, how do we interpret the news article itself? Here, we can make use of findings from the sociology of media. For a long time, sociologists tried to code up the "frame" of the article, attributing a lot of control to the journalist herself. And this went along with the idea that journalists "construct" certain issues, in an almost conspiratorial way. But journalists in the United States, at least those working for the larger dailies, don't really work this way, if only because they don't have time. They often try to master an issue over the weekend, sometimes overnight, and what they are looking for in their daytime hours are people on whom they can hang the opinions that they want to use, like washing on a line. In particular, in the United States, they are looking for "both sides," even when an issue really only has one, or has thirty different ones. Do they influence our general takeaway by the order in which they give the sides, or introduce the plot, or who they get to talk? Of course. But they tend to be following general editorial conventions. For example, if they are writing about a continuing story, they'll lead in with the most recent action, even if it's trivial, before rehashing the more important stuff. They will tend to play up disaster and negativity, and they'll have at least an attempt to get a second side for anything.

That means that journalists aren't really constructing the news; in the vast majority of cases, they're grabbing preconstructed pieces and quickly throwing them together in a familiar pattern. And so even if journalists write the stories, we shouldn't assume that they call the shots. This is key because, as I emphasized in chapter 2 (31–32) sociologists will often treat some facts as simple and unproblematic and others as constructed. This implies that the latter are of dubious truth—for example, that increased reporting of crime in an area doesn't correspond to an actual increase in crime. That might well be—there are definitely times when crime waves, say, are constructed by what we call social movement entrepreneurs, even though nothing on the ground is changing. But just using the word "constructed" doesn't make it so.

The final story is often the product of three corresponding and cumulative processes: first, an *event* that took place; second, a *frame* that interested parties (pundits, activists, experts, witnesses) tried to put on the event shortly after it happened or during the occurrence; third, there's the *journalistic editing* to take these and piece them together to make a gripping but comprehensible story (and there's how editors cut and rearrange text and add headlines). If we see a change over time in the final product, we don't immediately know where the change is originating.

Still, in most cases, the idea that there was a sudden change in what journalists are trying to do is the least likely explanation. Yet that's often our first guess. It sounds dumb when I put it this way, but those sociologists who aren't married to journalists and never worked as one can maintain a mental image in which once a month, journalists attend a meeting in which "the dominant culture" or "capitalism" or "patriarchy" or "hegemony" gives them their assignments for the month. But if something hegemonic out there does control the news (and I don't deny this possibility), it's control from the bottom up—because journalists are responding to pressures more than they are exerting them.

That's for the United States—in other countries, especially where newspapers are more closely tied to political parties, or to expert intellectuals, things are very different. But for the United States, the journalist, like most of us, is doing a convenience sample, letting ideas actively seek her or him out, as opposed to really taking control of the interpretive act. This isn't, then, a defense of journalists as being basically good guys—it's saying whatever they are, they aren't good (or bad) sociologists. The only question is, are you going to be a good one?

Who Had an Interest in Them?

We've seen the importance of correctly understanding why these documents are being made. But sometimes our problems arise not because of the document makers themselves, but because of other interested parties. A classic example is found in the literature following Durkheim's ([1897] 1951) excellent work on suicide. Durkheim argued that it made perfect sense, given his theoretical presuppositions, that the suicide rate of Catholics was much lower than that of Protestants. Even aside from the fact that Catholics tend to have larger families, theologically, they're more integrated into a community and, hence, preserved from egoistic suicide.

However, historians knew that there could be a bias here. In Catholic dogma, suicide is a mortal sin. By definition, you can't be absolved by a priest in between the act and your first intake interview with Saint Peter. As a result, suicides in old Catholic Europe were buried outside of the hallowed church ground... for everyone to see. It was very shaming for a family to have a member interred there. Therefore, families might put great pressure on officials of church and state to try to avoid a classification as suicide.

In fact, this is a more general pattern in the West, even today. Family members push hard for a ruling of "accident" from the coroner, and a lot of negotiation goes on. But it's very probable that in Europe, this pressure was stronger for Catholics than Protestants. Which makes comparing their suicide rates very difficult. But it isn't impossible, and we can, with some hard work, begin by seeing whether there is evidence of a bias. How do you do this? Well, we need to make some assumptions—most important, that Catholics don't differ from others in what types of people are most likely to have accidents. We might start by seeing what happens if all suicides were counted as accidents. Does the total of suicides plus accidents among Catholics look like that for Protestants? What if we look at different age groups? Do we see a bulge in the age distribution of deaths by accidents among Catholics where there's a bulge in suicides for non-Catholics, as opposed to where non-Catholics are more likely to have accidental deaths? What about if we use what we know about the likelihood of suicide at different ages to reallocate some accidents to suicide? And so on.

We can never get back to the true data once there has been strong selection. But, we can sort our theories of the selection into the more or less plausible, and then we can set bounds on the likely way the world looked before the selection. Then, we can say things like "it looks like 90 percent or more of the data would have had to have been destroyed for the relationship we see to be an artifact of selection," or, "with the misclassification of suicides being within the range of what others have estimated, the Catholic rate could have been anywhere from 0.8 times that of non-Catholics to 1.4 times." Disappointing, perhaps. But when you don't know something, it's comforting to know what you don't know.

What Kind of a Document Is This?

Thus we need to properly theorize the creation of the document. But we also need to consider what type of document we have at hand because some of the content of a document may be a direct reflection of its form, or genre.

Few people are very literate, and this includes us. That is, even though we can read and write (if you can't read, put this book down now!), there are types of documents most of us can't create, or even understand, most importantly, legal documents. Thus if you go to a lawyer to make a good-natured agreement with your neighbor, you might walk away with something that has a lot of implicit threats in it. Those are ascribable not to you but to the scribe—in this case, the lawyer.

In general, people often go to a professional scribe to make records, and these scribes use forms that they have learned somewhere. If we write something ourselves, as opposed to going to a professional scribe, we're still likely to rely on existing forms. And different forms have different structures. Many of the things we might attribute to the author really come from the narrative form. We therefore split up our interpretation into two parts. First, does the fact that *this* form was chosen have any information for us? Were there plausible alternatives? Second, *given* that this form was chosen, how was it adapted? What parts of the content *aren't* implied by the choice of form?

So back in the bad old days, historians were often suckered into having an extreme interpretation of the nature of some period because they relied on a set of documents all of the same genre; the accumulation of such documents therefore led historians to have a strong view of their particular period (such as "worst time for England *ever*," or "unprecedented turmoil!"). The problem was that when historians met, fisticuffs would break out because everyone had the same conclusion about his or her particular period being particularly different from all the others. Only when they systematically looked across all periods did they learn to take certain types of documents with a grain of salt. This happened more or less in the eighteenth century, but not all sociologists have learned this lesson yet.

Most famous are *Decline* narratives, where someone tells you about how much better things used to be, compared to how they are now. This is such a prevalent form of historiography that for quite some time Europeans assumed that the world had been going steadily downhill since Adam. Because even in the past, when things were obviously so much better, *they* thought things were getting worse! Many sermons take the form of decline narratives. Why? In part because there's an understanding that the preacher's job is to get people to ratchet things up, morality-wise, and a good way to shame them into doing this is to tell them that they're lagging their forebearers. Grandpa Noah would be disgusted with you.[6] And for big stretches of Christian history, what you have a lot of in the archives is ... sermons.

More subtle than *Decline* narratives, however, are critiques of the present (*Complaints*), which are usually more specific and targeted than general decline narratives. These are often taken as reliable indications of some sort of worsening conditions, though they can be interpreted in exactly the opposite way. When you get some people complaining about the immorality of their time, that could mean that their time is more immoral than others—or it could mean that there has been an increase in people's moral thresholds.

Now it would be counterproductive if we were to take any example of complaint and dismiss its value because we have labeled it a complaint narrative, and said that, given it is a complaint narrative, of course there are complaints in it! So how do we use this principle? For one, we understand that in many cases, the only ways in which political subjects can pursue their interests via governments are through complaint narratives. In a democracy, it's fine to say, "things are very good, but we'd like them to be even better." Where authority is traditionally legitimated, however, the only way to ask for change is to persuade your reader that the status quo has fallen away from the true principles (*Decline*), and that specific persons (never the *most* powerful) have abused and corrupted their rightful position (*Complaint*).

Further, once we recognize a complaint genre, we have a head start in understanding the particularities of the complaint. For example, those who study petitions (e.g., Zaret 2000) find that petitioners tend to be very sensitive to what seems to be within the realm of possible redress. You don't ask the king to get rid of all the armored buttheads going around stealing your food. You ask for a decrease in a particularly abusive tax. Thus studying the content doesn't tell us just about the desires or preferences of the writers, abstracted from all calculation—it tells us some-

---

6. There's also a tendency in this direction because history writers tend to be older than average. The early sixteenth-century writer Baldesar Castiglione ([1528] 2002, 65) noted that old people in every generation are convinced that everything is "continually going from bad to worse," which seemed implausible (since the cumulative decline should have led us to complete and utter bestiality). His explanation was that this was just like the error made by people on a departing ship keeping their eyes fixed on the shore, and thinking that the shore is receding. (That is, as people get older, it's their own lives that are getting worse, not the world.) This is, as we shall see, related to one of the "coding" issues we will deal with.

thing about their desires, as well as something about their assessment of the situation.

So we have a way of contextualizing complaint and decline narratives. There are, however, *Increase* narratives as well. Many things in history, at least since 1428, seem to have been increasing exponentially. That means that at any time, we have more of X than ever before! And even more, the *rate* of increase is greater than ever before!! And this leads people at any time to be sure that theirs is unique (because of the unprecedented increase). But for most of these cases, the rate of the rate of increase is constant.

And just as we have *Complaint* narratives, often addressed *to* powerholders, we have *Justification* narratives, given *by* powerholders, either to their higher-ups or their lower-downs (depending on whether they are in a democratic situation—and democracies have plenty of nondemocratic situations for powerholders). For example, police reports are often justifications for police actions. In an area in which police are basically containing a troublesome population, much of policing isn't response to crimes but, rather, is the negotiation of crime creation in response to the needs of policing (see, e.g., Stuart 2016). (That is, most offenses are minor infractions or misdemeanors, usually victimless, like having a bad taillight or having a joint or jaywalking, and there are plenty of potential "criminals" all over the nation if you wanted to find one.) If you use the resulting documents uncritically, you think the police come in response to crimes, when really, the crimes come—they are paid attention to, they are labeled and processed—in response to the needs of police.

> **"There is no problem, because there is no solution."**
> **Nam June Paik**

In between *Complaints* and *Justifications* are what we might call *Problematizations*. A problematization is when someone (we often call them entrepreneurs) has an argument that a certain existing or likely situation is problematic. This sounds crazy—why would anyone need to be convinced that, say, being at the mercy of vicious gangs is a problem? The reason is that it's a reasonable rule of thumb that most so-called problems only arise when there is a solution. Before the solution, it isn't a problem: it's just life. Further, it turns out that, sometimes even *with* the solution, people don't start seeing the potential problem as problematic. Someone has to go around and convince people that there's something wrong.

Randall Collins (1998) gives a great example here. If you study the history of Buddhism, you'd think that for years, Hindus were dragging their feet around, moping about the cycle of rebirth, and just resigned to not doing anything about it. That's the sorry situation they were in, until the Buddha figured out how to jump off the merry-go-round.

But in fact (says Collins), this problem only arose with Buddhism, which could only thrive if it successfully defined the previous condition as problematic. This sort of dynamic turns out to be rather common, which means that many documents are backward—we read them as telling us about the problem and how the author is here to solve it, but really, they're there to *create* the problem (by defining it as problematic).

This can sound very cynical—and dismissive. When we point out the role of a political entrepreneur, for instance, in problematizing an aspect of racial oppression (e.g., the location of environmental hazards), it might seem like we are saying "everything was just fine until those outside agitators came around, stirring everybody up." Not so at all. In many situations, it's just the opposite—there are so many plausible causes for grievance, and things are so bad, that it takes a tremendous amount of organizational work to get people to focus on one and to convince them that it isn't a fool's errand to try to change it. Thus *Problematization* very often requires empowerment (or, at least, the illusion of empowerment).

Finally, there are a wide variety of documents that are basically sales *Pitches* of some sort, at least metaphorically speaking. This requires empowerment of a different form—instead of the writer convincing the *reader* that the reader can change things, the writer convinces the reader that the *writer* has more power than might have been imagined. And of course, this does include actual advertisements, but it also can be found in religious literature used in evangelizing or in leaflets dropped behind the enemy lines. These documents often include claims and promises that are as absurd as those that are made by a toothpaste company. Yet sociologists often repeat them as if they were, shall we say, the gospel truth. In the 1970s there was a great deal of theorizing about the effect of advertising in creating new wants, basically because advertisers claimed this when they were talking to manufacturers. It isn't actually true that advertisers can do any of this (Schudson 1986), but advertisers don't actually need to sell products to survive—they only need to sell their own services. So the surviving advertisers are those that are best at that, and they make lots of documents. But many other internal organizational documents are sales pitches, and need to be taken as such.

So when we try to interpret things, we need to take into account the genre of the document. Anything that leads to a change in the composition of the genres that some group produces (e.g., they gain access to political power or control over a newspaper) can lead to a change in content. But there may have been no change in the underlying strategy or thoughts of the actors.

Who Saved Them and Why

We're now ready for the third layer of nonrandom selection—preservation. Most documents (thank God) are destroyed. Some are saved because they are made by famous people. Others are preserved merely out of organizational inertia—no one got around to shredding or burning them. But in all cases, we need to try to theorize the nonrandomness in preservation before we know how to interpret the documents.

It's worth noting that, all other things equal, selectivity increases with the age of documents. We need to think through the direction of this selectivity to determine whether it is, or is not, a problem for our particular question. Consider the stunning work of Winifred Rothenberg (1992) on the development of economic orientations in the early United States. She attempted to get a handle on whether eighteenth-century farmers in New England were rational actors by going over the account books. Before just assembling the data and making some conclusions, we want to make sure that we aren't confusing the likely processes of selection with those of historical change.

Who keeps account books? Probably the more rational farmers. Those who are most interested in analyzing their profit. This issue did not escape Rothenberg, and she focused on the possibility that she would have, in general, an oversampling of the farmers who were rational. The nonrational ones wouldn't even have account books in the first place! It turns out that keeping account books was a more widespread practice than we might fear. So the selectivity here might not be so high. That doesn't quite answer all our problems, for we might then ask, but whose account books survive? Those who don't have their farm burn down, who don't get bought out by someone else. Whose books get archived? Those whose descendants have their lives in order, and who are proud of their parentage. These might well likely be those who were relatively prosperous.

What might that imply about perceived patterns in response to her question? We might see some tendency to overstate price convergence, as we look at the sharper, more rational farmers. We're going to expect a bias toward more rational farmers, aren't we? That sounds reasonable. Does that argue against her conclusions? Well, we've assumed that the selection comes because the bad farmers (less rational) are going bankrupt, right? Doesn't that really support the phenomenon of an emerging market? We have to make sure that our theory of selectivity doesn't assume the very thing that we're trying to test, and so we reject the theory because we assume it.

How to Learn from Data

What Can Data Tell You?

Usually documents can give you multiple types of information, often indirect, and the indirect can be more important than the direct. So the account books studied by Rothenberg certainly tell you who was in debt to whom, and what they were borrowing, selling, and buying. But in the process of showing us patterns of indebtedness, they indicate class structure and the emergence of a landless class—if there wasn't one already. They can be used to examine possible factionalization (if there are divergent clusters of lending), family structure and inheritance, the age of marriage, and so on.

Many of the most important things we learn from documents aren't from what they say but what they don't say. Not in the sense of "they should have said X, and since they didn't, I have a big theory…" etcetera. Instead, I mean that if you say X, that strongly implies Y. How do we determine this? We use techniques that were, so far as I know, first worked out in the German new biblical criticism, which allowed for a pretty good reconstruction of the New Testament environment by figuring out who folks were likely arguing against. Of course, we then want to try to confirm our inferences, but even if we can't, we're probably better making them than not.

The obvious principles are:

1. People tend to focus on the things that are in dispute—maybe not with the person they're writing to, but still.
2. If they say, "X isn't true," you can bet that there is someone who is getting serious attention by going around and saying X.
3. If they try to link their argument Y to another one Z, which doesn't seem like an obvious link, presumably Z is an orthodoxy or is supported by someone with a lot of clout.

The less obvious ones are:

1. people keep records when they expect the relevance of something to be long,
2. or when they expect contestation,

3. and perhaps the most important ones pertain to possibility—when a document indicates that something you probably imagined didn't occur does occur.

A great example of this last, which we can call proof via anecdote, comes in one of the account books examined by Rothenberg. A farmer indicates that he had an altercation with a neighbor that led to blows. He himself took a big one to the head, which led to bleeding. He assigns the damage a *dollar figure* ($54)! Again, when he rented someone's oxen, he also tried to deduct an amount for the time they *stood still* (1992, 166). The existence of these anecdata is a proof via possibility—you can't reject the idea of a spread of a rational accounting culture after that. (For another classic example, see Ginzburg's [1992] examination of records of the Roman Inquisition.)

Using Comparisons

Of course, most of the time, we don't get a nice plum falling into our lap like this, with the reliance on good "anecdata," as we might call it. Thus the key creativity in using documents is how we link the data to the theoretical issues of concern to us. Above I talked about how we try to use documents to "measure" certain concepts. Now I want to talk about how we make clever comparisons to try to answer questions that don't have a direct answer in our data. That's often the case when we are trying to get at motivations.

It turns out that relatively straightforward comparisons of evidence gathered from documents can be used to get at our most abstruse theoretical issues, including questions of motivation—often in a way that we find more convincing than the use of personal documents (such as letters). Let's say there is a certain form of action that has taken place, and we are attempting to figure out *why*. If we use documents (newspaper reports, historians' compiled records, discussions in letters, court records) to establish a database, we can create comparisons that may neutralize the biases in the data and, at the same time, have strong implications for the likely motivations of actors. We can focus on what *types* of persons do things, what *conditions* lead people to do the acts in question, or what *combinations* of acts co-occur, and then use some reasonable assumptions to suggest what their motivation might be.

Here's a real example: There is a debate about the causes of hate crimes—why do, for example, white people kill black people when this homicide is not part of another crime (such as robbery)? Well, there are statistics on homicide, and if we believe that hate murder is an attempt to terrorize blacks who otherwise would be competing with whites on the job market, we can compare this murder rate to the white unemployment rate and the occupational overlap between whites and blacks. That's clearly a very indirect test of a motivational hypothesis, but there's not much data of other forms, and we're going to be suspicious of the accounts given by the murderers themselves.

Because we can't control what sort of data were recorded, piecing together an explanation is a bit like detective work. Often, we must jump back and forth from one type of data to another in order to really nail down a hypothesis. At the same time, we sometimes need to try out different hypotheses to figure out what some data are trying to tell us. That is, we try varying our linkage and seeing what other data we can bring to bear on the question by pursuing a different implication. It's that "running it to ground" approach that I talked about in the last chapter.

For example, above I mentioned John Markoff's work on the French Revolution. He was interested in what seemed to provoke rebellion—what the causes, or the motivations, were. One possible hypothesis, plausible given what people were complaining about at the time, is that rebellions were provoked by high taxes. It is certainly true that places with higher taxes in France had more rebellions. A bad analyst could stop here, but this is where Markoff gets going. Sure, the data are *compatible* with this hypothesis, but they're compatible with other ones too. For example, it isn't clear whether what provokes rebellions is the fact of taxes being high in absolute terms or the relative deprivation of knowing that others have lower taxes. To adjudicate between these two explanations, Markoff argues, we need to look at smaller areas than these regions, in this case, border areas between high- and low-tax regions (1996, 349).

Accept that gift horse. But inspect its mouth carefully.

In fact, it does turn out that rebellions are more likely in the border areas. But, Markoff realizes, there's another possible explanation. Wherever there is a border separating high- and low-tax areas, we expect smuggling. Because smuggling is illegal, and smugglers can't turn to the law for protection if they get robbed, they need to support their activities with violence, and so we imagine that there is a general climate of lawlessness around such borders. This could be the basis for the development of networks of organized resistance—since we already have a gang, why not use them against the nobles? But note that this would imply rebellions on *both* sides of the border, while if the cause is relative deprivation, you'd see it only on the side with high taxes (Markoff 1996, 350). Brilliant, right? So there are two regions where Markoff can investigate this—and it turns out that one region suggests one thing, the other, the opposite. "And there we must let this particular matter stand, at least as far as our statistical evidence is concerned" (351). Sometimes you know that you've done things right by the fact that the only thing you're sure of when you're done is that you can't be sure.

Biases and Comparisons

When we think through the logic of our data creation and preservation, we generally are going to suspect that there are biases present, and those biases are often relevant to our question. However, in some cases, there are questions for which the biases don't matter; these biases tend to "cancel out" in certain comparisons. Let's give an example. Newspapers are often used to assemble coverage of events, such as protest events. Sociologists have realized that events are more likely to get covered if they (1) are in the city that is the newspaper's home; (2) are in another major city; (3) involve injuries or destruction; or (4) occur at times with fewer competing stories.

For this reason, such sources aren't very good for a "point estimate" of how much stuff is happening at any time. And further, this means that some comparisons are biased—for example, one that uses the *New York Times* to determine whether there are more protests in New York City or in Pittsburgh. Other comparisons, however, aren't obviously biased—most importantly, temporal comparisons. Of course, with temporal comparisons, we always need to remember that we have to keep an eye out for changes in the production, dissemination, or preservation of documents.

What do you do when the biases are likely to be relevant for your question? Often we can use methodological triangulation: asking similar questions using different methods and data sets. In many cases, we can deliberately choose approaches that have biases in opposite directions. If we see the same pattern in both, we're more confident.

Does this seem obvious? It's always obvious in twenty-twenty hindsight. But it often takes a lot of discipline to force yourself to really question the data that seem to be giving you just what you want. Accept the gift horse, but look carefully in his mouth.

Questioning

The questioning of data (where did it come from, who made it, for what) must be made even for what seems like the "hardest" data, such as government data. Knowing who made them and why is often a good place to start. Some data (e.g., the cost-benefit studies produced by the Army Corps of Engineers) are widely understood as political rituals, despite the care that goes into them. They are, in many ways, *Justifications* (see Porter 1996). Other government data are routinely readjusted, and during these times, those who understand the stakes will descend on otherwise lonely bureaucrats to determine whether our indicators become the sorts of things that will indicate the sorts of realities that are in their interests or not (see Innes 1989). For example, adding those in the military to the numerator and denominator of employment ratios in 1983 "reduced" unemployment.

Often sociologists suspect that these numbers are up for some hanky-panky but figure that the census data can be treated as nonproblematic. While the census data are probably the least susceptible to meddling, and are generally of incredibly high quality, there are puzzles here that require questioning.

A surprising dip or jump in a series can alert us to when we need to go back to the original documents and figure out how they were produced. Often what seems to be a change in what is being documented is actually a change in procedures of documentation. For example, if you look at official data, there appears to be a jump in American women's labor force participation in the 1910s, but it is due to a change in the instructions given to census workers (Oppenheimer 1970, 4, 9). It seems that, previously, working women were being undercounted; this census tried in particular to enumerate women workers. Census workers were instructed not to overlook female agricultural workers, and to count them even if they are unpaid family workers.

So it's great to use these sorts of high-quality, premade data. But in many cases, we need to go beneath the surface, and triangulation is the best way to resolve doubts. Census data suggest that there was no shortage of women eager to enter the labor force, at least, as Oppenheimer reads them. Well, what do the women themselves say about this? Can we examine diaries and letters where women talk about the prospects of gaining employment?

Dealing with Data

We've considered how to link documents, or aggregate data that originated in documents, to theoretical claims. There's one key part of this endeavor that I've avoided touching, namely, "coding." Now in many cases, there isn't much you can do beyond close reading of the original documents, and so you should do this. But when there are too many to read and present, you may want to do something to reduce complexity and make possible the construction of a sociological database. And here, it's been very common for us to code documents—to assign each a value for a set of variables (such as, *main content, theme* X *is present*, and so on).

I'm going to be arguing against that. But not against all data reduction. In recent years, there has been a revolution in computational technology, which has fundamentally changed how we think about dealing systematically with documents, and it's a current tragedy that we have a set of students well in the middle of ad hoc coding plans who will be unemployable by the time they are done.

What Is This a Case Of?

Although in this chapter I've been mostly emphasizing the use of documents in the context of historical analysis, coding is a common practice in other subfields as well, especially in the study of social movements and in the political sociology of the present. To an even greater degree, it's the same problem that confronts the field-worker when she decides to go over and try to grapple with the complexity of her field notes. She reads a bunch of them, gets a set of ideas, and then goes through each document, asking, "What this is a case of?" And then she does some analyses of the resulting codes. *Almost all of the resulting findings are worthless.* The reason for this is that all the findings came once she decided "what this was a case of" (see Biernacki 2012).

We often teach you that you should start with a theory and that a theory implies concepts. And so each concept has a definition. I won't argue that this is always wrong. But it certainly sometimes is—it leads us to "conclusions" that are just our assumptions. I've used William Whyte's wonderful work *Streetcorner Society* ([1943] 1981) as an example in earlier chapters. Here, Whyte studied a slum closely and concluded that most sociologists were wrong—they said that slums were "disorganized," when in fact, they had their own principles of organization.

I would say, "Good job." But he almost got refused a PhD from the University of Chicago. Why? Because Louis Wirth pointed out (correctly) that he and his crew *defined* a slum as a "disorganized community." If Whyte happened to go somewhere that *looked* like a slum (which is how he chose), and indeed, it could even *sound* like a slum, and *smell* like a slum, and *feel* like a slum, but it wasn't disorganized, we know he just happened to find something that wasn't a true slum. If you agree with me that that reaction is sort of cracked, then you're accepting that sometimes we need to move away from our knee-jerk nominalism and realize that it's not always up to us to decide how to define things. Maybe theory is OK if it guides your research, but it can't determine your findings.

But that's what generally happens when we "code." For example, in a magnificent and pathbreaking work of history, Jackson T. Main (1973) attempted to sketch the outlines of the de facto party system in state legislatures right after the American War of Independence (but before the new constitution). He needed a term to express these sides, and he chose "locals" versus "cosmopolitans." The "cosmopolitans" tended to be in richer coastal areas, to be merchants or tied to international trade, and to be wealthier. The "locals" tended to be inland, to be farmers with relatively small holdings, and to come from less prestigious families. Most of the votes that Main finds dividing these sides seem to be related to relatively straightforward political and economic concerns (what should we tax? should we favor borrowers or lenders?). Yet when summarizing these patterns, and wondering why farmers were more likely to be "locals," Main (388) mused, "Farmers as here defined generally lived a restricted existence, well described as parochial or narrow. Circumstances forced them to concentrate on farming, to think of little but farming.... Large landowners, doctors lawyers, judges, and most traders generally had a much broader view—continental, cosmopolitan, urbane."

Now that might well be true—and presumably that's why Main decided to call the groups what he did—but that isn't at all relevant for his findings. He has a lot of data demonstrating economic interest, and nothing about their conceptual horizon. Yet his own labeling led him to think he had found something he hadn't. That can happen to you as well. And in fact, when it does, you may believe that you have the best and strongest findings ever. Because you'll get just the trends or comparisons you expect.

For example, suppose you are interested in something that you think of as "the new fascism" and you define it in some way as the presence of this, that, and the other. So, using, say, newspaper articles from 1885 to 2015, you code up every time you see any of the things on your list. You then make a graph and, what do you know, you have strong evidence of an increase in this new fascism...just as you had suspected.

But, most probably, there isn't any such thing. We know *you* think there is, but since this list includes all the things now that bug you, the increase just means that the world is getting closer to the time when you made your ideas. This is very common—people who start with a theoretical coding find their hunch confirmed that whatever they are coding for has increased over time.

And this returns us to Castiglione's point discussed above (n. 6)—that every generation may see things getting worse. There's an interesting sonic artifact called a "Shepard tone," which gives the listener the impossible sensation that the tone is continuously descending in pitch—yet getting nowhere. (The trick is that different overtones change in volume so there is a timbre replacement that allows the escalator steps to move down while the escalator stays in place.) So, too, in history there is often something similar in which certain standards are being phased out and new ones phased in. Every new thing is lower in the old standards, yet the oldest standards are decreasing in weight and new ones (in which the new things are "high") are coming in. Thus everything individually gets worse, yet everyone is equally happy with the way things are.

In sum, you absolutely need to stay away from coding in which you decide to count some things as indications of a theoretical abstraction that not all others accept. I understand that we often teach you a philosophy of science that convinces you that there really isn't any other option. You always need a theory, you always need to define things, and so on. Maybe it's true, maybe it's not, that you always need some theory, but I'm absolutely convinced that you don't always need to be a dumbass. But that's what you are when you walk away from years of hard work with a conclusion that only depends on what you decided to call things.

So does that mean you can't ever reduce the complexity of your documents? Of course not, but you don't want to do exclusive coding ("this is a case of that") that replaces the originals in your mind (Biernacki 2012). Instead, you want to *tag*, just as with field notes (see chapter 5). The exception may be when you have a two-level data set, with one level having an *N* in the terrible twos (see chapter 7), and the other much larger. An example might be when you have debate in the congressional record about various bills, and you have many bits of talk for each bill. In this case, you may need to code the smaller set of bills by hand. The best thing, however, is when you can employ codes or tags that correspond to those that you would develop for the larger set. And how will you do this, if not by coding? Send in the computers.

Scanning and Word Recognition

There was a time when coding made some sense, because it was too hard to count all the stuff in a complex document. But there has been a revolution in character recognition and the treatment of texts. Now instead of reading through each article and saying, "Oh, this strikes me as poor-are-bad framing," you can scan in every article, if they're not already in electronic form, and search the document for a count of every single word. And figure out how far each word is from other words. And what order they are in. There are still analytic choices to be made and they will involve theory. But you don't need to just code things up.

Is this a fad? Sure. Is a big chunk of the stuff being done with these techniques meaningless? Of course. But there's nothing to be ashamed of when it comes to using a new technique whose capacities aren't yet known. Some people will do meaningless things as a result, but no one *has* to, and even those who do so are learning. That's quite different from using a tried-and-true technique that is well understood to produce meaningless results. There's no excuse for that.

Whether automated or not, close attention to word use can get at complex issues of culture much more convincingly than when we use the brute force of coding, which simply declares that such and such is this or that (see Lee and Martin 2015). For example, Paul McLean (2007) studied the personal letters by Renaissance Florentines to understand the ways in which they created social relationships. He counted up the number of times they called one another "friend" or "father" or "brother" and showed the changes in how they seemed to navigate, if not understand, their relationships. He didn't so much "operationalize" his idea of a multiplex personality, he *displayed* it with noncontestable data on counts and co-occurrences.

> **Bad sociologists code.**
> **Good sociologists count.**

Further, there are new techniques that go beyond just looking at raw counts or co-occurrences of words. Now there is software (often developed for the purpose of automatically writing abstracts of scientific papers) that is getting decent at condensing an argument, and there are special-purpose ones that seem to do OK at assigning a score to any text reflecting the complexity or emotional tone of its argument. More will be out before this book hits the shelves.

New Relations to Documents

New Types of Documents

I've noted that digitization has made possible new research techniques. I want to say more about these techniques, since students now have little guidance and often teach themselves. Although overall, this aspect of the digitization revolution is good news for researchers, there are some temptations here that need to be watched. In particular, it is tempting to never leave home—to "grab data" somehow, and start messing around, trying this and trying that, and next thing you know, it's 3 A.M. the next day and you're still in your pajamas with nothing but an empty roll of cookie dough and a weird graph you can't remember how you made.

What have you done? Very often, you've found what seems a new, untapped data set—for example, a peer-created, open source, database on, say, fans' descriptions and ratings of every last character in the Harry Potter series, and you realize—hey! I bet no one has done *this* (yet!)—you could attempt to apply some social theory to this world. First, probably some other kid *is* doing it this very minute (it sounds like a pretty good idea to me, at any rate), so you want to do a good job. You don't have to be the first, but you shouldn't be the worst.

> **You don't have to be the first.**
> **But you shouldn't be the worst.**

Second, you might be delighted to find that some website has thoughtfully made an interface that allows you to download all the data through an automated query. But that doesn't mean that it's guaranteed to work properly! Check your results by hand. Trust no one—even government websites can malfunction and give you incorrect data.

And even with all this, chances are, you'll have lots of temptations to do a terrible job. Why? For one, the fact that you don't have to do much to get the data set up except tap on a computer means you are less likely to really have a sense of the extensive and intensive quality of the data. Your assumption that you can trust the data, and the fact that you can do everything without leaving your chair, is likely to guide you toward inventive data exploration techniques, as opposed to a more conventional, more disciplined, and simpler data exploration. So when you plunge in, it's easy to spend a lot of time analyzing them in ways that encourage you to get lost in a labyrinth of complexity, as opposed to getting some sort of bird's-eye view (which is what exploratory methods are supposed to be good for).

Further, it's still often the case that... you get what you pay for. Free data usually aren't as good as the harder-to-collect kind. It can be tempting for you to "look under the lamppost"—that is, to study whatever is easy to get, even at the cost of ignoring the more important aspects of life. For example, real social network data are very hard to collect; computer-mediated networks like Facebook are much easier (if you can get permission). So we stop looking at actual social networks and start looking only at computer-mediated stuff. Make sure you aren't trying to convince yourself that the found data are better than they are. Because the rest of us will prove harder to convince.

So, homesteaders—before the allure of new territory leads you to plunge headfirst into the woods, let's do a survey and see if we know where the stumps are likely to be. How is the digitization revolution changing the nature of the documents we might want to analyze?

The biggest stump of all has to do with law. One of the most unproblematically welcome aspects of digitization is that old archives are being scanned or recorded and made accessible to researchers who no longer need to travel to get their hands on it. Data that was once in print volumes that, if you wanted to analyze as a database, you'd enter by hand—for example, yearly economics reports—are now online, as are many government documents, genealogies, and special archives, like the Abraham Lincoln papers. Further, a number of federal oral history projects are now available for citizens to peruse. That's great. They're there for you, and they're 100 percent legal and free.

And as we all know, old books have been scanned, now often with character recognition so that their text is searchable. But your rights to this aren't clear. Google, in particular, has done this (and is keeping their greedy little hands on too much of it), and now also JSTOR, the shared digital library of academic journals, has searchable text (though if you download all of it, the government will kill you). And more generally, you might find websites that have just the data you want, and which are eminently scrapable, but that doesn't mean you might not be allowed to. In some cases, the provider may simply state that you aren't allowed to take the data. Whether this is legally binding is left for you and your university to talk about (see chapter 6). But in some cases, to get access to the data, you had to check a box saying that you agreed to certain terms. If those terms include not doing what you are about to do, you'd better stop.

Look, I agree with you—information wants to be free. It's messed up that corporations get their hands on this stuff and claim they own it. But your university is probably entangled with these types of corporations to a degree you don't appreciate. Don't f——k around with this—even if it's for science, if the Supreme Court says you don't have the right to download MP3 files for sonic analysis even of works in the public domain, then you are vulnerable. And chances are, your university will not hesitate to put you on the auction block if you piss off Sony, and if you go up against Disney™, Minnie Mouse will personally break your kneecaps.[7] Stay away.

Networked Data

There are also databases that yield important information *as* databases—that is, the connections that allow us to move through them are themselves of interest. Most famous are citation networks, which became a

---

7. And I mean that in a good way, Uncle Walt! It's all good! No lawsuits, please!

staple of the traditional sociology of science in the 1970s. But it isn't just articles that cite one another. So do patents. And so do legal cases. All of these are now easily available to you.

Even more, it is now often possible to link these networks to abstracts, keywords, and sometimes the full text. With a bit more work, articles in journals can be linked to data on authors, to dates, to status rankings of journals, and so on. In other words, documents pull in other documents. As long as you understand that you are doing the equivalent of a snowball sample, this can be a great way of understanding the organization of cultural production. It's easy to screw this up, but done right, the results can be truly tremendous.

Perhaps the biggest problem is that there is a huge gradient in going from the data as they are handed to you to the data as you need them to make rigorous conclusions. It might take you a month of time to check over transcriptions of all your interviews, if that's what you did. Ouch. But it might take that long just to try to disambiguate the C. Kims (who have around thirty thousand articles in the Web of Science database—considerably more than the twenty-six thousand of we J. Martins). When you think of all the duplicate names out there, you would tear out your hair. Of course, you can rely on programs that others have written—but if you don't check the checkers, you really don't know what you are dealing with.

Finally, be cautious in using the little bits of proprietary data that a company might offer. The reason is simple. Google, Facebook, Microsoft, and their ilk now have their own universities. They have people who are asking the same questions sociologists ask, and publishing in academic journals. It's pretty hard to beat them out because they deal the cards, and they get to look at them before they decide which ones to give you. You might need to winnow your way into their organization before you have a fighting chance. You might be better off doing a smaller study where you get to collect much more intensive data (such as by giving people cell phones, which are incredible all-in-one spy devices) than by getting the shallower data offered for, say, some contest.[8] Here, as elsewhere, the time you save in the beginning may be dwarfed by the time you spend trying to sort out your analyses, when you took something convenient instead of something that really would work for your particular question.

And that brings us to the issues of how to interpret and how to write up your results. And then we're done.

---

8. A competition is a very cost effective way of buying a service; that means it's almost never rational for you to participate—you only do it to get your hands on the data. As for cell phones as data-gathering devices, a great example can be found in Wyatt et al. (2011).

TAKEAWAYS

- Just because a document is personal or private does not mean it is a direct data dump from someone's head.
- Words don't mean anything. People mean things with words, and you need to know what they are trying to do to know what their words mean.
- Seek research designs that encourage you do to more, and better, work.
- Computers and robots are your enemy; you only need to watch a few good movies to learn this lesson. The world they will bring with them when they triumph is a colorless and efficient one; they have poker faces and no sense of humor. If you are going to tangle with them, you need someone on your side who knows them well.

If you were going to read more...
If you wanted to go further, you could look at *Using Documents in Social Research,* by Lindsay Prior; Matthew Salganik's (forthcoming) book on new computer intensive ways of gathering data; Richard Biernacki's *Reinventing Evidence* (2012); and then my piece with Monica Lee (Lee and Martin 2015).

* 9 *

Interpreting It and Writing It Up

You can't salvage things after making fundamental mistakes. But it can be that there is still discovery to be made after the data are in. Make sure you know what you have learned, and what others should pay attention to.

We're getting near the end. What's left are two intertwined tasks—interpreting things correctly and writing them up in a way that doesn't drive other people crazy.

Interpreting Subjectivity

What Is Interpretation?

By interpretation, either of a particular datum or your analysis as a whole, I mean how you link your findings to things about human life that have significance on either a scientific or human level. You know, in other words, what the patterns *mean*.[1] I'll also distinguish between interpretation and analysis, though the two bleed into one another. That's because in many cases, our overall analysis—our plan of how to connect all the data we have to a claim that we would like to make—first requires interpreting our data, and our interpretation of one datum can, at least in some cases, be partially independent of our other interpretations. So I want to focus first on the interpretation side, and then turn to analysis. In both cases, we'll be bumping into basic issues of research design.

Why deal with this at the end, and not the beginning? Because sometimes, even if you had a plausible research design when you started out, life has tricked you, for better or worse. For worse, your project may sim-

---

1. Some social scientists use a somewhat different vocabulary to talk about the same basic issues; they'd talk about figuring out "what your story is." That works sometimes, but you won't necessarily have a story with a beginning, middle, and end.

ply not have worked out the way you wanted, and you are hoping that you have something salvageable in your work. For better, your research uncovers something promising that you had never dreamed of. In either case, you find something interesting that you hadn't quite prepared for, and so you can still make new mistakes now—although you have successfully uncovered something, you need to correctly figure out *what* it is.

Losing Analytic Independence

The most obvious problems of interpretation arise when we need to interpret the subjectivity of others—what's going on in their heads. On the one hand, everyone will tell you, you don't want to be a sucker and simply accept the self-understandings of your subjects. And I agree, but not, if you remember from chapter 5, because of a fear that you'll "go native" and accept the ideas of "the group." And that's because the group includes the doubter, the malcontent, the one with a foot out the door, and the person trying to study *you* and adopt *your* culture because she thinks it will improve her life. The problem isn't when you adopt the views of the group as a whole, but when you adopt the views of a subset that you think is the true group—often the leaders. Adopting their general analysis means you interpret each datum to fit their "line."

Bosk, whose work on physicians I discussed in chapters 3 and 6, realized that he had fallen into this error. He had noted that senior attending surgeons (the bosses in the groups he studied) often saw (or at least, claimed they saw) the training as a "stress test" that could determine whether aspiring surgeons could "take the pressure" ([1979] 2003, 223). Some attendings explained that there were times when it was actually important for them to deliberately *increase* the stress on their underlings. To do this, an attending might insist that the student had made a terrible error, even though this wasn't true, simply to see what would happen if he badgered and criticized the underling (228). It is far from clear that there was any legitimate pedagogical reason for this sort of behavior, as opposed to the "stress" doctrine serving as a convenient justification for sadistic behavior. Indeed, you wouldn't have guessed it from Bosk's dissertation or the first edition of his book, but (as I noted in chapter 3) one of his two main informants, and the one who was responsible for Bosk generating his key idea of quasi-normative errors, was a complete, utter asshole, who thought it was fun to start a group meeting with his subordinates by making a holocaust "joke" to the Jewish student, a lynching "joke" to the black student, a rape "joke" to the woman student, and so on.

Bosk initially accepted the account given by the a-hole physician for this behavior, but not because he had "gone native." There's no evidence that the *underlings* agreed as to how important this part of their socialization was. *They* probably thought that this guy was a complete dick. In fact, at the time, Bosk didn't realize that he followed the dominant physicians in defining as blameworthy only errors that by definition *only underlings* could make ([1979] 2003, 57–58).

Recall (see chapter 3) that Bosk did this study to see whether doctors deserved their exemption from oversight because they were good at policing themselves. And he had concluded that they were, even though he actually had found that they can't really control each other once they are full surgeons, and they don't even try to protect the public from the incompetent. Bosk never saw them police each other, only others, and (in one case) police them with the same relish that a paramilitary commander in Chile might police a village. Yet he initially provided "functional" explanations of why this was necessary or good for medical training. Why? Instead of asking himself, "What's going on here? Why is this happening?" he gave up analytic independence to a *particular* set of persons, those who were used to framing their accounts authoritatively and punishing those who dissented. And, as I've been emphasizing, that's partly because he hadn't thought through the processes that brought him to *this* site, to *this* floor, and to be dutifully taking down as facts that claims of *this* respondent. In retrospect, he seemed to think it had more to do with the allure of surgeons than with the scientific characteristics of the site.

Partial Sampling

Thus we want to make sure we're not only seeing things through some actors' eyes and not others. Of course, sometimes it seems we agree with *all* our informants—but only because we have been selective in our sampling. We've gotten the same sorts of people, or caught them at the same point in a process. That can mean that we are trying to get a sense of a social interaction from only one side. That isn't necessarily a problem— some interactions, like some objects (say a sphere), look pretty much the same no matter what your point of view, and others (like a cube) you can also see properly from most angles if you can rotate them in your head. But there are plenty of interactions that (like a weird or very long shape) are impossible to understand from only one view (here, see Desmond 2014). And remember, as we learned in chapter 4, we shouldn't try to get our respondents to solve this problem by telling us about *others'* views.

Unfortunately, when we mess this up, and, ignoring the strictures in chapter 4, provoke people into giving us *accounts*, it's very hard for us, both emotionally and interactionally, to reject these accounts. Unless we have data from someone else that contradict the first account, we probably won't. And so we'll treat these as a form of data that we shouldn't.

A great example here is seen in Ebaugh's (1988) *Becoming an Ex*, which I brought up in chapter 6. If you recall, it's about the processes whereby people exit a role that is important to them. One of the most gripping portions of this work is Ebaugh's analysis of mothers who gave up custody of their children. Ebaugh is careful to repeatedly qualify her arguments by indicating that she doesn't actually know what happened, and that she is only analyzing how the actors *thought* about their transitions. Yet it is also clear that her analysis assumes the fundamental accuracy of these accounts; if they weren't accurate, we'd be very confused as to what was going on.[2]

For example, the majority of mothers report that they had low self-esteem because of their "strong, domineering husbands." Ebaugh points out that we can't be sure that they didn't have low self-esteem *before* the marriage. For this reason, as I said, she is careful to qualify her findings as reports, not facts. Thus she says that these "women had husbands *whom they described* as aggressive, ego-centered, domineering men who wanted control of the house, wife, and children. The husbands *reportedly* tended to downplay, derogate, and humiliate their wives by telling them how weak, incompetent, and/or dependent they were" (emphasis added). Now even though Ebaugh is being admirable in qualifying her statements, her own interpretation seems to have been based on accepting these as factual.

Why? Because her modal reproduction of the process is that the women did not mean to give up custody, but were tricked by their husbands (1988, 88–89). "As soon as the papers were signed, verbal promises were forgotten and the mothers found themselves cut off from their children." She also talks about how they supposedly were hoping in later years to regain custody, but "learned tragically that it is almost impossible to reverse that decision" (186). Other details that do not fit so well with this story (such as that the mothers may blame their children for problems in their marriages, "and, as they reject commitment to marriage, they also reject commitment to ongoing care of children" [189]) were dutifully noted, but they seemed not to bear the same weight when she had to piece it all together.

There are two things to emphasize. First, if you don't have the facts, don't think that it's OK to bulldoze ahead with an interpretation that requires them. You don't make this scientifically acceptable by (1) qualifying your claim (as does Ebaugh); (2) claiming that you don't care about the facts, if

2. Ebaugh employs what Goffman (1959, 25) calls "protective practices" to help her conversation partners save face, even in her analysis. Most notably, her discussion of the role exit from motherhood tends to tiptoe around the actual act of giving up custody, instead concentrating on the times before and after the act. She also never mentions any negative consequences of the decision (one woman felt guilty, we learn, but then was relieved to find the father wanted custody "and saw his having custody as a way out of a bad situation" [1988, 63]).

you really do; and (3) assuming that even if the respondents can't be trusted to tell you the true facts, they *can* be trusted to tell you "how they think about things." People whose way of thinking about things has no relation to what they believe to be the facts are those whom we call *insane*.

In many of Ebaugh's analyses, the facts *don't* matter. But in some of them, they do, and there, she was in a bind, because she only had reports from one side, and she wasn't willing to treat these reports skeptically. And this brings us to the second key point.

It isn't that Ebaugh sympathized with the mothers-without-custody because they are women.[3] It's that she sympathizes with them because they are the ones who provided the accounts—and these are incredibly painful events. We see glimpses of possible stories from the man's side, and she is never particularly rejecting of these, as she would be if she had a gender bias. For example, we read about a man who went to therapy to get advice about his marriage. "After interviewing both him and his wife, the therapist said she was a bitch and that he ought to leave her to preserve his own sanity" (1988, 100). Even better, a man that she studied because he was an ex-CIA agent turned out to also be a divorcé, and his wife (not in the study), a mother-without-custody. Here's what we learn about their relationship: "His wife had left him to marry another man and did not want to have custody of their daughter" (127). You can easily imagine the ex-CIA agent's wife being in this sample and having *her* version also sympathetically relayed as if there was no contradiction.

> Two men who have a dispute take it to the rabbi to settle. The first one tells his side of the story from the very beginning, and the rabbi listens attentively. When the first is finished, the rabbi says: "Hmm... yes, you are quite right." Then the second one tells his story, at the end of which, the rabbi says: "Yes, yes, you are indeed right." The rabbi's wife, who has been in the room the whole time and has overheard this, finally explodes at him: "You numbskull! The two stories are totally in contradiction! It is impossible for them both to be right!" The rabbi thinks and tugs thoughtfully at his beard: "It seems that you, too, are right."

3. And in case it isn't clear, Ebaugh is generally very up front about explaining how many cases fall into any particular pattern at any time, and she is also admirable at providing a full range of stories, even if they complicate the attribution of responsibility. In no way does she have a single or simple story for any of her subjects.

I don't think that Ebaugh could have done a better job here—the problem is that she took on the wrong job. You can't wade into account land, get accounts from one side, and come back with anything about the events themselves. You can't even really understand the events as seen from one side. You can't study the seeing of things you don't also see, for seeing is not hallucination.

We're going to call this the rebbetzin principle (see box; "rebbetzin" is the Jewish word for a rabbi's wife). If you wade into a sort of project that pits sides against one another, unless you figure out how to transform your question, you will end up siding with one and produce asymmetric interpretations, whether through ignorance of the other or through callous dismissal.

Two-Sided Interpretations

We've bumped into what is going to be the focus of my discussion of this sort of analysis, which is to say, the problems that come with certain forms of asymmetry in our interpretation. It's vital that you not get this confused with being fair. This isn't about sharing the blame, splitting the difference, or listening to all sides. It's about you actually doing your work properly and, in particular, making a distinction between the experiences your subjects can report to you, on the one hand, and their interpretations, on the other. You want, first of all, to be able to distinguish these and, second, for events where there are multiple sides, to make sure you aren't relying on just one.

However, with more sides, you can still get a lot of confusing disagreement—but at least now your subjects will be less likely to disagree on *what* happened (though you can get this as well), and more on *why* people did what they did (see, e.g., Goffman 2014, 131–35). And although you might want to try to get *the* right interpretation, you usually don't have to. You can let the differences be—the different accounts in which each respondent was the good one. As actors, our moral evaluations tend to cling to our interests as best they can. We aren't being dishonest—at least initially—when we fight for one interpretation that just so happens to be convenient for us. The key thing is for you to be able to get enough of them to reassemble the interaction... and not to promote some of your respondents to informants who you let tell you about things that they really can't, like what others were trying to do.

Of course, most of us, as actors, have *theories* of others' actions, but they're often based on remarkably few data. Sometimes, as actors, we work hard to get better data, and we really expose our theories of others to the evidence. But those times are few and far between: most of us are happy to stop with an explanation of others' action if it makes us feel better. And we're happy to report it to others, including researchers. And so if you ignored some of my points in chapter 4, you may be staring at data that you'd like to interpret as if they were matters of fact. But you can't.

"Why didn't you get the job?" "They found my awesomeness too threatening." "Why did he dump you for that other girl?" "He had a lot of insecurities and couldn't really deal with deep feelings." "Why was your article rejected?" "It was really too complex an argument for them to comprehend." And so on. Even if they were to try, people aren't good at telling you about what's in *other* people's heads, even their close friends.

When we get to look at an interaction from multiple sides, we're not there to get "the" true story. Think of "de-cide" here to mean "de-side," to throw out one side. You don't want to "de-side" what happened and return to a nice one-dimensional account. Rather, the true story *is* that tangle of different perspectives, interpretations, perceptions, and accounts. You almost always know when you don't have it, because people seem like cardboard cutouts. And then there's not much you can do, except remind yourself that they aren't.

Tell Us What You Really Think

Somewhat related, we often misinterpret things when we look not so much for "the" true account of an interaction, but the one true opinion. That is, we can make errors when we assume that there is a single, base subjectivity, which is what people *really* think, and we need to get at it. The other things we get from them *aren't* the real ideas. Now I won't deny that there might sometimes be screens we need to get behind. But I suspect people's ideas are a bit more tangled or ambivalent than we sometimes would have it. And I here I want to draw on some great work by Sniderman and Carmines (1999), who were interested in the relation between racism and opposition to affirmative action.

Explicit racism has definitely declined since the 1930s or so: public discourse and public opinion shows very few whites voicing opinions that blacks are innately inferior to whites. But this could be due to desirability effects. For this reason, many political psychologists have been working on clever experiments to get around this. Sniderman and Carmines suspected that not only are white Americans less likely to voice any racist beliefs they might have, but, more importantly, political liberals were less likely to admit that they actually weren't happy with affirmative action policies. And indeed, their experiments suggest that more liberals are angry about affirmative action than you would guess if you asked them if they were for or against it. Sniderman and Carmines then used this to make an argument about policy: that Americans really believe in fairness on the individual level, not the group level.

The work is great. But perhaps there is an assumption we shouldn't be so sure about. Just because people get angry about affirmative action doesn't mean they don't support it. As I noted in chapter 4, we tend to think that contradictory ideas mean that one is real and one isn't, and that the real one is the one we express in private, not the one in public. But if in the middle of the night you sneak down to the kitchen and finish off a pint of Phish Food ice cream, does that mean that you were lying when you refused dessert at dinner because you said you were on a diet? Maybe, but it might also be that you really *wanted* not to eat dessert, but you needed the public support to be firm in that conclusion. It isn't clear that our first-order preferences are realer than our second-order preferences (what we would prefer that we prefer... though we don't).

In sum, even if you aren't off to expose hypocrisy (a dreadful error that I'll get to in a second), you need to recognize that there might not be any particular opinion that you want to consider the "true" one. The variability is part of the opinion itself, just like the different perspectives were part of the interaction. Your job is to understand this, not to erase it.

Asymmetric Interpretations

You're actually most likely to do this erasing if, when you sit down to interpret people's beliefs, you just can't get past your own. That is, you have a dog in the fight. I've heard every argument for why there's no such thing as neutrality, values don't interfere with science, commitments are necessary for social science, and so on. Whatever. What I'm saying is that if you can't rise above your position (which isn't the same thing as giving it up), you will not do your job right. You will have an asymmetric approach, which means that you treat your data differently depending on whether you see the source as on your side, or on the other one.

Part of the reason for asymmetric analyses is that we do tend to see things from our position, but another part comes from our idea of what it means to "explain" what people believe. This might be a good time to refresh yourself on the points made in chapter 2 about "why" questions. We have a built-in two-road approach for explaining beliefs—the high road of motivation for our friends (who happen to be right), and the low road of causality for our enemies (who are wrong). (Yes, I talked about this in chapter 2. But you might not have listened then.)

> **Your enemies may be no better than you think they are, but your friends are probably worse than you think they are.**

Now of course, you *might* be able to investigate others' beliefs with the same care and respect you would use on your own. But you need to be ready for it, and if you find your very concepts trivializing others' ideas, you're not ready. What are the signs of this? Well, characterizing others' beliefs as "phobias" or "reactions" or "holdovers" or, perhaps especially, "myths." If you are using any of these words to describe the beliefs of folks who you wouldn't invite over for a barbeque, chances are, you're not ready to study them. As I said in chapter 6, even if the bad guys aren't any better than they appear, the ideas of the other side, the one you like, probably aren't quite as consistent and selfless as you'll make it seem. Because by trivializing some, you'll give the others a Get Out of Critique Free card. And remind yourself what you learned in chapter 4—if you asked vague, decontextualized questions, you basically handed your friends just that sort of Get Out of Critique Free card that now will mess up your analysis.

Well, From Here, It Looks . . .

Asymmetric interpretations often make themselves known because you have heroes to counterpoise to your villains. But there can be times when you carry out some of the same type of interpretive distortions when you don't have this sort of comparison—indeed, even on people that you think of as basically being good guys.

In particular, I find it fascinating how often I see sociologists attribute fear and anxiety to others to explain their actions. While this is sometimes done deliberately to trivialize others (see Martin 2001 for a discussion), it isn't only done for this reason. But few of us recognize all these fears within ourselves in settings that are homologous to those we are analyzing. In a nutshell, what we do is recognize that (1) person A has carried out a set of actions that lead to result X and not Y; (2) there are a number of noxious qualities of Y; and so we think that we can explain the action parsimoniously by (3) proposing that Y itself basically drove A away by inducing fear. But there are many possible ways in which a preference for X can be developed by an actor, even recognizing the formidable constraint imposed by the environment, other than "fear" of Y.

Let me give a great example. Some studies of poor people find that many make a clear distinction between themselves and good-for-nothing poor. Although the speaker may currently be on assistance, say, that doesn't mean that she is a bum like those other folks. We frequently imagine that, in saying this, the respondent is carrying out a kind of distancing work, pushing those others away or, better, *trying* to push them away, to prevent their stigma from infecting herself.

What's wrong with this? Well, it's that people often don't feel that they need to distance themselves—in their minds, they already *have* distanced themselves, successfully. They're *informing* you, as opposed to *enlisting* you. Now I'm not saying that the other never happens—that you are witnessing distancing work being done, and that if the work were to fail, the respondent would be threatened by stigma. But simply assuming that one homeless person is anxious to avoid being tarred with the same brush as others isn't really much different from you saying, "Since you all look pretty much the same to *me*, I'm just going to assume that that's more important data than anything *you* have to say." Ouch.

I mentioned the asymmetric dismissal of some actor's ideas as being due to "myths." This attribution indicates a problem, and not just because today's science (i.e., your beliefs) become tomorrow's myths. Rather, it usually indicates that you aren't doing a good job of contextualization. Real people aren't owned by their beliefs. And so they can act according to a set of ideas that, at least sometimes, they'll grudgingly admit are pretty stupid, but not because they are blinded and accepting ideology or myths. It's just that, in the situation they're in, they've got a pretty constrained choice set. This is because, as Swidler (2001) in particular has emphasized (following Mead [1934]), the thing about the meaning of some act isn't what *you* mean by it, but how it is interpreted by others. If it would be hard for your daughter to get married if you didn't bind her feet when she was younger, you might well bind her feet. And, if you had to defend it to a social scientist who seemed intent on making you feel bad about it, you might marshal all the arguments in its favor you could think of or insist that it was just your culture and that he should bug off. But a good sociologist wouldn't be going down that road in an interview.

In sum, when you sit down to interpret, you simply will not do a good job if you have an asymmetry, whether that comes because you are treating some but not all as informants, because you've only sampled people in one structural position in an interaction you are trying to study, because you see some as friends and others as enemies, or just because you use ways of thinking about *others* that you would never use on yourself. Convincing yourself there's no other way of doing it is using what brain power you have to stay bad, as opposed to getting better.

Fixing Interpretations

Fighting Back against Your Research Design

Usually, the best fix for bad interpretations is having a good research design up front: understanding what data you need to answer your questions, as opposed to simply vacuuming up "lots of great data" that you then have to pull something out of. But you also need to be aware of the ways that certain research designs will channel your conclusions. Some are so strong that I've urged you not even to go down that road—especially the type of question that asks, "Does X matter for Y?" Still, there may be times, even if you took most of my warnings seriously, when you may find that you built your interpretations into your concepts, and now you have to undo them. But you can begin to avoid being dragged to a bad place by understanding that even basically good research designs can force your brain in a certain direction.

For example, let's say you examined two different sites. Even if you didn't intend a rigorous compare-and-contrast scheme, there's a good chance you'll end up doing a fair amount of this sort of tabular analysis, especially when you are asking yourself, "What did I learn? What can I explain?" One of the virtues of the multiple cases is that the disjunctions will rise to the forefront easily. But that means that areas of overlap can be overlooked as "natural"—even though it might just be chance that both cases agree on this or that. Further, you'll tend to assume that any disjunction in each is fundamentally going to be explained by something that obviously varies across the two. It just isn't necessarily that way. And if you try to put this into a rigid format, using a Millsian comparison, you almost certainly will come up with *something*. (See chapter 7, where I strongly urged you away from any method that automates such a search for a Millsian difference—it's voodoo, not social science.) But even if you don't fall prey to a simple "explanation," a comparison is still likely to lead you to exaggerate the differences between your cases, because that's what you'll focus on.

For another example, if there are different possible levels or axes of differentiation of your cases, and you use only one, you'll probably begin to forget about possibly relevant processes that you'd only see if you had chosen a different level. Let's say you are interested in organizational culture, and you think that Americans and Germans have different ideas. You compare an American apparel firm to a German white goods firm and find they're different. Chances are, you want to focus on a cultural explanation (which is why you picked an American and a German firm). But of course, it might be that the difference springs from something about the difference of industry (apparel versus white goods), and not the firms across nations. Or it could be simply about the styles of the individual bosses.

When people remind you of this, you'll be tempted to come up with sophistical arguments as to why these other things can't possibly matter. If these arguments are as good as you think they are, go make them to your dean or provost. She or he will be delighted that they can save a lot of money by getting rid of psychology, or history, or whatever you've just "proved" can't matter. Knowing what you didn't see, and what you couldn't see, is crucial for understanding what you *did* see.

We may also confuse variation *within* and variation *across* our units. If we have compared richer versus poorer people within some countries and found differences in religion, this doesn't answer the question of whether some countries are more secular because their wealth leads to a new value system. As you probably learned in your stats class, sometimes the variation within your units has the opposite association with another variable than does the variation across your larger units. We can "know" this, but forget it when we are excited that a pattern that seems to explain something people are very interested in, even if really answering that question requires a different research design from the one used.

Other times, even if we have the level of analysis right, we may confuse variation in degree with presence or absence. We might notice that at times when there is more institutional separation of gender spheres of action, there is greater inequality of control of offspring. That's interesting, but it isn't the same as whether patriarchy is caused by the gendered division of labor. And, finally, this might be a good time to reread chapter 3 on ceiling and floor effects before making any arguments about change.

Outcome, Exposure, and Preference

Another common confusion is that between *outcome, preference,* and *exposure* (or *opportunity*). Given that we often have only observed outcomes, we can misinterpret our data as telling us about preferences, because we don't get to see the set of opportunities.[4] For example, we might be interested in patterns of intermarriage. And we might take these patterns to indicate something about people's racial ideas or sentiments. Most simply, imagine that there is one group *A* that is a small slice of the population, and that everyone only marries once for life. That means every time an *A* member gets married, a lot of other people who might *like* to marry an *A* are going to have a much harder time. If they end up marrying a *B*, we can't assume that this was their first choice.

In general, we can say that *Outcome = Preferences × Opportunity*. In quantitative demography this is well understood, but it's an issue relevant for all sorts of problems where we really have two moving parts for one observation. Remember in the last chapter, when we were considering how to interpret newspapers, we realized that *Story = Event × Activist Frame ×*

---

4. A great recent example of a rethinking of previous approaches will be found in Hagen, Makovi, and Bearman (2013).

Journalistic Editing, so that changes in stories couldn't necessarily be ascribed to changes in only one of these? We had to hold two constant? So too, more generally, when there's a change or difference in outcome, we can't ascribe it to changes (or differences) in preferences unless we know something about the opportunities (also called "exposure" in statistics). We need to hold off making an assumption that is basically equating outcome and preference, and ignoring opportunity.

And I think I need to take this opportunity to make a second excursus, returning to that issue of constructionism, reiterating and expanding the point made in the last chapter.

Proximate versus Distal Explanations

1. "It isn't the reality that determines political movements, it's the subjective sense."
2. "Interests aren't material, they are ideal."
3. "News isn't a passive reflection of what happened, it is a construct."
4. "Strict religions don't increase conservatism, it is a traditionalistic orientation that increases conservatism."
5. "Guns don't kill people—bullets kill people."

What do all these claims have in common? Two things. First, they are true. Second, they are misleading and lead to bad research. Why? Because each one makes a mistake of not thinking about what the Buddhists might call the "conditioned origin" (or "dependent arising") of things. By dependent arising, I mean that sometimes one phenomenon assumes a different one. By ignoring this, we read a statement that has an implicit condition as if it didn't.

Let's take the last one—guns don't kill people, bullets kill people. Let's imagine that there's a chain of dependent arising going a bit like this:

> Liberal gun laws → people have guns → people carry guns → people shoot guns → bullets leave guns → bullets go into people → bullets make holes in people → blood comes out → people die.

The earlier events are more "distal" from the eventual effect (death), and the later ones are more proximate. Unless you live in a really crisp and deterministic world, in a face-off, proximate events will have more explanatory power than distal ones. But they shouldn't ever be used in a face-off against distal ones. And that's because, in many cases, the reason that the more proximate things have their oomph in the first place is that they incorporate all the oomph of the more distal ones. That is all the more true when it isn't clear that our different stages in this chain are really separable; when it comes to example 4, we might be slicing up a single subjectivity into complexes that aren't well separable.[5]

Now let's return to example 3, which we explored in the previous chapter. There we saw that the constructionist answer properly trumped what we can call the naive realist one—but that it was misleading because people tended to use it to reject the naive realist one and that they tended to do this asymmetrically. Now we see that not only is it not that the two accounts aren't necessarily opposed: often the constructionist one only works *because* of the realist one. That is, the reason the construction of the "moral panic" of global warming worked so well is that the globe *is* warming, which is why you can read about it in the paper. That doesn't mean everything you read is true, but it means that you can't say that "it's because we read it in the news" and imply that it isn't true. In fact, we might find that the effect of the construction on the outcome is much greater when it isn't a bunch of hooey.

We see this same problem when it comes to interpreting people's interests (example 2). It is absolutely the case that people's actions aren't guided by their material interests but rather by their subjective understanding of these. But this isn't an *opposition* of two possibilities—it's simply shifting further to the right in the chain of dependent arising. The question isn't whether people's material interests directly shape their political behavior, but what the relation between their subjective and their material interests actually is. We can imagine a continuum: on one side, their subjective idea of their interests is totally detached from their material interests (such as "I want to impose crazy beliefs on everyone"); on the other, it is nothing but these interests (such as "I want a bigger paycheck"). Since both of those are equally subjective, the false face-off of material versus ideal is bound to play out badly.

And it's especially bad because some research techniques tend to put you further on the right side of the chain than others. You can't use the location of your research project in this chain to be the basis of an interpretive strategy that leads you to make strong conclusions. You need to think it through—why am I seeing this, focusing on that? So bearing in mind the tendencies that come with even the best research designs can help you avoid analytic errors to the end. What can we do for more deeply flawed designs?

Forgetting and Assuming

Very often, the biggest problem in our interpretations is that we've basically assumed—from the very beginning—the most problematic aspects

5. This way of seeing has additional problems: much of social psychology simply has made weird assumptions about the internal relations of elements within the head that just don't make any sense (Martin 2000; Borsboom, Mellenbergh, and van Heerden 2003).

of our whole approach. For example, we've assumed that we know the cause of a phenomenon, and we just want to document it or to look more closely at the mechanism involved. Or we've used theoretical concepts that make strong assumptions about the constitution of the world. Or, even worse, we've done both of these ("How do advertisements for cheese reproduce gender relations?").

I've urged you not to formulate questions that build in *assumptions*, and not to use procedures that make it impossible to find out you're wrong, but still, it happens. As you start writing up your research, you may suddenly realize that you can't justify all those assumptions. Is it too late to save your research project, now that the data are in, just because without this or that unprovable assumption, your finding isn't compelling? Yes. Yes it is too late. *That's why I told you not to do this!*

Burnt Toast

Here I don't know who first said this; I heard it second hand from someone who received this advice on one of his projects: "You know when you burn the toast, you can go to the sink, and scrape and scrape away at it… but sometimes it makes sense just to put in a new slice of bread." Very wise words. You need to know when you have burnt toast. It isn't rational to respond to sunk costs. If you wasted three years of your life, that doesn't mean you should waste three years and two weeks. I've seen students spend two years revising a flawed master's project when they are at a point where now they could do a great one from scratch in less time. Let it go.

> **If your project can't really be salvaged,
> don't waste another second on it. Next!**

But even if there's something there in your data, you might not yet know quite what it is. You need to analyze data in an open-ended fashion to construct your interpretation.

Analytic Approaches

Wading Through Data

Especially if you had a "back-loaded" (open-ended) research design, it's sometimes only toward the end of your project that you really confront some of the core principles of research. It comes when you find yourself tackling a mass of data that you're not quite sure how to analyze. No matter what you do, you will need to organize these data before going on. This seems to be the situation in which many researchers who have used in-depth interviews find themselves, and so for this section, I'm going to use this as an example. But similar problems are encountered by, say, textual analysts, including synthetic theorists and, all too often, historical sociologists and ethnographers (who often bitterly repent how complete their note taking was!).

When you try to impose some order on your materials, there is a fork in the road: your analysis can be about an *issue* or *theme* (and so you use cases to get at this theme) or about particular *cases* (and you allow different themes to give you a better sense of the case). Although any thematic analysis is by its nature general, case-based analysis can be more or less general. When it is more general, we move away from a case study and tend to be developing a typology. We might talk about egalitarian versus traditional marriages, say. As Weiss (1995, 174) says, the problem with typologies is that they make use of tendencies that are probably inherent in our limited minds, to make sense of the world by simplifying, by stereotyping.

Put this way, typologizing seems so bad that you'd wonder why people ever do it. But in fact even issue-oriented studies often are powered by invisible typologies. The typology may start as a contrast between two or three key cases (e.g., respondents you interviewed) who *stand out*, and who then start to *stand for* others, for a whole type of respondent. If things go well, we find that our central cases are ideal typical, even if not prototypical. The problem can be, however, that when we are making general claims we are still thinking of one or two particular cases. Typologizing, which can seem like outrageous simplification, can be the only thing that keeps us from simplifying utterly. That's because we may find that our interesting cases share some characteristics with one another that they don't share with the others. The typology allows us to bring in the full variation of the data, even if in simplified form.

> **Just because a case *stands out* from others doesn't mean it should *stand for* others.**

We don't always need to typologize in order to begin an analysis of themes, but even if we don't typologize, we're likely to use related analytic techniques. And that's because, like typologizing, such analysis is a struggle to answer the question: "This is a case of . . . what?" And here, many analysts will seek to code their notes—to take each particularity and subsume it into a more abstract concept. As you remember from chapter 8, I don't think you should code, but you should *tag*—place multiple simplifying mnemonics on your data so that you can begin arranging them and rearranging them.

In sum, typologizing can be an end in itself, but it can also be a means to an end, and can lead to conceptual simplification—and the same goes for coding up themes. Further, there are commonalities in how the work is done. In general, analysis involves a lot of typing and a lot of thinking, and a lot of things winding up in the trash. There are actually books on how to analyze textual results, but I think there are really only two or three principles that are invariably used.

First, *organize*—interviewers and field-workers generally spend a great deal of time organizing their notes to make sure that they don't lose track of things that are important. The most general way of organizing, or tagging, is just attaching a flag that allows you to pull up certain documents; then, if you can organize some subset of tags, you are well on your way to getting a hold over the data. Generally, speed is of the essence, so people try to put down, in some simple fashion, themes or statements found in an article or an interview or field note, so that they can find that document later to use. There are good reasons to do this in the middle of data collection,[6] but as your research progresses, you may well decide that your original way of looking at things, and hence your way of attaching tags, was wrong. Back to the beginning—but the exercise might have helped you move past your initial ideas more quickly.

For this reason, I think we almost always find we need to leave ourselves time for two passes through the data. The chance that the first try falls apart under its own weight is too great for you to assume that you can make a single pass.

There are a number of well-thought-of computer programs to aid such analysis. I won't specifically warn you away from them, but I've met plenty of successful analysts who admit that they have never used anything more advanced than Control+F to organize their data. And I see a lot of students spending a great deal of time conscientiously going through their work and putting it all into nested boxes, almost none of which would ever be

6. Some people have personalities where they really like to segregate stages of the work process, and if that's you, work with your strengths, not against them. And some projects, especially ethnographic and archival work, can force that segregation on you. But if there are pauses between interviews, or visits to your field sites, going over your notes and trying to code is great. Not only can it be a real wake-up call to problems in your technique, but you can also start to form provisional hypotheses that you can explore as you go along.

used. If you're the type of person who loves organizing, watch out—you can trick yourself into wasting time neatening up when you need to be thinking, making the organization an end in itself, as opposed to a means to an end. If that's what you really like, drop out of sociology now and go into a more appropriate field. You cannot succeed as a sociologist on the strength of the database procedures you designed![7]

And you can be too neat. Unless you have a set-up like Houston Mission Control or the Pentagon war room, your screen is too small to use for organizing data, at least, without burying the originals and completely replacing them with your tags. Your floor, or if you live in Manhattan, your loft bed, might be better. Because after you have tagged your notes, you can use these to make provisional boxes to put them in. But there's a good chance that as you do this, you'll find that the materials refuse to stay in their boxes. You wanted to have, say, five boxes, but you keep on finding things that are, say, between boxes number 2 and number 3, and so you make some new boxes (now you have nine), but find that you still can't fit everything in; now you have in your hand examples that seem to want to sit between numbers 5, 8, and 9. As you puzzle over how to fit the nine piles on your mattress, you arrange them in a square and it suddenly hits you—instead of nine boxes, or even five, you have just two dimensions. That's a good day.

The second major theme is *generalization*—to go from the many specifics to a sense of what is going on in general. Despite this being the core of the whole method, it is harder to say much about this part. Except perhaps that the whole point of organization is to make this generalization easy— once things are organized properly, the general lessons are apparent when you go back over the data. That's what happens when you literally see the square of piles of notes on your bed. If you can turn your data into figures in which you can see the patterns, you'll have a head start in reaching general principles, compared to someone who is still dealing with long strings of text, even if they're now in the syntaxless language of tags.

Now if you've spent three years getting to know each of thirty-two people as complex individuals, it might seem hard to generalize. Indeed, you might even have read some self-identified theoretical argument that implies that generalization is inherently pernicious. You may be afraid that you'll be criticized for overgeneralization if you generalize. You need to get over it. That's what we do in sociology. Here, business is wholesale, not retail. If you don't like it, it's time for a different career.

7. This might sound odd, but every year I am contacted by students who do think that this is a plausible claim to fame, or who think that they can make a bundle selling what worked for *them* and *their* project to *you* for *yours*.

Sociology is wholesale, not retail.
Go ahead and generalize.

Then the third major theme is to *illustrate*—once they have a general claim to make, researchers who can will generally go back to the data (interviews, documents, field notes) and use these (e.g., the voices of the respondents) to illustrate points. That might seem very unscientific; certainly, illustrating isn't *sufficient* to support a point, but it is *necessary*. There are plenty of graduate students who have interpretations for which they cannot actually supply a single unambiguous illustration from their data. That's usually an interpretation that is dead in the water.

When they can find at least some illustrations to demonstrate that these aren't selective, unrepresentative quotations (for the case of interviewers), researchers will also count. That is, they'll say something like "fifteen of the twenty women spontaneously mentioned neighbors when asked what were the main stresses in their family. Two of the remaining five also acknowledged that neighbors had been a source of stress in the past year."

This is good because it helps keep researchers (without really intending to) from just saying whatever it is they want to say and illustrating it with a few juicy quotations. If you interviewed twenty people but are always quoting the same one or two, that's probably because you're basically wrong and ignoring what eighteen of the people tell you. (And for this reason, never use more than one pseudonym for the same respondent. Readers deserve to know if you rely heavily on one or two.) The importance of reporting numbers holds true for any "small *N*" study. If you have more than one unit of analysis, there are numbers attachable to your statements. Saying "three out of six" isn't "mistaking" your "approach" for a "quantitative" one, making some sort of "error," as students often seem to think. It's being honest. If you won't tell us the numbers, chances are it's because you're afraid to.

From Why to How

Sometimes you sort through the data, looking for what it tells you, and you realize it's telling you something important and powerful, such as that *x* causes *y*. You are delighted, confident and excited, until you realize that what you've found, after all the work, is pretty well known. (Why didn't you know it before? Probably because you hadn't set out to explain *y* and so you weren't conversant with *y*-ology.) Now you are crushed. But actually, it can be that this is the best news you could hear. If you've done a "small" study, such as hanging out over the summer with two groups of eight middle-school students each, true, no one will use your research to conclude that, say, educational disparities between middle-class and working-class children increase over the summer. But given that the "big N" studies show this, people may be very interested in understanding why, and looking more closely.

So if you're picking up on a causal story (whatever that means to you), you might find you are not in a position to *demonstrate* the fact of a causal connection (perhaps you haven't had the right sampling frame). But if you've studied the "treated," say, you can look closely at what intervenes between them "getting the treatment" and the appearance of the effect. If it's not a causal story—in that you are pretty sure it doesn't make sense to try to rule out self-selection—no problem. You do the same thing. In fact, it's all the better for you. The statistician will pull out his hair over the fact that many kids get to decide how to spend their summers, but you can contribute to the issue of how schools produce, decrease, or increase social inequality with your investigation of what the kids are doing. Indeed, you can make a contribution to the study of very difficult—indeed, insoluble—issues of causality like the "effects" of schooling just by studying those who are doing badly in school, and see how they react to it and make subsequent choices, even if you aren't comparing to those who do well in school. You won't be able to do it all, but you will have a contribution.

We often call this examining "mechanisms," but I think what is key here is not mechanism but focus. Different things are easier or harder to see at different scales. And there are plenty of reasons to think that sometimes your small N study, whether or not it finds what others have argued, is more important than the supposedly decisive big N studies. For example, there's been, and still is, a debate over whether immigration takes away jobs from certain kinds of people. As a statistical problem, it's delightfully complex and perhaps insoluble. Because immigrants can bring spending power or help create new areas of growth, compensating for the employment they require. Determining the causal impact from longitudinal data is a very subtle and creative problem.

But then imagine a Hispanic researcher (a real but as-of-yet unpublished anecdote) went to work in plants that relied on African American employees and was taken aside by a manager on the first day and asked, "Can you bring your whole family here? I'll fire all these black guys and give you their jobs if you do." That doesn't prove that the net effect on employment, or even on black employment, is negative—the spending power of any hired immigrants might generate new employment, and so on—but at least we know where to look next.

From How to What

Further, this looking-more-closely can be important in issues where there isn't a causal relation that researchers are attempting to explain. While it isn't a particular virtue to show that things are more complicated than we thought, it often is a virtue to give people a better sense of what is going on at key junctures of the processes that they care about—how people choose whether to have abortions, what different kinds of people might get grouped together as juvenile delinquents, and so on. Find the clumpiness in the world and tell us about what's going on. There's plenty to explore.

When in doubt, look more closely.

One way of telling us what's going on is to subsume your findings as a "case of" something else. And it's often seems extremely exciting and daring to try to show that your phenomenon can be subsumed in a category no one had imagined. This general notion is quite reasonable—it's one way of explaining a case, namely, to show that it is like something else we understand. And when social science is working properly, this can be immensely important. For example, in many ways Milgram's experiment (see chapter 7) was saying that certain ethical actions can be subsumed in the more general class of situations that social psychologists had been studying for a while.

In no way do I deny that this can be an important form of analysis. Still, subsumption is a dangerous game to play, and easy to lose. The worst version of this is the "unmasking" approach, in which you try to show that something we think is good (giving to charity) can be subsumed into something not good (egoism, as in an economic analysis assuming a utility for feeling charitable). Sometimes this resolves into a trivial application of tautology; other times it involves those sorts of distortions that follow from an asymmetric analysis.

And even if you are able to avoid the unmasking version of subsumption, there are serious traps on the way. First, you have to recognize that no one else will accept your applying a label to your case as itself a great accomplishment. And don't count on the cuteness and/or shock value of your subsumption (like, "atheism is a religion!") to carry you. Older people have gotten inured to that sort of stimulus by now. You can't stop with the application of the label, nor ever working it through as an allegory; you'll need to show that doing so gets us something we didn't have before. And that something can't be "insight," because that just means "seeing A as a kind of X is good, because it gives you the insight that A is a kind of X."

So if you say that A is a kind of X, you're actually going to go ahead and analyze it *as* a X. If you claim that kindergarten social behavior is political, read up on theories of political action and then try to study the kids' behavior the same way you would (say) congressional committees. Same for "sexual prices" (analyzed *as* prices) or "religious work" (analyzed *as* work). Take the claim seriously, and figure out what this does for us in analytic terms.

The problem is that, very often, once we do this, we find that we want to go back and say that the theories of prices, or of work, are wrong. It's almost as if you said: "This here tall guy is a guy of average height, but my study leads me to revise the concept of average height somewhat in the upward direction." You aren't finding that *they* were wrong about their theory of political action—*you* were wrong in your "clever" subsumption. But here we are moving to problems of writing, more than of analysis. And so I'm going to turn to this issue—how do we write up what we found—and return to this issue in that context.

Writing

Now all that's left is to write it up. The best projects write themselves. In the real sciences, there are articles with titles that say exactly what they are, and the writing is fast. Here's the title of today's article on *PLOS ONE*: "Elimination of Chromosomal Island SpyCIM1 from *Streptococcus pyogenes* Strain SF370 Reverses the Mutator Phenotype and Alters Global Transcription." I think you have a good idea of what's in this article: whatever this SpyCIM1 is, if you manage to get it out of some strain of strep, this reverses the mutator phenotype. There's a short introduction, a lot describing exactly what they did, and then a brief conclusion (Hendrickson et al. 2015).

Of course, not all discoveries are so crisp, even in science, and so they often do need more writing. But this is the key: the cleaner your actual work, the less writing you need. Some statisticians would say all their work was just to make up for bad (i.e., nonexperimental) data. So too about all our theory writing: we use it to make the connection between the key elements of our argument—the further apart these are, the more writing we need. For this reason, too much writing suggests a problem.

There are ways of doing this writing that might at first glance seem to solve your problems very neatly. Such writing methods seem to explain why the research you did, which might at first blush seem weak, idiosyncratic, or ambiguous, is actually very theoretically powerful. But these fixes bring with them their own problems. Let me steer you away from some intrinsically problematic ways of writing, and/or ways of "framing," your research. In particular, you should never try to handle substantive, methodological, or theoretical problems *rhetorically* if there is a practical way of handling them. Don't ask me, or anyone else, how to frame a problematic project. That's like asking the Food and Drug Administration how to sell rotten fish. We're in charge of *preventing* this from happening, and if someone is colluding with you to pass bad goods, they're corrupt.

But sometimes the problems that arise in writing just indicate a mismatch of what you've learned and what you'd like to say about it. That's good. That means your work is just a little bent, but not broken. It might seem implausible, but it turns out that quite often, we still aren't quite sure as to what we've accomplished until we are rereading our first draft. In these cases, we need to retroactively figure out what question we should have been asking. Determining this is an occult art; I can't state it exactly, but I'll try to show the bounds you should work within.

I Meant to Do That

In chapter 2, I referred to the *Jeopardy* move of just stating your answer as if it were a question. I don't think that's an impressive move. In fact, one of the reasons why we have such a hard time writing our results up is that we've been indoctrinated with a particularly stupid way of writing an article. I learned this in eighth grade, as the "lab report." We had a mimeographed form: on the top, three lines: hypothesis. Under that, on the left, a big box: materials and procedures. On the right side, a box: observations. On the back side, more lines: conclusions and new hypothesis.[8] I know that we like this ceremony; it's sort of like the white wedding that people still go through, for comfort's sake. But everyone knows that you didn't formulate that hypothesis before you did your procedures, and everyone knows that the two of them are no strangers to each other's apartments.

I'm not going to talk about all the problems with our atavistic attachment to this ritual because I'd be starting another book. In most cases, it is at best meaningless duplication—instead of saying "I found *X*," first you say "I bet I'll find *X*" and then you say, "guess what? I found *X*!" And at worst, it is a classic conditioning experiment in antiscientific procedure: we repeatedly combine every "revealing of a finding" with a "saying of an untruth."

8. I am not making this up. I know because I found in my old room one that I had saved. On the left side, where the write up of the procedures was supposed to be, was a very nice picture, drawn by me, of a child with a welding helmet holding a test tube via tongs over a raging fire. On the top, in nice red pen, written by my teacher, was the letter D.

Call me an idealist, but I think science has something to do with the pursuit of truth. And I think lying is incompatible with truth. So pretending to do something you aren't doing isn't the right way to start. Of course, you may disagree. But I suggest you lie about it in public.

Or you could, you might think, try to bring your practice into line with what we claim to do. And there's a movement in social sciences, though relatively weak in sociology, for us to really formulate a hypothesis before collecting the data, tell everyone what it is ("register" it), and how we are going to (mechanically) test it with the data, and then do just that. It will all be on the up and up.

> **Sky Matheson [from *Guys and Dolls*]: On the day I left home to make my way in the world, my daddy took me to one side. "Son," my daddy says to me, "I am sorry I am not able to bankroll you to a large start, but not having the necessary lettuce to get you rolling, instead, I'm going to stake you to some very valuable advice.**
>
> **"One of these days, a guy is going to show you a brand-new deck of cards on which the seal is not yet broken. Then this guy is going to offer to bet you that he can make the jack of spades jump out of this brand-new deck of cards and squirt cider in your ear.**
>
> **"But, son, you do not accept this bet because, as sure as you stand there, you're going to wind up with an ear full of cider."**

But it won't be good sociology, at least, not most of the time. Why? Because it's absolutely true that the way science works is through hypothesis formation—making a tentative extrapolation, checking if the world agrees, correcting, making a new extrapolation, just as John Dewey, for one, would say. But it's something that you should be doing *a dozen times a week*. Otherwise, you don't have much of a chance of learning anything really new. If you are only going to do basically five to ten hypothesis tests in your career—which is what a serious use of the registration method implies for most people—then you'll be damn sure that you'll be right. You'll play it safe. And indeed, most of the "hypotheses" that I see students formulating are so painfully obvious that they make an excellent case for not even bothering to do the research.

So don't try to squeeze exploratory results into a deductive format. Remember how when little kids trip and do something silly, they sometimes try to save face by saying "I meant to do that!" ("I think it's funny you think I didn't mean to do that.") It doesn't fool anyone, though, does it? Well, when you first go over vague theories, and then claim general hypotheses, and then say that this implies in your data that we expect such and such to be positive, and such and such an interaction to be negative.... it's basically saying, "uh... I meant to do that."

So if you think that the punch in your article is going to be that you correctly predicted at the beginning of your paper the exact patterns that we would see at the end, you have to understand that most of us will not be impressed. We get it. Cider in the ear (see box).

So What?

Worst of all, even if you actually do what your teachers probably tell you to do—first formulate a theory, then find a way to test it, and then have the world accept your predictions—you can find that you're not allowed to walk away with the prize. Huh? Misled by all the talk of theory testing, you might have diligently tested your own theory... but did not rule out the most plausible alternatives. In the most obvious cases of this sort of useless theory testing, there's wide agreement that a certain phenomenon or pattern exists. (For example, we usually don't want to be dead, mostly.) This phenomenon might be consonant with a researcher's elaborate theory (say, that we have discrete psychological mechanisms that were selected for in the Pleistocene), so in a mechanical way, testing the implications of her theory (we won't deliberately forgo dinner every night, mostly) means that she has tested her theory and it has not been falsified. But it's basically a waste of time.

In subtler cases, although there might not be widespread agreement that a certain phenomenon exists in certain situations, still there are many plausible explanations, and your data don't really speak to which of these is right. And even though no one else predicted your phenomenon, once they see it, they aren't buying your explanation, because they have another one they like better. And you go home empty-handed. The reason you didn't understand that you weren't engaging with the alternatives is usually that you weren't in dialogue with experts when you were doing your work. Only when you submit it for publication—or give a job talk—does someone say "but we all know that this is a common result of X." There's no rhetorical fix. Try to adjudicate if you can. If not, move on (see "Burnt Toast," above).

Your Theory Doesn't Explain My Case

So it doesn't help to say that you have (mirabile dictu!) confirmed your theory, given that your theory is invariably a generalization of the patterns you've found in your case. But perhaps you're more ambitious—you think you aren't going to support your own theory, but challenge someone else's. Now if that's what you set out to do, and you've succeeded, it's wonderful. As I said in chapter 2, theories are like zombies, and if you can put a bolt through one's cranium, more power to you.

But I find that it's rare that students are actually setting off, early in the morning, on a zombie hunt, armed with the tools of the trade. It's in the write-up stage that they decide that they grazed that zombie on the way back and have every right to claim the bounty. What happened? How might you end up in this tenuous position? First, you very possibly chose your site for the reasons I said you shouldn't (personal interest). Then, you found (just like I warned you) that you couldn't get other people interested. So you tried to figure out how to subsume it as a case of something else that they *would* find interesting. Because, you think, your case C is very much like a case of X, indeed, a very interesting one. You were very relieved. But then—even better—you realized that the dominant theory for X's, namely, T, didn't fit C. So now you have a very strong argument: theory T is wrong and must be adapted!

Unfortunately for you, when confronted with a face-off in which they have to choose to abandon a well-loved theory that seems to do OK for the core cases or to determine that your case C isn't in fact a member of the set X, most readers will go with the latter. And that makes a lot of sense as a rule of thumb for a scientific community: where scope conditions are unclear, draw them empirically far from the weird cases where the theories don't work. Lawyers have a saying: "Bad cases make bad law"—meaning that if you really try to craft the law so that it fits that crazy, weird, unusual case, you'll have law that will set up terrible precedents for the more run-of-the-mill cases. And I think that's our gut feeling, too. Bad cases make bad theory. So to the extent that your C is explained by theory T, well then, X-ologists will be all chummy with you. They'll slap you on the back, buy you drinks, and introduce you to their friends. ("This is Ricky! He showed that T theory covers cases like C.") But if you say that, in fact, T is wrong, suddenly your friends are gone and the bartender is giving you the tab.

You might think that's unfair. But it's not. It's totally fair. And that's the thing about our nominalism—our belief that we all get to define things the way we want. It's a free country. *You* can define X so that it includes C. But *they* can define X so that it *doesn't* include C—and so that you don't have a job.

Where did you go wrong? In essence, you went backward from your case to find "what it might be a case of," and you stopped after finding X with its theory T. But you then need to go forward—and ask yourself if we really cared about X and theory T, would we ever go to site C to answer it? If not, there's a problem.

To summarize: social science, like most forms of real science, occurs in communities whose members are in communication, cooperation, and competition with one another. Sociology students often take this first in an outraged fashion, then in a cynical one—as if they were assuming the very unsociological possibility of a nonsocial organization to scientific production. But as I said, it's a free country. You can do what you want. And the others can do what they want. Sure, you can try to trick them into channeling resources toward you because you say you're really working on the same thing they are, even though you're not. And God bless you, you might even succeed. But if they see through this, and reject all your work, it's hard to get the rest of us to see this as some sort of injustice.

Z Is Also a Case of X

Finally, there's a version of this in which we first loosen a definition so that it includes our case, and then claim to have clarified our understanding of some concept. So we begin with a concept, especially a consensually dis- valued one—say, terrorism, racism, fascism, paranoia. Some of these are crisper than others, but you might still need to do work to get it to cover a case that it doesn't obviously subsume—say (respectively), carrying out military attacks with little regard for civilian casualties, being unwilling to support affirmative action, believing that civil liberties don't allow offenses to public decency, and active concern for extremely unlikely risks, such as stranger abduction. We accept moves like this as part of the rough and tumble of politics, but even if they're fine, it doesn't make it social science.

So if you think that your argument is going to first require that you change our definition of a concept, and then, once you've done that, you'll show that your case fits that concept, again, we're not surprised. This is just as true when the category in question isn't a politicized or morally blameworthy one, but only a sociological one. We know what to expect—cider in the ear.

Further Bad Frames

Overselling

Now let me turn to a set of problems with writing that come from overzeal- ous attempts to "frame" your work. We use the term "frame"—generally in an indefensible and rather appalling way—to mean how we explain the relevance of what we have done. When frames work best, they are not creative—they're obvious linkages to the relevant issues and problems. When they work worst, they are convoluted attempts to sell something to a reluctant buyer.

Here's the simple fact—good things sell themselves. A long, complex frame is like the long sales pitch a car salesman gives you when he is trying to unload a lemon on you. It is absolutely true that you can have a piece-of-s——t study, paint it up with a bunch of b.s., and get it published. You know that's true because you read that sort of crap in the journals every now and then. But what you don't see is that for every one that slipped through, there are twenty that didn't make the first cut. Students who haven't really done one of those projects that sell themselves often underestimate the intelligence of the average sociologist and think that they can wrap their stinky findings in a more attractive wrapper and sell them that way. Even worse, they sometimes believe their own grand pitches and make wild claims—in crude terms, they oversell what they have to offer.

Someone has perhaps interviewed twenty-five people about their experiences raising toddlers while students. That's cool. But to say, "There has always been a debate about structure and agency.... no one has quite done it right.... and I am going to wrap this up," just isn't convincing. In fact, it raises suspicions and usually creates more problems; solving these problems leads, in turn, to more problems—in particular, a ballooning of the introductory section and a top-heavy paper in terms of the ratio of talk to substance.

I tell my students to imagine being a paratrooper in, say, World War II or the Korean War, told to get to the top of a hill and get into an empty bunker under hostile fire. (They immediately stop listening, but maybe you'll get it.) You need to aim for a decent clearing in which to land, but you want to be as close as you can to your eventual goal. All the time you are running on the ground, you are an easy target. You might wince at the metaphor, but I wince when I see people doing just this: insisting on being dropped in the middle of a beach, taking evasive action from potshots while they are still a mile from their data. Start close. Move in a straight line. Don't oversell.

So overpromising is itself a bad frame. But there are other frames or wrappers that might seem appealing to you, yet turn out to have identifiable problems built into their very form.

X Matters

Perhaps the most common problematic frame along these lines is the "X matters" one. (When I was at Berkeley, we all wanted to do "culture matters"—there are equivalent ones floating around today, though they of course have different *X*'s.) If you can show precisely *how* it matters for something in particular, that's great, but just that it *does*... no sale. The problem with this is almost always that if you've just spent, say, four years studying *X*, we know you feel sure it matters and that you'd never entertain the opposite thought for a second. Further, by spending four years studying *X*, you've got a lot of information about it, and so it will be hard to say that it doesn't matter. This is even true if you are arguing that *X* matters for *Y*... if you've done a research design that basically just looks at *X* in *Y*. For example, if you study the importance of religious sentiment for immigrant incorporation, you're going to staple together all your religion-influenced immigrant-incorporation stories and say "religion matters for immigrant incorporation." And, as we saw in chapter 3, by choosing your site carefully, you can probably make *X* matter if you want, or not matter if you don't. In this case, it will matter or not depending on which nationality of immigrants you pick.

So the reason most readers don't care when you think you've shown that *X* matters is that they know that whatever you went looking for, you'd find. So spare us the claim that "we must not overlook *X* anymore." I'm actually going to go right out and overlook it just to spite you.

It's More Complicated Than That

Sometimes students mistakenly think that they are making a contribution just because they are showing that things are actually more complicated than *T* makes it seem, where *T* is a theory, a tradition, a famous writer, or what have you. Right. We know that. That's why we do science, to get a handle on the complexity. As I said in the previous chapter, if you have a hang-up about generalization, don't become a sociologist, just like you wouldn't become a gardener if you don't like plants. It's kinda built into the occupation.

So you're not "helping" by showing that reality is more complex, any more than a toddler helps his parents pack by taking everything out of the boxes. It isn't even always a contribution just to show that there is internal variation in some phenomenon. Sticking with the case of immigrant incorporation, you might argue that previous researchers haven't really understood the importance of the difference in experiences between poor and rich. But this is only important if you can get some theoretical grip on the nature of this difference. It can't simply be that previous researchers were stupid/bad/crude to treat all immigrants the same because presumably if you necessarily pool "rich immigrants" as a type, in order to compare them to poor ones, the same criticism applies to you. You've started down a road that ends in the destruction of sociology. If you wanted to be consistent, you'd end up splitting every group until each person is in his or her own category.

The point isn't that you should never explore internal variation or heterogeneity. You should. And if you can show precisely *what* complicated things are going on, kudos. But the virtue isn't simply in the negation of pooling. That can't be it, so don't imply that it is.

Danger Flags

Finally... a few small tips. While you are writing, if you notice yourself typing any of these, it is a danger flag that things are going wrong with your writing.

1. "In fact" or "obviously"

    This usually means that you are making a claim for which you have no evidence.[9]

2. "is not nuanced enough" or "I add nuance"

    "Nuance" is basically part of the hate speech of academia. When someone else says something clear and direct, and you don't like it but can't disprove it, you're tempted to criticize it precisely for being clear and direct. You aren't doing anyone a favor by adding vagueness (see above).[10]

3. "can be seen as"

    Anything can be seen as anything you want.

4. "Although... I still am confident"

    Your subjective state of confidence is not persuasive to others. Instead, it just suggests that you can't be trusted. If you have identified a problem, solve it. If you can't, admit it.

5. "The point is" or "Why I am saying this?"

    Probably when you started writing this section, you weren't quite clear as to what your point is. Take what you are going to say now and put it at the top.

6. Splitting the difference

    Finally, as I've said above, never let yourself think that, in a world with two theories, call them A and B, where $B = \sim A$, that your contribution is showing that things are somewhere in between.

---

9. I was alerted to this by David Gibson, and now check my own writing carefully. Thanks David!

10. Recently one of my favorite sociologists entered the lists against this, to great acclaim, but I do wish to caution youth that we should strive to avoid not only pretention but also vulgarity.

Coda: Writing about People

Before I leave the subject of writing, I want to say something about an issue that might seem trivial. And it's this: how do we quote and write about what people say? First, a little bit about recording versus reconstruction is a good starting place for this topic. Sociologists used to be very loose about this, in part because tape recorders were cumbersome and so there was more shorthand note taking. And so researchers would "quote" informants based on their reconstructions of the conversation.

That's not OK anymore. For one thing, as I've said in chapter 4, you should be recording conversations if you possibly can. But if you can't, and you do reconstruct, don't put the words in quotation marks—or if you do, make it very clear (in the text, not a footnote) that these are reconstructions. Because everything we know about memory suggests that such reconstructions are tendentious.

Although reconstruction is scientifically unacceptable, that doesn't mean you can't "clean up" speech. Because most people use lots of "ums" and overlays and false starts, if you don't clean up speech, almost everyone looks like a moron. There's nothing wrong with changing "They wa—they were, I mean, already, uh, already *there* an' ... like, it wasn't, ummm, I mean, it wasn't, uh, even *around*" to "They were already *there*, and it wasn't even *around*." You've only taken out the failures, not the successes, in verbal communication. If you do this, you should note that you have cleaned up repetitions, but these are almost always nontendentious changes in that they take the text further in the way the speaker would have wanted. Of course, if you do it for some, do it for all.

What about trying to capture the intonation of speakers? Sometimes, doing this seems necessary to correctly communicate the denotation of the words. That's because some terms, often originating in slang, are popularly spelled with dropped consonants, like rock 'n' roll. "Rock and roll" might be something different, perhaps anachronistic. Similarly, if a subject was quoted as saying that he was "just hangin'," we might not read it as an attempt to capture his sound but just his meaning, because in California (maybe) that is something a bit different from "hanging." But is it a good idea if you wrote "jus' hangin'" to give more of a sense of the accent?

There was a big debate in the field of folklore over this. Some argued that it was important when capturing oral speech to give a sense of the lilt of spoken words. Others emphasized that this implicitly makes one kind of speech unmarked—or accentless. Now while there *is* a way in which there is an unmarked accent—a generic American English, in that it's very hard to place the person in geographic but also social terms—writers don't restrict their lack of sonic marking to this one case.[11]

That is, when writing up data that come from an interview with a white Midwestern banker, I don't think any sociologist will write "I saw myself in the meeror," even though that's the somewhat grating way that Midwesterners talk (no offense!). Why? Basically, because, as they say, white is right. Even though this person does have a recognizable accent, writers don't think they need to pay attention to it. And the ambiguity of what is "neutral" can lead to an attempt to be faithful to the sounds of spoken English to make the words of some respondents—and, given who sociologists interview, especially African American respondents—stand out greatly from the text. If you make your respondents' words look on paper like Uncle Remus, your readers will be freaked out.

Maybe they are freaked out for the wrong reasons, but I think their instincts are right. Those writers who think they really need to capture the whole "feel" of the quoted person, often are basically trying to paint their theory into the data—watch for them also trying to describe the mentality of the speaker (e.g., "his eyes flashing with righteous anger as he remembered the event"). I'm all for description—but description shouldn't be explanation pretending to be a matter of fact, and that's what often happens when we allow ourselves a full palette to paint our subjects.

My sense is that you should communicate the kinds of people you have, report their words as words, not as speech acts, unless you are going to use conversation analytic notation. Italics are awesome, but only to reproduce emphasis.

In sum, try to be straight with us. And be straight with the people you studied. It might be a lot harder than twisting data into an unrecognizable monstrosity and dressing it up as something it isn't, but it's a lot more fun in the end.

TAKEAWAYS

- Any philosophy of science that encourages you to do asymmetric interpretations is not your friend.
- You cannot necessarily salvage a bad research design. Sometimes you just need to move on.

---

11. Such "accentlessness," like the absence of dialectic in languages, doesn't require a value judgment—it's usually related to the speed at which some dialects or accents have spread. We recognize an accent or a dialect in areas in which there has been both resistance to incoming speechways but also no effective transmission outward.

- Do not pay more attention to the wrapper you are trying to put on your findings than to your actual findings themselves. Sociology is a lot more like a science than we let on.

If you were going to read more...
Do you really want to learn how to write? The place to start is *How I Wrote Certain of My Books* by J. Raymond Roussel.

Conclusion

A book like this doesn't need much of a conclusion. If you want a recapitulation, go back and refresh yourself on the takeaway points. Let me just say one thing about the guiding principle of this work. We need methodology because sociology is hard. It's easy to think you've learned something that you haven't, and hard to uncover something new. There might be an upper limit on how good we can get, and that is sure to be far short of perfection.

But I've been impressed by how easy it is to improve the quality of our research if we are willing to do so. That usually involves only four things:

1. We should think through the steps that take us to our question, our site, our subjects, our themes, and so on.
2. We have to understand what phenomenon it is that we are actually studying and refraining from relabeling it as something different. This allows us to catch up on what social and behavioral sciences already know about this phenomenon. And...
3. It lets us understand our production of data as a situation and a relationship, cross-embedded in one another.
4. We need to recognize what we haven't done, and when we're wrong, to refrain from trying to paper it over or to confuse things with a flurry of words.

And most important, we recognize that our biggest problems usually enter as solutions to other problems. Your problem is you can't think of a topic—so you decide to study something you are already interested in. You can't get access to a site—but then someone you know invites you to a group. You are having trouble finding people to talk to—but then a popular person befriends you and brokers contacts for you. You are having trouble getting data relevant to your theoretical interest—so you find ways to get "good material" by dropping loaded words into your questions. You have too much data—so you code it on the basis of your a priori conceptions. Your findings don't seem intrinsically important—so you find a subfield and make a deductive chain of reasoning as to why your site fits here. Your findings are actually compatible with an opposing theory—so you have yet another lengthy chain of reasoning at the beginning of your work trying to explain why this isn't true.

All of this can, profitably I think, be brought together in the idea of thinking through our methods. Without mystification or wishful thinking, we figure out where we are and what we are doing, as well as what we are not doing. And in particular, we question every solution that appears. Funny though this will sound, the truth is most of us *can* do this, but we don't *want* to do it, because we're frightened. We are afraid of what we might learn.

This isn't because sociology is a worse science than others. It's because we teachers give our students a lot more freedom to improvise their own research designs. Experimental psychology is hard, but it's easier to know what the potential problems are going to be and easier to do research that you can be reasonably sure won't be embarrassingly wrong. In sociology, you're often in a trickier position, with more moving parts, even if they seem individually pretty straightforward.

So I think we're worried that if we look down, we'll notice that there's no support for what we're doing, and like Wile E. Coyote, we'll suddenly plunge to our (near) deaths. And so for that same reason, we try to attach safety lines to the clouds, with implausible promises to test this or that grand theory.

But here's the thing. Since this isn't Warner Brothers, you don't actually get to stay hovering in the air until you look down. *You're already falling.* You are only forced to admit it when you touch down.

References

Adorno, T. W., Else Frenkel-Brunswik, Daniel J. Levinson, and R. Nevitt Sanford. 1950. *The Authoritarian Personality*. New York: Harper and Row.

Altemeyer, Bob. 1981. *Right-Wing Authoritarianism*. Manitoba: University of Manitoba Press.

Bailyn, Bernard. 1967. *The Ideological Origins of the American Revolution*. Cambridge, MA: Belknap Press.

Bakker, Janel, and Jenell Paris. 2013. "Bereavement and Religion Online: Stillbirth, Neonatal Loss, and Parental Religiosity." *Journal for the Scientific Study of Religion* 52:657–74.

Baldassari, Delia, and Guy Grossman. 2013. "The Effect of Group Attachment and Social Position on Prosocial Behavior: Evidence from Lab-in-the-Field Experiments," *PLOS ONE*, 8(3).

Ball, Hugo. (1920–21) 1996. *Flight Out of Time: A Dada Diary*. Translated by Ann Raimes. Berkeley: University of California Press.

Barton, Allen H. 1968. "Bringing Society Back In: Survey Research and Macro-Methodology." *American Behavioral Scientist* 12:1–9.

Becker, Howard S. 1992. "Cases, Causes, Conjunctures, Stories, and Imagery." In *What Is a Case?* edited by Charles C. Ragin and Howard S. Becker, 205–16. Cambridge: Cambridge University Press.

Becker, Howard S. 1998. *Tricks of the Trade: How to Think about Your Research While You're Doing It*. Chicago: University of Chicago Press.

Best, Joel. 2012. *Damned Lies and Statistics: Untangling Numbers from the Media, Politicians, and Activists*. Updated ed. Berkeley: University of California Press.

Biernacki, Richard. 1997. *The Fabrication of Labor: Germany and Britain, 1640–1914*. Berkeley: University of California Press.

———. 2012. *Reinventing Evidence in Social Inquiry*. New York: Palgrave Macmillan.

Blau, Peter Michael. 1955. *The Dynamics of Bureaucracy: A Study of Interpersonal Relations in Two Government Agencies*. Chicago: University of Chicago Press.

Borsboom, Denny, Gideon J. Mellenbergh, and Jaap van Heerden. 2003. "The Theoretical Status of Latent Variables." *Psychological Review* 110:203–19.

Bosk, Charles L. (1979) 2003. *Forgive and Remember: Managing Medical Failure*. 2nd ed. Chicago: University of Chicago Press.

Bourdieu, Pierre. (1984) 1988. *Homo Academicus*. Translated by Peter Collier. Stanford, CA: Stanford University Press.

Bourdieu, Pierre, and Loïc J. D. Wacquant. 1992. *An Invitation to Reflexive Sociology*. Chicago: University of Chicago Press.

Breiger, Ronald L. 2009. "On the Duality of Cases and Variables: Correspondence Analysis (CA) and Qualitative Comparative Analysis (QCA)." In *The SAGE Handbook of Case-Based Methods*, edited by David Byrne and Charles C. Ragin, 243–59. London: Sage.

Brown, Robert. 1984. *The Nature of Social Laws*. Cambridge: Cambridge University Press.

Burawoy, Michael. 1982. *Manufacturing Consent: Changes in the Labor Process under Monopoly Capitalism*. Chicago: University of Chicago Press.

Burt, Ronald S. 2012. "Network-Related Personality and the Agency Question: Multirole Evidence from a Virtual World." *American Journal of Sociology* 118:543–91.

Butler, Samuel. (1903) 1945. *The Way of All Flesh*. New York: Literary Classics Book Club.

Cage, John. 1961. *Silence*. Middletown, CT: Wesleyan University Press.

Castiglione, Baldesar. (1528) 2002. *The Book of the Courtier*. Translated by Charles Singleton. New York: Norton.

Cherry, Elizabeth, Colter Ellis, and Michaela DeSoucey. 2011. "Food for Thought, Thought for Food: Consumption, Identity, and Ethnography." *Journal of Contemporary Ethnography* 40:231–58.

Cohen, Miriam. 1967. *Will I Have a Friend?* New York: Macmillan.

Collins, Randall. 1998. *The Sociology of Philosophies*. Cambridge, MA: Harvard University Press.

Correll, Joshua, Bernadette Park, Charles M. Judd, and Bernd Wittenbrink. 2002. "The Police Officer's Dilemma: Using Ethnicity to Disambiguate Potentially Threatening Individuals." *Journal of Personality and Social Psychology* 83:1314–29.

Coxon, Anthony P. M. 1995. "Networks and Sex: The Use of Social Networks as Method and Substance in Researching Gay Men's Response to HIV/AIDS." In *Conceiving Sexuality*, edited by R. G. Parker and J. H. Gagnon, 215–34. New York: Routledge.

D'Andrade, Roy. 1995. *The Development of Cognitive Anthropology*. Cambridge: Cambridge University Press.

Davidson, R. Theodore. 1983. *Chicano Prisoners: The Key to San Quentin*. Prospect Heights, IL: Waveland Press.

Dean, John P., and William Foote Whyte. 1958. "How Do You Know If the Informant is Telling the Truth?" *Human Organization* 17:34–38.

Desmond, Matthew. 2014. "Relational Ethnography." *Theory and Society* 43:547–79.

———. 2016. *Evicted*. New York: Crown Publishing.

Duneier, Mitchell. 2000. *Sidewalk*. New York: Farrar, Straus and Giroux.

———. 2011. "How Not to Lie with Ethnography." *Sociological Methodology* 41:1–11.

Durkheim, Emile. (1897) 1951. *Suicide*. Translated by John A. Spaulding and George Simpson. New York: Free Press.

Ebaugh, Helen Rose Fuchs. 1988. *Becoming an Ex: The Process of Role Exit*. Chicago: University of Chicago Press.

Effler, Erika Summers. 2010. *Laughing Saints and Righteous Heroes: Emotional Rhythms in Social Movement Groups*. Chicago: University of Chicago Press.

Ellis, Carolyn. 1986. *Fisher Folk: Two Communities on Chesapeake Bay*. Lexington: University Press of Kentucky.

———. 1995. "Emotional and Ethical Quagmires in Returning to the Field." *Journal of Contemporary Ethnography* 24:68–98.

Emerson, Robert M., Rachel I. Fretz, and Linda L. Shaw. 1995. *Writing Ethnographic Fieldnotes*. Chicago: University of Chicago Press.

Erikson, Kai T. 1966. *Wayward Puritans: A Study in the Sociology of Deviance*. New York: John Wiley & Sons.

———. 1995. "Commentary." *American Sociologist* 26:4–11.

Evans-Pritchard, E. E. 1940. *The Nuer*. Oxford: Clarendon Press.

Fearon, James D., and David D. Laitin. 2003. "Ethnicity, Insurgency and Civil War." *American Political Science Review* 97:75–90.

Feld, Scott L. 1991. "Why Your Friends Have More Friends Than You Do." *American Journal of Sociology* 96:1464–77.

Festinger, Leon. 1957. *A Theory of Cognitive Dissonance*. Stanford, CA: Stanford University Press.

Fine, Gary Alan. 2008. *Kitchens: The Culture of Restaurant Work*. 2nd edition. Berkeley: University of California Press.

Freeman, Derek. 1988. *Margaret Mead and Samoa: The Making of an Anthropological Myth*. Cambridge, MA: Harvard University Press.

———. 1998. *The Fateful Hoaxing of Margaret Mead: A Historical Analysis of Her Samoan Research*. Boulder, CO: Westview Press.

Gaskell, George D., Colm A. O'Muircheartaigh, and Daniel B. Wright. 1994. "Survey Questions about the Frequency of Vaguely Defined Events." *Public Opinion Quarterly* 58:241–54.

Gellman, Andrew, and Thomas C. Little. 1998. "Improving on Probability Weighting for Household Size." *Public Opinion Quarterly* 62:398–404.

Gibson, David R. 2012. *Talk at the Brink: Deliberation and Decision during the Cuban Missile Crisis*. Princeton, NJ: Princeton University Press.

Ginzburg, Carlo. 1992. *The Cheese and the Worms: The Cosmos of a Sixteenth-Century Miller*. Translated by John Tedeschi and Anne C. Tedeschi. Baltimore: Johns Hopkins University Press.

Glazier, Stephen D. 1993. "Responding to the Anthropologist: When the Spiritual Baptists of Trinidad Read What I Write about Them." In *When They Read What We Write: The Politics of Ethnography*, edited by Caroline B. Brettell, 37–48. New York: Bergin and Garvey.

Goethe, Johann Wolfgang von. 1987. *From My Life: Poetry and Truth*. Translated by Robert R. Heitner. Princeton, NJ: Princeton University Press.

Goffman, Alice. 2014. *On the Run*. Chicago: University of Chicago Press.

Goffman, Erving. 1959. *The Presentation of Self in Everyday Life*. New York: Anchor Books.

Goldthorpe, John H. 2007. *On Sociology*. 2nd ed. 2 vols. Stanford, CA: Stanford University Press.

Goodman, Philip. 2014. "Race in California's Prison Fire Camps for Men: Prison Politics, Space, and the Racialization of Everyday Life." *American Journal of Sociology* 120:352–94.

Gottschalk, Louis. 1950. *Understanding History: A Primer of Historical Method*. New York: Alfred A. Knopf.

Habermas, Jürgen. 1987. *The Theory of Communicative Action*. Vol. 2: *Lifeworld and System: A Critique of Functionalist Reason*. Translated by Thomas McCarthy. Boston: Beacon Press.

Hadaway, C. Kirk, Penny Long Marler, and Mark Chaves. 1993. "What the Polls Don't Show: A Closer Look at U.S. Church Attendance." *American Sociological Review* 58:741–52.

Hagen, Ryan, Kinga Makovi, and Peter Bearman. 2013. "The Influence of Political Dynamics on Southern Lynch Mob Formation and Lethality." *Social Forces* 92:757–87.

Hallpike, C. R. 1977. *Bloodshed and Vengeance in the Papuan Mountains*. Oxford: Oxford University Press.

Hendrickson, Christina et al. 2015. "Elimination of Chromosomal Island SpyCIM1 from *Streptococcus pyogenes* Strain SF370 Reverses the Mutator Phenotype and Alters Global Transcription." *PLOS-ONE*. DOI: 10.1371/journal.pone.0145884.

Humphreys, Laud. (1970) 1975. *Tearoom Trade: Impersonal Sex in Public Places*. Chicago: Aldine.

Hyman, Herbert H., with William J. Cobb, Jacob J. Feldman, Clyde W. Hart, and Charles Herbert Stember. 1954. *Interviewing in Social Research*. Chicago: University of Chicago Press.

Innes, Judith Eleanor. 1989. *Knowledge and Public Policy: The Search for Meaningful Indicators*. New Brunswick, NJ: Transaction Publishers.

Jankowski, Martín Sánchez. 1991. *Islands in the Street: Gangs and American Urban Society*. Berkeley: University of California Press.

Janus, Samuel, and Cynthia Janus. 1993. *The Janus Report on Sexual Behavior*. New York: James Wiley and Sons.

Jerolmack, Colin, and Shamus Khan. 2014. "Talk Is Cheap: Ethnography and the Attitudinal Fallacy." *Sociological Methods and Research* 43:178–209.

Jones, Edward E., and Victor A. Harris. 1967. "The Attributions of Attitudes." *Journal of Experimental Social Psychology* 3:1–24.

Katz, Jack. 1999. *How Emotions Work*. Chicago: University of Chicago Press.

Keller, Evelyn Fox. 1983. *A Feeling for the Organism: The Life and Work of Barbara McClintock*. New York: W. H. Freeman

Kelley, Harold H. 1973. "The Processes of Causal Attribution." *American Psychologist* 28:107–28.

Kurzman, Charles. 1991. "Convincing Sociologists: Values and Interests in the Sociology of Knowledge." In *Ethnography Unbound: Power and Resistance in the Modern Metropolis*, edited by Michael. Burawoy, 250–68. Berkeley: University of California Press.

Latour, Bruno. 1987. *Science in Action*. Cambridge, MA: Harvard University Press.

———. 2004. "Why Has Critique Run out of Steam? From Matters of Fact to Matters of Concern." *Critical Inquiry* 30:225–48.

———. 2005. *Reassembling the Social*. New York: Oxford University Press.

Laumann, Edward O., John H. Gagnon, Robert T. Michael, and Stuart Michaels. 1994. *The Social Organization of Sexuality: Sexual Practices in the United States*. Chicago: University of Chicago Press.

Lawson, Matthew. 1999. "The Holy Spirit as Conscience Collective." *Sociology of Religion* 60:341–61.

Lee, Monica, and John Levi Martin. 2015. "Coding, Counting and Cultural Cartography." *American Journal of Cultural Sociology* 3:1–33.

Le Play, Frédéric. (1862) 1982. *Instruction sur la method d'observation*, excerpted and translated by Catherine Bodard Silver. In *On Family, Work and Social Change*, by Frédéric Le Play, 163–83. Chicago: University of Chicago Press.

Leschziner, Vanina. 2015. *At the Chef's Table: Culinary Creativity in Elite Restaurants*. Stanford, CA: Stanford University Press.

Lieberson, Stanley. 1991. "Small *N*'s and Big Conclusions: An Examination of the Reasoning in Comparative Studies Based on a Small Number of Cases." *Social Forces* 71:307–20.

Long, Theodore E., and Jeffrey K. Hadden. 1983. "Religious Conversion and the Concept of Socialization: Integrating the Brainwashing and Drift Models." *Journal for the Scientific Study of Religion* 22:1–14.

Mahoney, James. 1999. "Nominal, Ordinal, and Narrative Appraisal in Macro-causal Analysis." *American Journal of Sociology* 104:1154–96.

Main, Jackson Turner. 1973. *Political Parties before the Constitution*. Chapel Hill: University of North Carolina Press.

Markoff, John. 1996. *The Abolition of Feudalism*. University Park: Pennsylvania State University Press.

Marlor, Chantelle. 2011. "Ways of Knowing: Epistemology, Ontology, and Community among Ecologists, Biologists and First Nations Clam Diggers." PhD diss. Rutgers University, New Brunswick, NJ.

Martin, John Levi. 2000. "The Relation of Aggregate Statistics on Belief to Culture and Cognition." *Poetics* 28:5–20.

———. 2001. "*The Authoritarian Personality*, 50 Years Later: What Lessons Are There for Political Psychology?" *Political Psychology* 22:1–26.

———. 2015. *Thinking Through Theory*. New York: Norton.

Mazur, Allan. 2005. *Biosociology of Dominance and Deference*. Lanham, MD: Rowman & Littlefield Publishers.

McGrew, W. C. 1972. *An Ethological Study of Children's Behavior*. New York: Academic Press.

McLean, Paul D. 2007. *The Art of the Network: Strategic Interaction and Patronage in Renaissance Florence*. Durham, NC: Duke University Press.

Mead, George H. 1934. *Mind, Self, and Society: From the Standpoint of a Social Behaviorist*. Edited by Charles W. Morris. Chicago: University of Chicago Press.

Mead, Margaret. (1928) 1967. *Coming of Age in Samoa*. New York: William Morrow and Company.

Meredith, George. 1909. *The Ordeal of Richard Feverel*. Vol. 2 of *The Works of George Meredith*. New York: C. Scribner's Sons.

Merton, Robert K. 1968. *Social Theory and Social Structure*. 2nd ed. New York: Free Press.

———. 1987. "Three Fragments from a Sociologist's Notebooks: Establishing the Phenomenon, Specified Ignorance, and Strategic Research Materials." *Annual Review of Sociology* 13:1–29.

Milgram, Stanley. 1974. *Obedience to Authority*. New York: Harper and Row.

Mill, John Stuart. 1872. *A System of Logic, Ratiocinative and Inductive*. London: Longman.

Milroy, Leslie. 1987. *Language and Social Networks*. 2nd ed. Oxford: Basil Blackwell.

Mohr, John W. 1994. "Soldiers, Mothers, Tramps and Others: Discourse Roles in the 1907 New York City Charity Directory." *Poetics* 22:327–57.

Moskos, Peter. 2009. *Cop in the Hood*. Princeton, NJ: Princeton University Press.

Nichols, Elizabeth. 1986. "Skocpol on Revolution: Comparative Analysis vs. Historical Conjuncture." *Comparative Social Research* 9:163–86.

Nippert-Eng, Christena. 2015. *Watching Closely: A Guide to Ethnographic Observation*. New York: Oxford University Press.

Oberschall, Anthony. 2000. Review of *Theory and Progress in Social Science*, by James B. Rule. *Social Forces* 78:1188–90.

Orne, Jason and Michael M. Bell. 2015. *An Invitation to Qualitative Fieldwork*. New York: Routledge.

Oppenheimer, Valerie Kincade. 1970. *The Female Labor Force in the United States*. Berkeley, CA: Institute of International Studies.

Payne, Stanley L. 1951. *The Art of Asking Questions*. Princeton, NJ: Princeton. University Press,

Peterson, David. 2015. "All That Is Solid: Bench-Building at the Frontiers of Two Experimental Sciences." *American Sociological Review* 80:1201–25.

Pinderhughes, Howard. 1997. *Race in the Hood: Conflict and Violence among Urban Youth*. Minneapolis: University of Minnesota Press.

Porter, Theodore M. 1996. *Trust in Numbers*. Princeton, NJ: Princeton University Press.

Ragin, Charles C. 1987. *The Comparative Method*. Berkeley: University of California Press.

Riecken, H. W. 1962. "A Program for Research on Experiments in Social Psychology." In *Decisions, Values and Groups*, edited by N. F. Washbume, 2:25–41. New York: Pergamon Press.

Riley, Dylan. 2010. *The Civic Foundations of Fascism in Europe: Italy, Spain, and Romania, 1870–1945*. Baltimore: Johns Hopkins University Press.

Rogin, Michael Paul. 1969. *The Intellectuals and McCarthy: The Radical Specter*. Cambridge, MA: MIT Press.

Rosenthal, Robert. 1969. "Interpersonal Expectations: Effects of the Experimenter's Hypothesis." In *Artifact in Behavioral Research*, edited by Robert Rosenthal and Ralph L. Rosnow, 181–277. New York: Academic Press.

Rosenthal, Robert, and Lenore Jacobson. 1968. *Pygmalion in the Classroom*. New York: Holt, Rinehart & Winston.

Rosenthal, Robert, and Ralph L. Rosnow. 1969. "The Volunteer Subject." In *Artifact in Behavioral Research*, edited by Robert Rosenthal and Ralph L. Rosnow, 59–118. New York: Academic Press.

Rothenberg, Winifred Barr. 1992. *From Market-Places to a Market Economy: The Transformation of Rural Massachusetts, 1750–1850*. Chicago: University of Chicago Press.

Roussel, J. Raymond. 2005. *How I Wrote Certain of My Books*. Translated by Trevor Winkfield. Cambridge, MA: Exact Change.

Salganik, Matthew. Forthcoming. *Bit by Bit: Social Research in the Digital Age*. Princeton, NJ: Princeton University Press.

Schaeffer, Nora Cate. 1991. "Hardly Ever or Constantly: Group Comparisons Using Vague Quantifiers." *Public Opinion Quarterly* 55:395–423.

Schaffer, Simon, Trevor Pinch, and David Gooding. 1989. *The Uses of Experiment: Studies in the Natural Sciences*. Cambridge: Cambridge University Press.

Schopenhauer, Arthur. (1847) 1974. *On the Fourfold Root of the Principle of Sufficient Reason*. LaSalle, IL: Open Court Publishing.

Schudson, Michael. 1986. *Advertising: The Uneasy Persuasion*. New York: Basic Books.

Shivley, Jo Ellen. 1992. "Perceptions of Western Films among American Indians and Anglos." *American Sociological Review* 57:725–34.

Short, James F., Jr., and Fred L. Strodtbeck. 1965. *Group Process and Gang Delinquency*. Chicago: University of Chicago Press.

Skocpol, Theda. 1979. *States and Social Revolutions*. Cambridge: Cambridge University Press.

———. 1984. "Emerging Agendas and Recurring Strategies in Historical Sociology." In *Vision and Method in Historical Sociology*, edited by Theda Skocpol, 356–91. Cambridge: Cambridge University Press.

Sniderman, Paul M., and Edward G. Carmines. 1999. *Reaching beyond Race*. Cambridge, MA: Harvard University Press.

Spencer-Brown, G. 1957. *Probability and Scientific Inference*. London: Longmans, Green and Co.

Stuart, Forrest. 2016. *Down, Out, and Under Arrest: Policing and Everyday Life in Skid Row*. Chicago: University of Chicago Press.

Swanson, Guy. E. 1967. *Religion and Regime*. Ann Arbor: University of Michigan Press.

Swidler, Ann. 2001. *Talk of Love*. Chicago: University of Chicago Press.

Thorne, Barrie. 1993. *Gender Play: Girls and Boys in School*. New Brunswick, NJ: Rutgers University Press.

Tourangeau, Roger, Lance J. Rips, and Kenneth Rasinski. 2000. *The Psychology of Survey Response*. New York: Cambridge University Press.

Turnbull, Colin. 1961. *The Forest People*. Bungay, Suffolk: Reprint Society.

Turner, Victor. 1970. *The Forest of Symbols: Aspects of Ndembu Ritual*. Ithaca, NY: Cornell University Press.

Vaisey, Stephen. 2009. "Motivation and Justification: A Dual-Process Model of Culture in Action." *American Journal of Sociology* 114:1675–1715.

Vaughan, Diane. 1990. *Uncoupling: Turning Points in Intimate Relationships*. New York: Vintage.

Venkatesh, Sudhir Alladi. 2008. *Gang Leader for a Day: A Rogue Sociologist Takes to the Streets*. New York: Penguin Press.

———. 2013. *Floating City: A Rogue Sociologist Lost and Found in New York's Underground Economy*. New York: Penguin Press.

Viterna, Jocelyn. 2013. *Women in War*. New York: Oxford University Press.

von Greyerz, Kaspar. 1987. "Biographical Evidence on Predestination, Covenant and Special Providence." In *Weber's Protestant Ethic: Origins, Evidence, Contexts*, edited by Hartmut Lehmann and Guenther Roth, 273–284. Cambridge: Cambridge University Press.

Wacquant, Loïc. 2005. "Carnal Connections: On Embodiment, Apprenticeship, and Membership." *Qualitative Sociology* 28:445–74.

Weber, Max. (1905) 1949b. "Critical Studies in the Logic of the Cultural Sciences." In *The Methodology of the Social Sciences*, translated and edited by Edward A. Shils and Henry A. Finch, 113–88. New York: Free Press.

Weinberg, Jill D., Jeremy Freese, and David McElhattan. 2014. "Comparing Data Characteristics and Results of an Online Factorial Survey between a Population-Based and Crowdsource-Recruited Sample." *Sociological Science* 1:292–310.

Weinreb, Alexander A. 2006. "Limitations of Stranger-Interviewers in Rural Kenya." *American Sociological Review* 71:1014–39.

Weiss, Robert S. 1995. *Learning from Strangers: The Art and Method of Qualitative Interview*. New York: Free Press.

Whewell, William. [1860] 1971. *On the Philosophy of Discovery*. New York: Burt Franklin, Orig. Publishers. Reprinted from original by Lenox Hill Publishers, New York.

White, Harrison C. 1995. "Network Switchings and Bayesian Forks: Reconstructing the Social and Behavioral Sciences." *Social Research* 62:1035–63.

Whyte, William Foote. (1943) 1981. *Street Corner Society*. 3rd ed. Chicago: University of Chicago Press.

Willis, Paul. 1981. *Learning to Labor: How Working Class Kids Get Working Class Jobs*. New York: Columbia University Press.

Wyatt, Danny, Tanzeem Choudhury, Jeff Bilmes, and James A. Kitts. 2011. "Inferring Colocation and Conversational Networks Using Privacy-Sensitive Audio." *ACM Transactions on Intelligent Systems and Technology*, vol. 2, no. 1.

Yeung, King-To. 2007. "Suppressing Rebels, Managing Bureaucrats: State-Building during the Taiping Rebellion, 1850–1864." PhD diss. Rutgers University, New Brunswick, NJ.

Zaret, David. 2000. *Origins of Democratic Culture: Printing, Petitions and the Public Sphere in Early-Modern England*. Princeton, NJ: Princeton University Press.

Zelditch, Morris, Jr., and Anthony S. Floyd. 1998. "Consensus, Dissensus, and Justification." In *Status, Power and Legitimacy*, edited by Joseph Berger and Morris Zelditch Jr., 339–68. New Brunswick, NJ: Transaction Publishers.

Index